SELLING is dEAD

Moving Beyond Traditional
Sales Roles and Practices
To Revitalize Growth

Marc Miller
and
Jason Sinkovitz

WILEY

John Wiley & Sons, Inc.

Published by John Wiley & Sons, Inc., Hoboken, New Jersey
Published simultaneously in Canada

For general information on our other products and services or for technical support,
please contact our Customer Care Department within the United States at (800) 762-2974,
outside the United States at (317) 572-3993 or fax (317) 572-4002.

Wiley also publishes its books in a variety of electronic formats. Some content that appears in
print may not be available in electronic books. For more information about Wiley products,
visit our web site at www.wiley.com.

Library of Congress Cataloging-in-Publication Data:

Miller, Marc S., 1947–
Selling is dead : moving beyond traditional sales roles & practices to
revitalize growth / Marc Miller, Jason Sinkovitz.
p. cm.
ISBN-10 0-471-72111-5 (cloth)
ISBN-13 978-0-471-72111-6 (cloth)
1. Selling. 2. Success in business. I. Sinkovitz, Jason. II. Title.
HF5438.25.M5655 2005
658.85—dc22
2005003084

Printed in the United States of America

10 9 8 7 6 5 4 3 2 1

I dedicate this book to my wife, Janet, for her support in spite of all my deficiencies. To my parents, Jack and Ann, who taught me the value of discipline, hard work, and purpose. To my sister, Kathy, and my talented niece and nephew, Lauren and Danny. To my mother-in-law Louise—a great lady. And last, to my wonderful children who make my life fun, spontaneous, and meaningful: Jennifer, Jason, James, Marc, Jeanette, and Julia.

Marc Miller

I dedicate my efforts on this book to my family of entrepreneurs: especially my brother Matt, my father Bruce, and my mother Marge, who have each started businesses and inspired my interest in how companies go to market. My four grandparents, my uncles Bob and Chick, and my cousin Matt are also entrepreneurs who have taught me the value of creating and managing relationships with clients. Lastly, I dedicate this book to my stepfather Ray (who reminded me each morning while I was in college that 50 years of work awaited me) and William Henning (my high school English teacher who encouraged me to write and to be focused on the readers' perspective).

And to you Katie, I hope you know how much you mean to me.

Jason Sinkovitz

Contents

II Igniting Your Growth Engine

III Sustaining Your Growth Engine

Foreword

Neil Rackham, Author of *SPIN Selling*

It's now 25 years since my team set out to be the first serious researchers to investigate success in complex sales. Looking back, it's hard to imagine how unsophisticated selling was in those days. Along with tips on how to dress to impress, IBM was putting great emphasis on the initial few seconds of the sales call. "It's what you do in the first 20 seconds that will make or break your success" they assured a generation of salespeople selling multimillion dollar mainframe computers. So the firm handshake, but not *too* firm, and the wide smile, but not *too* wide, were recipes for success. Xerox, generally admired at the time for its sales training, was still teaching its top major account salespeople primitive closing techniques that today even the proverbial used car salesperson would be ashamed to use. And most other companies were worse. I kid you not. A 5,000-person business-to-business sales force I worked with was advised by its "experts" never to allow customers to speak because "if you let customers talk they will create their own doubts."

   Were these companies crazy? That sort of advice sounds unbelievable to us today. How could people possibly be so naïve? The answer is simple. Twenty five years ago, everybody assumed that selling was selling. Nobody made any distinction between large sales and small. So, for example, perfectly good research, based on college students going door to door selling magazine subscriptions, had shown that if you don't make a good impression in the first 20 seconds, there will be no sale. And, selling being selling, there was no reason to suppose that a complex IBM mainframe sale would be any different.

The easy part of our research was showing the ineffectiveness of much of this simplistic conventional wisdom that had been imported into the business-to-business sale from studies of low-value door-to-door selling. The hard part was putting something better in its place. By studying 10,000 salespeople, during 35,000 sales calls, we collected by far the largest body of information about effective selling that the world had ever known. We studied 116 behaviors that we suspected might relate to success. We worked in 23 countries, in a dozen languages, and across a wide variety of B2B sales. The next step was to use this mountain of data to create new and radically different ways of looking at sales effectiveness.

Our first attempts met with a predictable hostility and rejection from those with a vested interest in the conventional wisdom. The first of a series of books I published based on this research was *SPIN Selling,* now regarded as a classic. To give you some flavor of the sales climate at the time, it was rejected by Prentice Hall, the publisher who commissioned it, as too radical. Seven other publishers subsequently rejected it on similar grounds.

I tell you all this to explain one of the great disappointments of my research career. In order to get my research published I had to work at relentless simplification. I had to remove a lot of material that was either too controversial or too complex. In *Major Account Sales Strategy,* for example, I wrote about the three generic stages buyers go through in making a major purchase. What I *didn't* write about were all the tantalizing strands of evidence suggesting that there were a number of different buying processes each influenced by factors such as buyer sophistication, product familiarity, competition, and purchase size.

The basic models I created have since become well accepted and used by major corporations all over the world. But over the years I've hoped that others would take my original concepts much further. In particular, I hoped to see deeper thinking about buying cycles. So I've been looking with interest to see when new ideas would emerge. Because of some unspeakable sin committed in a former life, I am condemned to reading the manuscripts of dozens of new sales books every year. I'm lucky if two weeks go by without someone sending me their "breakthrough" contribution to the advancement of selling. Most of these books rehash old thinking. I usually look in vain for original thought.

In this book I've finally found some of the new thinking I've been searching for. The central idea of concurrent offerings and divergent offerings is particularly interesting. It gives a framework around which new models of the buying process can be created. Concurrent offerings are those currently being used by the buyer. They are the accepted norm, and the perceived risk of making purchasing decisions is low. In contrast, divergent offerings are those that fall outside the buyer's familiar way of doing things. There is evidence from my own research that buyers act differently when purchasing divergent offerings. For one thing, the perceived level of risk is much higher. In *Account Strategy for Major Sales,* there's a chapter on how buyers react to risk. It's an important determinant of purchasing behavior, and I'm delighted to see *Selling Is Dead* looking at this area in depth.

Another aspect of selling divergent offerings is the need for a more aspirational selling model. For some years I've felt that classic selling skills models, including many that I have created, rely too heavily on selling solutions to problems. Two changes in particular have made this solution selling approach less useful.

- The shift from the executive as a problem fixer to the executive as an opportunity creator.
- The shift from selling as value communication to selling as value creation.

Twenty years ago, growth came from fixing problems, so selling models that focused only on uncovering and developing problems was entirely appropriate. Today, the most dramatic growth opportunities come from divergent offerings. Salespeople following problem-based models often fail to uncover opportunities until very late in the call—if at all. What is needed is an approach that encourages discussion of opportunities much earlier in the sales process. The frameworks proposed here marry very well with new thinking about more aspirational concepts of selling.

You'll find this a thoughtful book. It's provocative and insightful. *Selling Is Dead* presents a new and useful perspective on creating and managing large selling opportunities. And like most books that make you think, it's not a quick read. But its ideas are worthwhile and will repay the effort.

Neil Rackham is a world-renowned consultant and business thinker. He has written multiple books, including SPIN Selling, Major Account Sales Strategy, *and* Rethinking the Sales Force.

Acknowledgments

Yikes! When we decided to write *Selling Is Dead,* we dramatically underestimated the time and effort that would be involved with researching and writing this book. Throughout the lengthy process, we have relied on many gracious individuals for ideas, feedback, experiences, and assistance.

Lisa Banach, a colleague of ours at Sogistics, deserves to be singled out for her contributions to this work. Not only did she supply us with the epilogue and drive the selection of the title *Selling Is Dead,* but she also played a key role in refining the content and turning our thousands of annual sales assessments into a powerful research engine.

We also owe a tremendous amount of gratitude to Neil Rackham. Neil is one of the most interesting and thoughtful people we have ever met. His wisdom, research, publications, and advice have helped thousands of organizations achieve new levels of sales performance. At Sogistics, we have been loyal disciples of Neil's work since the late 1980s. In spring 2004, when Neil was in Cleveland to speak with a group of area executives, we approached him for some advice and to get his feedback on some of the new models we developed from our research. While we were simply pursuing some helpful hints, we were fortunate enough to get much more. Over the months that followed, Neil shared his boundless insight and related experiences with us. His generosity is something we may never be able to repay. His support, and the value and merit he sees in our work, means a great deal to us. Thanks, Neil.

We were very fortunate in how we found a publisher for *Selling Is Dead*. John Wiley & Sons was our first choice and the only publisher to which we fully submitted our work for consideration. The good folks at Wiley obviously decided to publish it. We have benefited from a wonderful working relationship with our editor, Matthew Holt. Matt, thanks for your patience, your belief in our project, and all of your work and responsiveness. Micheline Frederick, the senior production editor at Wiley who was assigned to our book, commands both our respect and sincere appreciation. Thanks, Micheline, for helping us complete and polish our book. We would also like to express our gratitude to all of the people at Wiley who were involved with our book, and most notably Laurie Harting and Tamara Hummel.

Danielle Lake played a major role in the editing of *Selling Is Dead*. We appreciate her efforts and acknowledge her for improving our language and making the book more concise and easy to read. Great work, Danielle. You added instant and immeasurable value.

We would also like to thank Mike Salemi from Telstar Productions and Michael Terry and Stacey Simonton from Sanctuary Software Studio (the firm that provided some wonderful web development in support of our book).

During the process of creating *Selling Is Dead,* we have come to understand the necessity of good design for communicating concepts and for general appeal. Lindsay Gormish at Akhia Public Relations is a talented, creative, and efficient designer who made significant contributions to our book. We relied heavily on Lindsay, and the vast majority of the figures in this book were created by her. Jennifer Kelnhofer, another designer who helped with the book, initially brought our words to life with a beautiful design concept and wonderful illustrations. Several of her graphics are in the version you see today. We also thank David

Randall, a third designer who supplied us with some key ideas early in the process.

Dozens of our associates were instrumental in reviewing our work and concepts, contributing case study stories, selecting a title, and challenging our thinking. We have learned a great deal from these bright and successful people over the years. This wonderful group includes Joe Palmisano, John Robertson, Laura Leggett, Jim Daley, Katerina Ostovsky, Dolf Kahle, Mike Bechtold, Bruce Harris, Tim Reynolds, Frank Piunno, Martin "Chuck" Neath, Dave Powell, Ken Thompson, John Magyari, Scott Joseph, Jim Scaparotti, Ted Wetzel, Bob Teichart, Diana Schumacher, Don Philabaum, Dan Richards, Bill Burke, Bill Hodge, Scott Rickert, Doug Grossman, Brad Bowers, Sue Thomas, Jim Elsey, Dave Gilbert, Dan Wallace, Mark Sinreich, Harry Schoenfeld, Charlie Gray, Ed Gabbert, Fred Ode, Jan Gusich, Kevin Reichley, Dennis Castiglione, Jeff Concepcion, Bob Fritz, Ruth Coleman, David Inglis, Jim Hornyak, Norman Fairman, Ken Pim, Patt Cretu-Ball, Marybeth Whelan, Nathalie Petri, Vicki Porter, Tim Travis, Peter Flood, Kristen Swantek (an intern at Sogistics), Matt Sinkovitz, and Jason Mitchell.

The people, though, who have truly pushed our work to new heights and who were inspirational to us in crafting this book are Mark Woodka, David Peckinpaugh, Jeff Fugate, David Kelly, Bill Horrigan, Ed Bachman, Ron Newcomb, and Dana Harris. Larry Kronick and Gary Giller at Lincoln Financial were also tremendous supporters in the early years, and good friends still today. Thanks to each of you, and we hope that you feel some ownership of *Selling Is Dead* as well.

MTM and JMS
2005

Building Your New Growth Engine

Is Selling Dead?

Three small words. One powerful and provocative question. The answer has potentially severe consequences for a corporate America dependent on sales teams for not just growth but survival.

The premise behind this book is that the business and profession of selling are about to change. Soon. Dramatically. Forever.

After decades of inspired productivity advances throughout the enterprise (production, distribution, back office, product development, communication, etc.), selling units on the whole have found themselves lagging pathetically behind in the race for more with less.

In an article titled "Measuring Up" in the March 2005 issue of *Sales and Marketing Management,* several reports and studies about the under-performance and unacceptable productivity levels of sales teams were discussed.[1] One of the studies was conducted by Accenture, a management consulting firm. Accenture had administered a survey finding that senior executives rated sales as the most critical department from a value perspective. Yet, 56 percent of these same executives felt their sales teams performed at only a mediocre, undifferentiated level, while an additional 28 percent felt their teams were performing either below average or at a catastrophically bad level.

Accenture's conclusion about the cause of disturbingly low levels of sales productivity? It wasn't due to inefficiencies. Nor was it caused by generating an insufficient volume of selling leads. Not from poor retention of customers, either. Rather, the culprit that caused 84 percent of senior executives to feel their sales teams were lagging behind on the productivity curve was "an inability [of salespeople] to effectively manage sales opportunities." Ineffectiveness is the key constraint.

Why? Why has corporate America allowed its selling units to function in a business as usual manner? Why has corporate America failed to demand the same productivity gains from its sales teams as it has demanded from other business units?

A partial explanation comes from the brilliant and renowned Peter Drucker, who has been widely quoted with the following insight: "*Marketing and innovation make money. Everything else in a business is a cost.*" In other words, product development, marketing, and sales (a subset of marketing) are the drivers of revenue and profit. Everything else is a profit-killing drain on a profit-motivated organization.

Drucker's statement reflects a prevailing sentiment in corporate America. The result has been an ongoing productivity revolution . . . a war primarily waged against non-money-multiplying uses of cash. The area most unaffected by this growing revolution, and the area that has recently begun to actually do less and less with more and more, is sales. Because sales is the area of a business that most directly correlates to revenue in the collective business psyche, it's been the last area to be right-sized and purged of unessential costs and inefficiencies. Although executives recognize the underoptimized performance of their selling teams, they have either lacked the formula for making improvements or the discipline to carry them out.

The old equation for increasing profits (cut non-market-driving costs + invest more in sales & marketing = increased profits) no longer holds true. Increased investment in the sales arena, at least with sales being in its current apathetic condition, is often a mistake. A big mistake. The most egregious and dubious example was former IBM CEO John Akers' strategy in the early 1990s to turn thousands of IBM employees ("overhead") into salespeople ("growth drivers"). The ill-fated attempt nearly sank the ship.

The primary reason why investing in sales is no longer a safe way to grow profits, and a second major culprit in why sales mediocrity has been tolerated, is that there have been no new, disruptive, and (most important) accurate ideas about dramatic sales effectiveness improvement since Neil Rackham authored *SPIN Selling* and *Major Account Sales Strategy* in the late 1980s. Conventional sales investments such as training, adding more salespeople, intensifying marketing support, disseminating sales-automation technology, and improving sales management practices do little more than recycle the same ideas and methodologies that are powering today's mediocre-to-disappointing results. Such conventional investments will add cost at a faster pace than profitability can match.

The cost of sales is already much too expensive. For example, corporate America has bid up the total compensation of free agent sellers to the point where it well exceeds the true value those sellers deliver back to their organizations. Pay has increased well beyond and much more rapidly than the depth and speed of sales productivity gains. Even those sellers who lack discipline, skill, effective strategy, and threshold talent get to eat and live well from the charitable overpayments of their employers. We see many $125,000-plus salaries being paid to glorified account managers and customer service people who bear the title of *salesperson,* but who are incapable of actually being consistent creators of business value and new business revenue. That's a lot of money to pay for a cream-skimming, easily replaced, noncreator of demand and growth.

The cost versus productivity of salespeople has become so high that the aforementioned Peter Drucker has commented: "*People are simply too expensive to be used for selling. We cannot, by and large, sell anymore—we must market, i.e., we must create the desire to buy which we then can satisfy without a great deal of selling.*"[2]

So, it's now time for selling to die. And it's time for all salespeople to lose their jobs. All 18 million of them here in the United States. The sooner the better.

Unfortunately, organizations cannot kill selling and dispense with their sales teams because organizations have *nothing* with which to replace selling and salespeople. No better means of creating and managing large selling opportunities exist. Moreover, no suitable replacements are on the horizon. The utopian marketing endeavors called for by Drucker are nonexistent. Generally, marketing alone is absolutely inadequate to drive new business in large, complex selling environments, especially where the product or service represents innovation or a new application for the buying organization.

This brings us to the answer of our question: *Is selling dead?* The answer, of course, is that selling is not literally dead. In fact, effective and efficient selling is needed more now than ever before—if only because there are no practical alternatives. However, traditional selling strategies and roles have lost relevance in today's marketplace. Because of this death of relevance, salespeople are ill-equipped to drive growth on the shifting surface of today's economic landscape. They are only prepared to excel in market conditions that no longer exist, and that will probably never return again.

Selling is broken. Because selling is the business of doing business, we are all affected. Returning to Drucker one last time to articulate the importance and priority of fixing sales, he wrote, *"The purpose of a business is to create and keep a customer."* In other words, the purpose is sales and everything else just supports sales. Although Drucker gave us this simple logic over 30 years ago, it has continued to resonate despite the last 30 years of wrenching economic change, massive job shifts, and multiple bubble bursts. How do we create and keep new customers when selling is broken . . . and increasingly irrelevant? We must have an answer. We must have that answer now.

Before offering mechanisms to revitalize growth and ignite a productivity boom in the sales arena, let us first explain the dynamics at play that have devalued salespeople and selling as a whole—at least in their current state. Before you can understand these new mechanisms, you must understand the market forces that have stolen relevance from the sales roles and strategies originally created for a no-longer-existent marketplace typified by slower innovation and higher demand.

Three primary market dynamics work together to reshape selling and devour the relevance of sellers operating on old paradigms:

- ◆ The Cadence of Commoditization
- ◆ The Bend in Buying
- ◆ The Dissipation of Distance

Market Dynamic 1: The Cadence of Commoditization

Few would disagree that we live in an age of rapid, accelerating, and endless innovation. The age of innovation, however, is still in its infancy, indicating further expansion of innovation is imminent.

An interesting repercussion associated with innovation is that one man's innovation creates another man's commodity. Innovation is an opportunity for one organization and a downfall for another. Think about it. Nearly every successful launch of an innovation simultaneously commoditizes another offering.

This corporate Darwinism used to occur every few years in a given industry. Today, the ever faster pace of innovation seems to make commoditization a yearly, quarterly, or sometimes even monthly occurrence in industry after industry.

The quickening cadence of commoditization places tremendous pressure on selling teams from two perspectives:

1. The pressure to sell the new innovation that represents the future of a company and achieve rapid market and financial success with the innovation before the next wave of innovation commoditizes it.
2. The simultaneous challenge to protect the organization's cash cow commodity, which is needed to sustain the company until the full transformation to the innovation has successfully been achieved.

Sales teams rarely falter when selling commodities because buyers see commodities as safe, comfortable, existing applications. However, once a company's core business has matured and the market for those commoditized offerings has become saturated, organizations must turn to innovation for growth and survival. Unfortunately, there is powerful evidence that the transition of sales teams from selling commodities to selling innovative new platforms is difficult and fraught with failure. *The real challenge in selling is selling innovation.*

The reason why selling innovation is so difficult is simple. Buyers are resistant to buying the "new." The "new" represents uncertainty, risk, and high potential for loss. It is a leap into the unknown that causes predictable buyer reluctance and steep resistance.

Nobel Prize–winning psychologist Daniel Kahneman, along with colleagues including Amos Tversky, has done significant research on how decisions are made. Their studies clearly demonstrate that fear is a much stronger and more intense motivator than the desire for gain.[3] In fact, the intensity of emotion around the fear of loss is over twice that of the emotion around opportunity for improvement. Since organizations are simply made up of people with the same fears as you and I, it is easy to understand why "buying the new" generates powerful fear and resistance with buyers. Similarly, it is easy to understand why selling the new (in the form of innovation) is such a difficult and imposing challenge.

How bad are sales teams at selling innovation? In their excellent book, *The Innovator's Solution,* Clayton Christensen and Michael Raynor found that only 1 in 10 companies can sustain growth that translates into above-average increases in owner and shareholder return for more than a few years.[4] The authors argue that, quite often, new growth initiatives cause a company to begin a downward spiral of failure from which most never recover.

Why? From a sales perspective, the following cycle of failure often occurs:

1. The core business approaches maturity and margins are threatened.
2. Executives develop strategies to generate new growth.
3. The company invests aggressively in creating or acquiring the new capabilities or offerings (a.k.a., innovation) that will lead to renewal.
4. The sales team is introduced to and trained on the innovative offerings.
5. The sales and marketing team sputters; they fail to make efficient and significant inroads in the market with the innovations.
6. Results are dismal.
7. Leadership is forced out.
8. New management refocuses the company back to its original core market, products, and services.
9. The result: slow growth, moderate margins, and a clouded future.

This cycle is repeated over and over, in company after company. Innovating is often easier done than selling innovation. New growth initiatives for going to market with innovation are highly successful on occasion, but there is an uneasy randomness to success.

The cadence of commoditization requires that selling teams get good at selling innovation. Consistently good. This is an essential competence. Why? Because being effective and efficient at selling innovation is simultaneously both an organization's best offense and defense. Unfortunately, at a time when selling innovative new applications is becoming more critical, most salespeople lack a process and framework for doing so. The roles, strategies, process, and skills possessed by most sellers are appropriate and effective for selling commodities and existing applications. These roles, strategies, processes, and skills don't translate into the effective and efficient selling of innovation and new applications.

Market Dynamic 2: The Bend in Buying

Technology advances, ever-mounting time constraints, and the drive for productivity gains in non-money-multiplying functional departments have converged to create what we call a bend in buying. To explain and articulate the bend in buying, we will recite a story about Wal-Mart recently shared with us by Neil Rackham.

Wal-Mart is perhaps the savviest of the savvy when it comes to purchasing. Many of you may even be familiar with the sign Wal-Mart posted above its purchasing agents' door decades ago that basically read, "Don't call on us unless you manufacture it." Wal-Mart executives knew early on that the company needed to buy direct if it was to be the low-cost retailer in its market.

Rackham tells us that, recently, Wal-Mart discovered that a large percentage of its purchasing agents' time was spent researching and purchasing products, which contributed to only a small percentage of Wal-Mart profits. Because Wal-Mart employed almost 4,000 buyers, this inefficiency was easily costing over $100 million annually.

Wal-Mart's solution: Use the Internet exclusively to purchase the large number of goods that are of low strategic impact to Wal-Mart's bottom line. By initiating this new purchasing protocol, Wal-Mart was able to significantly reduce the size of its purchasing staff and dramatically cut its $100 million annual inefficiency. Perhaps Wal-Mart has since replaced its previous sign with a new one for salespeople: "Don't call on us—period."

The lesson for sellers?

If you sell commodities and don't personally offer any additional source of bottom-line value, your buyers will need you less and less, and eventually (soon) not at all. Information and commerce technologies will make you an anchor to your clients and your employer.

Remember, when selling offerings that represent existing applications for your buyers, those offerings are viewed as nonstrategic procurements. Buyers know significant productivity advances come from new applications, not existing applications. At best, your existing applications will be seen as tactical, incremental sources of gain. Buyers won't have time to meet with sellers of tactical offerings.

The majority of sellers who can't effectively and consistently sell new applications (innovation) add less value to their organizations and their buyers' organizations. This is the majority. They are becoming obsolete. The bend in buying will force sellers upstream—or out.

The new acid test for a sales team: Can they sell the new applications that significantly impact a buyer's bottom line? Can they build a case for strategic change? Can they become *businesspeople who sell?*

Market Dynamic 3: The Dissipation of Distance

The third market dynamic that is stripping away the relevance of sellers is the dissipation of distance. Frances Cairncross wrote an intriguing book on this subject called *The Death of Distance.*[5] The book discusses how technology and the Internet will soon combine to erase the geographic boundaries that currently restrict commerce.

In simple terms, when "voice, video, and data" gradually achieve a critical-mass state, the sales call will change forever and on a broad scope. Sellers will digitally achieve the effect of knee-to-knee, belly-to-belly, face-to-face meetings. Such technological advances will dramatically increase time available to sell. The cost of sales (and sales calls) will also be significantly lowered due to the drastic reduction in travel expenses.

This is the weakest of the three market forces deteriorating the value of sales and sellers. It does not diminish all salespeople equally. Its impact will primarily be in the form of needing fewer salespeople to achieve the same results. The less talented and mediocre performers will be the ones cast out. The dissipation of distance will also introduce an era of increased specialization amongst sellers, with sellers focusing on more narrow niche markets unlimited by geography.

The combination of more sales time per salesperson, reduced travel costs, and greater specialization of roles represents one of the two possible drivers of sales productivity increases: *the efficiency driver.* The second, more powerful driver of sales productivity advances is improved effectiveness. However, if the efficiency driver occurs first (more time to sell + less travel cost = more sales at a lower cost), it will create organizational satisfaction that will be a disincentive for the second, more powerful driver . . . improved effectiveness. Without a push for improved effectiveness by corporate America, even the sellers who survive the dissipation of distance will continue to struggle selling innovation, thus adding less and less value to both buyer organizations and their own employers.

Revitalizing the Role and Relevance of Sales

Although you may be surprised, this book is not about the demise of selling. Rather, it's about the resurgence of selling. This book is an optimistic look about how to reinvigorate sales productivity through increased effectiveness. *Selling Is Dead* jumps right into solving the challenges created by the three market dynamics described here. *Selling Is Dead* presents a new role for sales units and a new strategic framework for achieving greater value for the buyer's and seller's organizations alike. It's a book about growth engines and customer abundance.

Again, more than ever before, corporate America will rely on its sales teams to survive, differentiate, grow, and create. Relevance must be restored and advanced, and *Selling Is Dead* provides a disciplined approach for doing just that.

Notes

1. Calabro, Sarah. "Measuring Up." *Sales & Marketing Management* (March, 2005)

2. Found in Kotler, P. (2003). *Marketing Insights from A to Z: 80 concepts every manager needs to know*. Hoboken, NJ: John Wiley & Sons.

3. Discussed in Schwartz, B. (2004). *The Paradox of Choice: Why More Is Less*. New York, NY: HarperCollins.

4. Christensen, C., and Raynor, M. (2003). *The innovator's solution: creating and sustaining successful growth*. Boston, MA: Harvard Business School Press.

5. Cairncross, F. (1997). *The death of distance: how the communications revolution is changing our lives*. Boston, MA: Harvard Business School Press.

1

Customer Abundance

To paraphrase Peter Drucker, the purpose of any business has always been to create and keep new customers. New customers drive real and significant growth for most companies, and ensure survival for others.

But something has changed. It's all very different now. The path to new opportunities—and customers—has been blurred. Fractured. Often ending in sharp, impassable chasms.

New business revenue has become increasingly scarce. Belts are getting tighter. And tighter.

The sweeping entrance of the so-called new economy has rendered the conventional growth strategies employed by most sales teams ineffective. Salespeople, the champions of growth, must adopt a new strategic framework; they must be reinvented and redeployed.

> *"My notion is that selling is dead. These days, [salespeople] have to be customer-productivity experts."*
>
> Jeff Immelt
> CEO, General Electric
> From *Customer Intimacy* by Fred Wiersema[1]

13

This is YOUR wakeup call.

This is a wake-up call. Many companies are behind the proverbial curve, and they don't know it . . . yet. But they soon will, and they will search for a new growth engine to help them catch up in terms of competitiveness and customer count.

Selling Is Dead is for major account sellers. You must become customer productivity experts. You must begin to add much more value, significant value beyond the product or service you currently offer. *But, in order to do so, you must first understand the very nature of buyer demand—and how it affects all your sales strategy and market-facing endeavors.*

By the time you turn the final page of this book, we hope you understand that customer scarcity is a self-inflicted epidemic. Although the paths to new customers may now be more fragile, more complex, and even more unforgiving, they are still there, somewhere. Just let buyers be your guides, your beacons.

Our research has found that most salespeople are strategically misaligned on several key levels. Because this misalignment is so common across a wide variety of industries, an enormous opportunity is available for sales teams to create competitive advantage by how they face the market. The sales organizations that adopt the strategic frameworks outlined in this book will be rewarded with an *enduring market advantage* and an *abundance of new customers*.

Why Is This Book So Important?

1. Previous Research and Sales Theory Are Not Sufficiently Precise

Past research has clearly proven that the skills and strategies that work in small sales are ineffective in larger sales. Large account selling is distinctive. It requires a unique effectiveness methodology. Applying short-cycle skills to larger, longer-cycle sales is a proven recipe for failure. This has been validated through years of exhaustive research by Neil Rackham, the renowned sales author, consultant, and founder of Huthwaite. We encourage you to learn about the disparities between small and large sales (and much more) in Rackham's bestseller, *SPIN Selling.*[2] However, although Rackham's research proves the disparities between proper small account and large account selling are significant, it does not break down major account sales into more precise subcategories that allow for more appropriate and accurate sales strategies.

Our research, and the premise of this book, is based on the fact that there are different types of large, major account sales. In fact, there are four categories of large sales (Figure 1.1). Most important, each category has its own set of best practices, requiring a separate set of selling skills and strategies for optimum sales effectiveness. That's due to two important elements: buying behavior and the buyer decision-making process. Both change from one type of large sale to another. This shift in behavior and decision processes from one major account category to the next can be severe, dramatic, and profound.

Selling Is Dead represents a major turning point in the discipline of selling because it claims using a singular, general set of major account sales strategies and skills is bad practice. This book contributes to sales literature by explaining the multiple sets of sales frameworks, each used situationally based upon the specific type of major account sale.

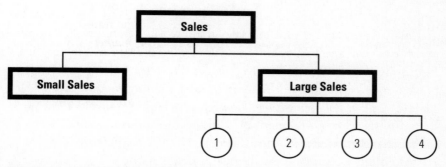

Figure 1.1 There are four different types of large sales, each with its own set of unique challenges.

The implications for major account sellers are significant. A selling team that adopts a generalist, large-sale strategic framework will most likely head down a path of high market resistance, wasted opportunities, and buyer inertia. Correspondingly, the selling team that adapts its tactics and strategies to the appropriate category of major account sales will gain a clear advantage in the market.

No longer will a broad, major account selling strategy be enough. A more focused framework that mirrors the demand type of the buyer is necessary to achieve the one goal of all sellers—market optimization.

2. Selling Is Dead *Introduces the Components of a Best-Practice Strategic Selling Framework for Large Sales*

Think Broad Sales Framework—Not Narrow Sales Training

For most organizations, their selling system essentially is little more than a specific sales training methodology. Unfortunately, sales training is no longer sufficient for those major account selling organizations that seek to build a best-practice growth foundation.

Instead, it is essential to implement a full *sales framework*. A framework is a broader, more complex mechanism that goes beyond the overly simplistic and constricting elements of sales training models. *A framework ultimately defines, dictates, and drives the manner in which a selling organization creates and manages its vital selling opportunities.*

Sales training systems typically comprise skills that are primarily taught to salespeople, while a sales framework goes well beyond skills taught to and applied by salespeople. This book explains the foundation and main components of a full sales framework. Therefore, it's important for us, the authors, to differentiate *Selling Is Dead* and its teachings from other books about sales. In fact, we chose the title of this book to prevent a perception that it's a narrow sales training methodology (e.g., *Strategic Selling, Solution Selling, Conceptual Selling, Selling to VITO*, etc.); such a misperception dramatically diminishes the scale, scope, and significance of this work.[3]

Although we provide much greater detail about selling frameworks in Chapter 4, here are the five major structural elements, each beginning with the letter *S* (Figure 1.2).

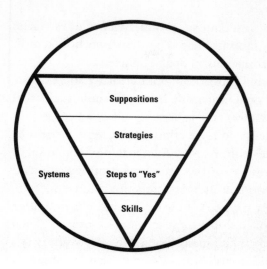

Figure 1.2 A proper major account selling framework has multiple elements, each ultimately tied together by systems.

1. *Suppositions.* Suppositions are those guiding *beliefs* that dictate how an organization philosophically chooses to face its market. Without including formal suppositions in the sales framework, every individual in the sales team will likely develop a unique set of beliefs. No uniformity. Many of these beliefs will run

Without an effective framework, sellers often degenerate into low-value-adding talking brochures that are despised by buyers.

counter to each other and damage productivity. Cohesiveness within a sales team begins with shared beliefs about how to sell. Therefore, sales leadership must manage beliefs.

2. *Strategies.* You will learn a great deal about creating and executing strategies in this book. For now, however, understand that strategies are the broad plans for achieving sales objectives.   As you will learn, strategies need to be adjusted throughout the selling cycle with each sales opportunity. A formal, disciplined set of strategies must be included in the broad sales framework, and employed uniformly and consistently across the sales team.

3. *Steps to "yes."* The best path to a buyer commitment in a large sale typically consists of multiple steps in the sales process. Each sales call that takes place when managing a sales opportunity is a step. These steps should be used in a sequence that is consistent with the overall strategies being employed. As you will learn, large sales are not linear. Rather, each sales opportunity has its own unique sequence because each buying entity is distinctive. This book discusses powerful sales steps that can be used to advance buyers toward "yes" decisions in the most efficient manner possible.

4. *Skills.* Best-practice skills are essential when faced with large selling opportunities. Selling larger offerings that represent moderate to high risk to buyers requires its own unique set of competencies. Neil Rackham made that point very clear in the late 1980s. However, because there are four different types of large sales, salespeople must be able to execute a wide variety of situation-specific skills. Our aim is to bring these skills to the forefront where they can be structured, taught, and leveraged across all market-facers in an organization.

5. *Systems.* Sales organizations must have management systems in place to hold the sales framework together—and to hold members of the sales team accountable to the framework. Without rigorous systems, breakdowns occur and the framework will fail. Best practices have recently been redefined as they relate to sales systems. *Selling Is Dead* discusses some of these important systems, which maintain a cohesive selling effort across an organization.

Case Study: The Impact of Implementing a Selling Framework at CGS

David Peckinpaugh joined Conferon Global Services in 1998 and is the company's executive vice president of sales and marketing. Between 1998 and 2004, Conferon Global Services became the largest meeting management firm in the world. During this period, the company more than tripled its revenue and more than doubled the size of its sales organization. Although much of this growth came from acquisitions, Conferon Global Services experienced unprecedented real growth from dramatically increasing its new business revenue each year under David's stewardship of the sales team.

The sales organization that David inherited in 1998 was not in need of a savior. The company was not in a turnaround mode or performing poorly. According to David, "We weren't broken as a company or as a sales team when I came aboard. The opposite was true. Our numbers were healthy and our growth was fairly steady."

However, David quickly realized that the sales effort at Conferon Global Services was far from optimized. "In order for us to reach the next level of growth, I knew we had to change. Primarily, we were too loose, casual, and unstructured as a sales team. That may not be highly detrimental to a small sales team, but I felt we had grown to a point where the lack of cohesiveness and uniformity would prevent us from optimizing our key markets and successfully adding new salespeople to our sales team."

Cohesiveness was lacking on multiple fronts:

- Members of the sales team had graduated from different schools of sales thought, which essentially meant that everyone spoke a different sales language. This problem grew with each new hire and acquisition. Everyone managed sales opportunities differently, so many opportunities were being managed poorly and lost.
- Sales managers also subscribed to their own sets of sales strategies, which led to members of the sales team receiving conflicting advice.
- No systems were in place to hold people accountable and to monitor sales activity. The sales team was geographically dispersed, so there was little opportunity for managers to spend time in the field or otherwise closely manage each person.

In order to establish some discipline and cohesiveness in the sales team, David and his lieutenants created a comprehensive sales framework, which was branded as the Conferon Global Services Way. This framework

(continued)

was phased in gradually between 1998 and 2004. Some of the components of this framework are as follows:

- A unified set of suppositions was actively instilled in members of the sales team. The mentality changed from everyone being relational product and service salespeople to value-multiplying businesspeople who sell total solutions and generate new business.
- The sales team adopted a single sales methodology that was based on buyer models. For the first time, every member of the sales team operated with the same set of strategies, skills, and process steps. A Conferon language emerged.
- David also created mechanisms to quickly ramp up new hires and newly acquired sales teams. Rapidly engraining these people in the Conferon Global Services Way prevented them from unknowingly tearing at the fabric of cohesiveness that David was seeking to create.
- Systems were in place to hold people accountable to the new methodologies. These systems included a customer relationship management (CRM) system that reinforced the methodologies while providing managers with key data, a revamped compensation system, and routine coaching programs.

"The sales framework really fostered a period of strong growth for us, even during some tough economic conditions for our industry," David told us. "What's interesting is that the framework has become a valuable part of our culture, and it's been embraced by leadership throughout our organization. It has also helped us soften the transition when acquiring companies and integrating their sales teams. In fact, these acquisitions are more successful. First of all, we can make the salespeople from these companies more effective by immediately plugging them into our framework. Second, because our existing people are experienced selling *business value,* not just products or services, they can quickly adapt to selling the offerings of the acquired organizations."

The impact of the Conferon Global Services Way framework is apparent in the *633 percent growth in new business revenue* (not total revenue) each year from new clients between 1999 and 2004:*

1999:	$1.5 million
2002:	$5.9 million
2004:	$9.5 million

*These numbers do not represent total revenue for CGS, but revenue from new clients each year.

3. **Selling Is Dead** *Integrates the Four Types of Large Sales into a New, Distinctive Framework*

If your sale is a large sale, your sales framework must be reconstructed to reflect the four types of large sales. Otherwise, your selling framework cannot be considered a best-practice, or even a good-practice, system.

The overall selling framework described in *Selling Is Dead* is the first to account for all four types of large selling opportunities and how buyers change the way they make buying decisions based on the type of offering they are buying. Buyers do not make all large buying decisions in the same way. The flexibility of this framework allows sellers to adjust their strategy and sales process appropriately from buyer to buyer.

We hope that you will see the importance of the flexible, comprehensive framework outlined in this book—and adopt it.

Even if you have a group of stars on your team, the majority of your sales team probably lags well behind optimum performance. They may be effective enough to keep their jobs, but lack the talent or self-development methodologies necessary to become optimum performers. However, if this group of moderate achievers can be plugged into an appropriate, learnable, and executable *sales framework,* their productivity can be enhanced significantly. A sales framework can serve as a compass, helping to guide sellers down proper strategic paths step-by-step. Moreover, sellers functioning in the same selling framework can more easily learn from each other and share best practices.

4. *A Forest or . . . Trees?*

Most sales books are purely tactical. They lack strategic value. We are confident that you will find this book to be strategically significant. Applying the models and ideas in this book should lead to strategic adjustments both inside and outside your traditional sales organization.

For an organization to extract the full benefit of the concepts presented in *Selling Is Dead,* these concepts should be understood and promoted by the most senior of management. These ideas must be applied to all market-facing units within a company: for example, sales, customer service/account management, marketing, product development, product managers, and project engineers.

In other words, because of the importance of these concepts, they should impact the processes, business rules, and decision making of all market-facing units. This book should challenge each of these nonsales units. In fact, many of our clients who initially implement these strategies within their sales domain soon want to realign their marketing strategies and account development efforts. Please consider these strategies as not just sales strategies, but broader market-facing strategies.

The additional strategic significance of *Selling Is Dead* includes:

- You will find a powerful weapon in the form of a process for differentiation that will drive success in competitive selling environments.
- This book provides insight into how sales and marketing strategies must be adjusted over the life cycles of products and services.
- This book shares concepts that represent the key to selling innovation and driving buyer change. Thus, if appropriately applied, these concepts increase the likelihood of success for new product and service offerings.

◆ You will learn a formula for dramatically and organically growing revenue and profits through seamless alignment with buyers and enhanced ability to deliver more impactful buying experiences to your market.

You're in Charge. What Are You Going to Do?

Okay, let's get busy. Here is an interesting case study for you to work through.

Congratulations, you are the new VP of sales for Axcellerant. You should be excited because Axcellerant is a very promising technology company with a solid business model and a genuinely good and experienced management team.

Your primary market consists of Fortune 1000 companies. The good news: All of them would benefit from Axcellerant offerings. So, what does Axcellerant do? As the VP of sales, what will you be selling?

Well . . . maybe this book isn't as important as some of these other books. Then again, if you're under pressure to hit your sales quota, you may want to keep reading this one.

Your primary revenue gen-
erator is *Axcellerant Blue,* a
knowledge management tool.
Axcellerant Blue allows various
work groups within the IT
department to better understand
the company's software assets, to
organize these assets, and then
to share and reuse these assets.
Each large company has hundreds or even thousands of programmers who write new code
every day for various applications. Previously, they had to
start from scratch each time
when writing code. *Axcellerant*

Here's your Board of Directors at Axcellerant. Not a patient bunch.

Blue allows programmers to search through existing software for the
purpose of identifying a program that can be leveraged for pending
needs. *Axcellerant Blue* then allows programmers to use the existing
program's proven code as a basis for new programs. No more starting
from scratch. No more reinventing the wheel. Much more reliable
code is used.

Don't worry if you do not understand what you just read. Just
understand that *Axcellerant Blue* is the type of innovation that can and
will lead to a productivity revolution within large IT departments. It can
save millions of dollars.

Axcellerant Blue should be easy to sell. It solves a wide range of problems for Fortune 1000 companies, such as:

- Reducing redundancy of effort, allowing programmers to get
  significantly more work done in less time.
- Dramatically decreasing the frequency and impact of painful
  quality problems that accompany new software programs.
- Providing faster turnaround of new programming initiatives and
  projects.

Even more exciting for you is that the sales team you have inherited
consists of veterans with tremendous success selling software solutions in

the late 1990s. A great fit for selling *Axcellerant Blue,* right? Your prede-cessor certainly thought so when hiring them. Axcellerant also has a strong market position versus competitors, although the market is highly underdeveloped.

Your new position with Axcellerant is a layup. A veteran sales team selling a customizable product that everyone needs and . . . I guess we forgot to mention . . . that generates a staggering and quantifiable ROI for most implementers in a reasonable period of time. This should be the easiest management position you've ever had—or will have.

But it isn't. Six months in, the pressure is mounting, you've missed conservative sales goals in two consecutive quarters, and the venture capitalists backing you are beginning to expect a bottom line anywhere in the black. What's going wrong?

Your salespeople are getting in plenty of new doors with high-ranking IT executives (people who can say "yes") and are entertaining a lot of interest. Unfortunately, this interest isn't turning into new busi-ness revenue.

Why?

To understand why your sales team is failing, let's identify some of the symptoms:

- *Your salespeople are still opportunistic, but they are blaming their poor results on the product, service, pricing, and the overall economy.* You are beginning to listen to their protests because you believe they have good skills and methodologies (everyone has been through SPIN Selling, Strategic Selling, and/or Solution Selling training programs).
- *You are clearly not losing sales to competitors.* That's good, isn't it? Most of the sales are being lost to buyer inaction. After what tends to be very lengthy selling cycles, you and your salespeople are constantly running into the same wall. Prospects tell you they are not ready to change. Are they feigning interest? Maybe. Buyers seem to prefer the status quo to your substantial and impressive value proposition.
- *Multiple and logical strategies that have worked for you in the past are failing.* You have tried selling to different vertical channels, enter-ing at various management levels, team selling versus having the

sales team face the market individually. You have also created multiple demonstration strategies, including tailoring demonstrations to each audience.

Okay, those are the primary symptoms. The clock is ticking. What is the illness? Just as important, what's the remedy?

Don't know? Take a few minutes to write down what the root cause is and what your next strategy will be to correct the Axcellerant ship. Remember, you may be frustrated, but as the VP of sales, you are paid to solve these problems. So . . . solve them. Quickly!

Just for fun, take your notes that you've just scribbled and paper clip them to the back cover of this book. When you have finished reading the book, look at these notes and ask, "Is my strategy appropriate for Axcellerant?" and "What is the best strategy based on what I now know?"

Our firm, Sogistics, works with selling and management teams on removing impediments to growth. Quite often, our clients know they have a sales productivity problem, but they're just not sure what is causing the undesirable outcome. This was the case at one of our Texas-based clients that we've named Axcellerant in order to protect its identity. Fortunately for Axcellerant and Sogistics, the real VP of sales and marketing is a strong leader who is open to new ideas and change. If its business model holds true, Axcellerant will be a profitable, fast-track company for a long time because of how he rebuilt the sales team's foundation with the concepts presented in this book.

Your Board of Directors needs your response now. They've formulated their own action plan just in case they don't like your answers.

Throughout the 17 years of Sogistics' existence, we have worked with more than a few organizations—all of whom market an offering that:

- Could make a critical impact on the buyer's situation.
- Requires a mid-to-long selling cycle.
- Is difficult to sell due to the buyer's resistance to incur the high costs of change.

For many of our clients, their offerings also represent a discretionary new application to the potential buyer.

Needless to say, the problems experienced by Axcellerant were not unique. In fact, they are far too common. We've witnessed these same problems in widely disparate, seemingly unrelated, companies and industries.

The problems faced by Axcellerant and most of our clients are not simply a result of a poor business model, ineffective marketing, or a lack of leadership. Nor are these constraints entirely due to having hired the wrong salespeople. It would be easy to blame any of these factors, but our instincts, research, and past experience clearly indicate otherwise.

Instead, Axcellerant's problems were due to one reason: strategic misalignment. That is, their sales process did not adapt to their buyers' cycles of demand. Most of the sales teams we work with don't realize that buyers' decision processes change dramatically from one demand type to the next.

The Strategy of Demand and Psychology

Being a good salesperson is no longer enough to be effective in a major account sales environment. Not even close. Not anymore.

Now, buyers will not buy from salespeople—nor give them their time. Buyers require salespeople to be more. Much more. To be *businesspeople who sell*. Remember, when you are selling an offering that commands a significant investment, forces buyers to incur high costs of change, and creates significant perceived risk for the buying organization, the decision maker isn't going to be a tactical, low-level manager. The decision maker

> For our purposes, *demand* is the means and intention of a population of buyers to purchase a given offering.

is going to be a high-level executive. Therefore, being a salesperson who is foremost a businessperson means being more strategic, and speaking the language of finance and economics.

The content of this book represents best practices. To develop your sales team into a differentiating, best-in-market force, your sales team must understand and adopt the concepts, methodologies, and strategic frameworks contained in the next 200-plus pages. It won't be easy, and it will certainly take some time. This book will stretch your people and accelerate the development of their business acumen.

With that being said, we introduce the definition of demand as it applies to major account selling, an important concept for *Selling Is Dead*.

Demand drives every company's economic engine. Interestingly, the demand for most offerings is cyclical. Understanding the *cycles of demand* can explain one company's growth and prosperity. It can also explain another company's decline and extinction.

Demand for specific products or services moves through distinct cycles (each later explored in greater detail):

1. *New application demand.* The first purchase of a category of product or service. It is a discontinuous purchase for the buyer. (By *discontinuous,* we mean there is typically no existing infrastructure in place at buying organizations to support such an application.)
2. *Aggregate demand.* Purchases of additional quantities of the new product or service.
3. *Continuous improvement demand.* Purchasing the bigger-better-faster version of a product or service.
4. *Economy demand.* Purchasing a down market, lower cost, no-frills version of a product or service already being used.

These four demand types create the four different types of large sales. As the buyer's demand type changes, the buyer's decision process changes. As buyers change the way they make decisions, sellers must adjust their sales process and strategies to realign with buyers and their decision-making process.

Salespeople are purveyors of demand. In essence, a salesperson is in the business of creating, servicing, and managing buyer demand—in many cases, all four types of demand. They serve no greater purpose for their organizations.

Yet, very few salespeople understand the nature of demand, let alone adjust from one type to another. From interviewing thousands of salespeople in our behavioral assessment business at Sogistics, we know that most salespeople apply the same rigid selling process over and over—regardless of the buyer demand type. This is the Number One killer of selling opportunities. With buyers moving through multiple demand types and sellers utilizing only one, inflexible process, it is obvious that sellers are often misaligned with buyers.

Sellers and their companies are not the only ones who suffer. Prospective buyers remain just that—prospects. These companies never realize the gains of new innovations that might lead to increased revenues, decreased cost structure, or strengthened competitive advantage. No win-win here. Instead, lose-lose.

Understanding the cycles of demand enables selling teams to create superior market-facing strategies that work better for both buyer and seller. These strategies are never based on a rigid, step-by-step, linear selling process. Rather, a cycles of demand strategy prefers flexibility, which manifests in two ways:

1. Adjustment to how a prospect's decision-making process changes from one demand type to another.
2. Alignment to the psychological needs of buyers—needs that are unique to the demand type currently unfulfilled.

In essence, understanding the cycles of demand—and each demand type's corresponding decision steps—gives salespeople a more solid strategic footing. This foundation allows selling teams to build a better path to new customers, maximize each selling opportunity, and experience customer abundance in a world of customer scarcity.

The Cycles of Demand

Let's dig into each of the cycles of demand a little further. Keep in mind that each requires its own selling strategy, tactics, and framework. With each type, we'll begin by briefly focusing on some basic consumer-related examples to help you understand the concepts. Subsequently, we'll move on to some larger, more relevant, demand-type examples.

Demand Type 1: New Application Demand

Most of you reading this book don't sell smaller-ticket offerings such as microwaves or phones to end users. You are major account sellers. The price tag for your products or services may be $10,000 on the low end or $1,000,000-plus on the high end. You already have one strike against you because a high price tag represents high perceived risk to the buyer. A poor decision to go forward would jeopardize a great deal of capital and be hard to sweep under the rug. Larger investments are higher profile within the buying organization and are expected to yield a healthy return. The greater the investment, the greater the buyer reluctance.

Remember your first cordless phone? If not, ask your neighbors. Your conversations were broadcast to every cordless phone owner within a 10-minute walk. Your first cell phone may be laughable now. It was basically a brick and it continuously dropped its signal, but you were glad you had it, anyway. How about your first desktop printer? It was a bubble jet. One color (black) and one page per minute. Then there was your first microwave. No revolving plate. No popcorn button.

Each of these firsts was significant. They each represented a new application for you. Despite their drawbacks and limitations by today's standards, they offered you new capabilities. A way to roam through a section of your house while talking to your sister-in-law from Baltimore. A way to conveniently communicate while you were mobile. A way to print hard copies of your work while at home or without having to leave your plush office chair. A way to prepare a warm dinner for your hungry kids more quickly before running off to ball practice. The cordless phone, the cell phone, the desktop printer, and the microwave were a means to an end: reducing personal productivity constraints, improving your quality of life, etc.

If, in addition to selling big-ticket offerings, they also represent new applications for buyers . . . Strike 2. Selling pricey new applications is the most challenging scenario in sales. It's also the most rewarding. New applications are the drivers behind significant productivity gains and markedly better business results. Simply, new applications demand is the economic catalyst that creates entire new industries. These new industries spur countless new companies, jobs, and wealth.

New applications can take many forms: a new process, system, technology, product, project, or service. Many salespeople spend the majority of their time in the domain of selling new applications. Selling new applications requires salespeople to convince individuals or organizations to *change* significantly or dramatically from the comfort of the status quo as a means to realize some desired result. The desired result is either the removal of a dissatisfaction or the achievement of some objective (in simple terms, of course).

Because change is inherent in selling new applications, the process of selling often becomes very complex. Prospects may be curious about the offering, but resistant to change. The wheels start spinning, but this change avoidance allows inertia to set in. Resistance to change can be caused by several factors. Implementation of a new application can take weeks or months of aggravation. Learning curves can be steep. The buyer may have to undergo a transformation—either departmentally or organizationally. Disruption. Disruption. Disruption. Furthermore, the buyer and seller must forge an intimate relationship for success to be achieved.

From the buyer's vantage point, the costs of change are usually significant enough that most prospects remain just that—prospects. In effect, the safety of the status quo is a stronger allure than the potential benefits of the solution. And the seller—well, the seller loses the frustrating battle to "no decision."

New application selling means that what is being sold meets two criteria:

- The offering is a new application to the buyer; it has currently not been adopted by the buyer.
- The new application is a new concept, often a paradigm shift, for the buyer.

Furthermore, in most new application scenarios, the buyer lacks the necessary knowledge, skills, expertise, or infrastructure to readily support the new application. Thus, adopting the new application requires serious commitment since the change costs accompanying the new application are so high.

An interesting example of companies facing the challenges of selling new applications are in order.

New Application Demand Case Study: PCi Corporation

Alternatively, and less frequently, a new application is not discretionary. For example, a new application may not be discretionary when a new state or federal regulation forces some industries to adopt a new technology or process. New regulations often force buyers to make a full commitment to a new application. For instance, in 2002, states and municipalities began proliferating their own predatory lending laws, forcing lending institutions to adhere to a rapidly expanding number of regional and local laws. PCi, a Boston-based company and the nation's dominant lending compliance software company, released a new product called Wiz Sentinel that helps banks adhere to the multitude of new state and local predatory lending laws. Large lending institutions had little or no choice but to fully commit to new predatory lending compliance products such as Wiz Sentinel. No opportunity for a beta existed.

New Application Triggers
New applications can originate from a variety of drivers. However, new applications often stem from disruptions in the market.

Our favorite classification of these disruptive new application triggers comes from Adams Capital Management, a national venture capital firm headquartered in Pittsburgh, Pennsylvania, that focuses on disruptive technologies in the information technology and telecommunications/semiconductors industries. Adams Capital Management's categorization system was described to us by Martin "Chuck" Neath, a general partner with the firm. This system, which serves as a basis for Adams' investment strategy, organizes disruptive technologies into four categories: technical discontinuity, regulatory discontinuity, standard discontinuity, and distribution discontinuity. On its website, Adams defines discontinuities as "rapid and permanent structural changes in established markets."

Bending Adams Capital Management's categories of disruptions to suit the purposes of this book, we describe the four most common triggers of new applications:

1. *Technical disruption.* This type of disruption comes from the introduction of innovative, new-to-the-world technologies. Software reuse technologies is a useful example. Never before were software programmers able to recycle and reuse code from previously written applications.
2. *Regulatory disruption.* The introduction of state, federal, and international regulations are common triggers for new applications. Regulations can force organizations to adopt new practices or alter existing practices. PCi's Wiz Sentinel is an example. The insurgence of state and local predatory lending laws began to force lending institutions to scrutinize their lending activities on a state and local basis and conform to those laws. Lenders had to turn to sophisticated software such as Wiz Sentinel to help them comply to the new legislation and avoid regulatory problems.
3. *Standard disruptions.* These disruptions occur as new applications or platforms gain acceptance, such as the Java programming language. Another example of a standard disruption is cellular technology, a platform currently accessed by over 1 billion cell phone users. New applications leveraging this new standard communication platform include wireless Internet service providers, wireless content providers, fleet-tracking systems, and corporate communications systems.
4. *Distribution disruptions.* New methods and mechanisms for distributing goods and services spawn new applications. The rise of sophisticated, e-commerce-enabled websites allowed Dell to innovate in marketing PCs. Other new applications stemming from e-commerce distribution disruption include selling books and other media online (Amazon), renting DVDs online (Netflix), and online auctions (eBay).

Demand Type 2: Aggregate Demand

Once an individual or organization embraces a new application, either after an initial beta or full commitment, they often want additional quantities of the same. The buyer has already received at least a taste. They have first-hand experience of a better way, and are now educated. If the buyer has only completed a beta, there may still be some costs of change for a full rollout. However, those costs are less significant than they were prior to the beta. Regardless of the nature of the first purchase, the buyer's perceived risk associated with additional scale or volume of the new application is substantially reduced.

A few examples are in order.

In the 1980s, I (Marc Miller) sold a dry-film laminating system to book printers. A laminating system applies a clear film onto book covers to improve gloss and scuff resistance. Back then, book printers such as RR Donnelley, Doubleday, and W.A. Kreuger would generally send out their covers to a trade laminating service. Our concept was simple: laminate in-house instead of farming the work outside. Our equipment was automated, fairly simple to operate, and produced a quality product.

Unfortunately, producing this type of work in-house was a new paradigm for book printers. Our dry-film technology was considered radical—adding to the skepticism and reticence of printers curious about laminating their work in-house with our equipment. It took a lot of hard work to convince printers to buy that first system. Buyers needed vast amounts of testing, demonstrations, etc. . . . It all added

You bought that second cordless phone despite your eavesdropping neighbors. You had one in the kitchen, but you thought it would be nice to have one in your bedroom as well. Despite their imperfections, you bought additional cell phones. You felt better knowing your spouse, your parents, or your children had access to a cell phone in the event of an emergency. You also purchased a second desktop printer. Your printer at work was a necessity, but one at home was a worthwhile luxury. How about that second microwave? You sent the old one off to college with your oldest daughter. You wanted the new one for yourself.

In each example, you were comfortable with the results of your first purchase, leading you to make additional purchases.

up to a fairly rigorous selling cycle before the first system sale was consummated.

However, once a book manufacturer bought one system and tried it, the manufacturer usually loved it. Book manufacturers began earning a reasonable ROI within 12 months. Job cycles sped up. Quality and control increased because the laminating process could be done more easily in-house. Often, this would lead to orders for additional systems. The real work for me was in selling the *first* system (which could take many months, even years). After that, it was simply a process of taking orders. Those reorders represent a classic example of *aggregate demand*.

Let's return to the Axcellerant example. Axcellerant sells a knowledge/software management tool that enables software reuse. For Axcellerant, once an initial software reuse project was successfully implemented with a new customer, aggregate demand would kick in. Buyers would want to make the tool available for more programmers and for different divisions and for different internal processes. For instance, software reuse might be originally purchased to speed up the engineering department's ability to design new products. Once successfully implemented, a Fortune 1000 company would often order additional systems in areas such as customer service, operations, or knowledge management. In essence, once a company was sold on the concept of reuse, it often ordered additional systems to satisfy its growing appetite for the application.

Demand isn't just proprietary to the business-to-business sale. On a consumer level, DVD players are a good example of both new application and aggregate demands. DVD players have clearly gone mainstream—gradually and then quickly replacing VCR technology. A first-time buyer of a DVD player is trying a new application. After that buyer experiences the DVD player, he eventually behaves exactly as Mitsubishi, Sony, and Panasonic desire by ordering additional systems to replace the remaining VCRs in the home. DVD manufacturers depend on aggregate demand, as do MGM and Universal Studios who produce the movie consumables played in the new DVD boxes.

DVD manufacturing companies have become less focused on convincing households to adopt the new application (DVD technology) with first-time purchases. Increasingly, their selling and marketing strategies are shifting to reflect the challenges of generating aggregate

demand, which is their new growth engine. Unless marketing and selling strategies shift to address aggregate demand, growth will not be
optimized.

Aggregate demand is a wonderful economic engine. Remember,
once a new application emerges, it often eradicates the old application
(dry-laminating systems replaced solvent systems and DVD players
replaced VCRs). And once buyers taste success from the new application, they often want more. As many salespeople have told us, the easiest sale is typically when buyers order additional quantities because it's
an easy decision for the buyer to want more success after initial achievement has been realized. Many sellers depend on the second, third . . .
twentieth order from the same buying organization.

Another factor that drives aggregate demand is *replacement*. Equipment, products, and services wear out over time through natural attrition
or planned obsolescence. When this occurs, many buyers simply reorder
the identical or upgraded offering. Also, many successful industries have
been built on the residuals around new applications. *Residuals*—those
products and services needed to support a new application—are another
form of aggregate demand. For example, the film supplies needed to run
our laminating system kept many plastic film companies busy.

Once an application has been fully adopted, buyers' resistance to
change is actually an advantage for salespeople who sell aggregate
demand. After buyers embrace and implement a new concept, process,
or technology, they must invest in the necessary infrastructure to support
it. Due to this investment, buyers are more apt to buy additional quantities of that same application than to go down the more difficult path of
changing to another new application.

Commoditization is the danger of reliance on aggregate demand.
Once close substitutes emerge, competition is realized and buyers can
begin shopping around. Buyers are now sophisticated and knowledgeable.

Demand Type 3: Continuous Improvement Demand

Buyers are almost always interested in bigger-better-faster ways of doing
existing applications. After all, they've invested in the new application
infrastructure. Keeping it current makes perfect sense.

You eventually bought a better cordless phone. It had such features as redial, speed dial, and large buttons. Even better, your neighbors could no longer listen in. New features were added to cell phones as well. You treated yourself to a high-end cell phone that was small, lightweight, and able to take digital pictures and access the Internet. You also purchased a new desktop printer at work. This time it was a color printer that used wax-emulsion ink. The quality was outstanding; the throughput a blazing six pages per minute. Your next microwave was no less impressive. It had a touch pad user interface. It was twice as big. Three times as powerful. You could watch your meal spin on a rotating plate. Oh, it had a popcorn button, too. With each of these purchases, your life got bigger-better-faster. You paid a bit more for the extra features—but it was worth it.

Continuous improvement demand, the third demand type, satisfies this need. In effect, once a new process, product, or service has been adopted (new application demand) and additional quantity has been satisfied (aggregate demand), the third type of demand may kick in—continuous improvement. We say *may* because there is a fourth—and final—demand type that a buyer sometimes prefers. We'll discuss this soon.

Continuous improvement demand is driven by a buyer's thirst for higher-quality solutions. This demand type is especially prevalent with buyers who see the application as important to their current or future situation. Because they view the application as somewhat critical, they are more apt to consider paying for improvements. In behavioral terms, after becoming aware of a new capability, the buyer becomes dissatisfied enough with the current situation to consider upgrading. Often, the existing version fails to totally meet their needs, so higher quality or additional features are desired. Examples:

- *CRM technology.* The senior VP of sales sees the current customer relationship manager database as key to future competitiveness. This individual is frustrated that the current CRM software is not web based and is more suited for contact—not account—management. A change is seriously considered.
- *Production line change.* An operations manager at a large food manufacturer is intrigued by a new packaging line that improves productivity by 40 percent. This would be a significant upgrade over

the existing line. Since the company considers packaging to be a core competency, this potential improvement is being seriously discussed.

- *Outsourced IT service.* A CIO is considering changing from the local vendor to a more expensive, national IT firm. Although the national firm is pricier, the CIO likes some of the new platforms and functionality of its service. Since this CIO's company is placing huge bets on using technology to create competitive advantage, the CIO seriously considers this continuous improvement change.

The key with all three examples is that an existing application is in place, but the buyer is considering a potentially better total solution for the application. In other words, the buyer is contemplating making a continuous change relative to the application in question.

Clayton Christensen, in his excellent book *The Innovator's Solution,* writes of sustaining innovations as one type of innovation.[4] Sustaining innovations are comparable to continuous improvement. They are neither radical nor discontinuous. They do not represent huge paradigm shifts. They are simply improvements of what is currently being used or done.

From a selling perspective, continuous improvement can take different forms:

- Trying to create a new customer by dislodging the existing incumbent with your better offering in a given application domain.
- Attempting to persuade an existing customer to adopt your improved product, service, or capability within a given application domain. This higher-quality version would make the buyer's situation more convenient, cost effective, easier, or more productive, and possibly expand the buyer's capabilities.

With continuous improvement demand, the buyer might experience significant resistance, stemming from both financial and change costs. However, expect this resistance to be much less severe than what is typically associated with new applications. The learning curve with a continuously improved offering is less steep, and the infrastructure around existing applications is usually more adaptable to a continuously improved offering than a completely new application.

Demand Type 4: Economy Demand

These scenarios describe our fourth, and final, demand type: *economy demand*. Economy demand occurs when buyers feel overserved by the current offering. As a result, a more cost–effective alternative better serves the buyer. The cheaper and more convenient offering may lack many of the features, benefits, and functionality of the original or other market alternatives, but the buyer is more than happy to trade off these extras for a reduced cost.

Economy demand has a simple value proposition: *lower cost!* People like the sticker price in this category. These buyers don't want

Last year, you completed an addition to your home. You built a small Florida room. You wanted a phone in this room. However, because you and your family will only be using the room occasionally to sit and relax, a feature-rich cordless phone was unnecessary. Instead, you bought an inexpensive corded phone.

Cell phones have become a necessity for your business. You decided to provide company cell phones for members of your sales team. The most advanced cell phones that incorporated extravagant features such as the ability to take pictures were not necessary. You purchased basic model cell phones that offered the lowest pricing for unlimited minutes.

Two years ago, you loved the new color printer you purchased for your work office. Recently, your home printer needed to be replaced. But you didn't use your previous printer nearly as much as you anticipated. And when you did, it was typically just to print a few digital pictures. The printer you use at work is a high-quality, fast machine, but ink supplies are almost double the cost you initially expected. You could have purchased the model you have at work, or the latest super deluxe 20-pages-per-minute printer, but you went with the bargain 4-pages-per-minute color printer with lower quality, but lower cost, consumables. It was good enough.

After destroying your large microwave with aluminum foil, you had to replace it. Because the kids have moved away and you and your spouse eat out more frequently, a large, automated unit that literally speaks to you was unnecessary. You chose the smallest, cheapest, and simplest to use model you could find.

You also fly Southwest Airlines now. Yes, it's no-frills, functional transportation. No meals or reserved seating. But it's significantly less expensive than the other two major airlines that fly out of your local airport. Your goal is to get from point A to point B—and Southwest fills the bill nicely.

fancy—just give them a functional, reliable alternative that saves them money.

What drives economy demand in the business world? In one word . . . change. Business climates change rapidly. New competitors, mergers, acquisitions, new innovations, leadership changes, and soft economies are all immediately disruptive elements to a business. As a result, a business application that is considered important one moment can quickly be perceived as less significant or less valuable the next. This type of disruption may cause an organization to immediately consider downsizing, downscaling, or dumbing down an application—all good descriptions of economy demand. For instance:

- A large manufacturer decides to shift its channel strategy from selling direct to selling through distributors. As a result, it has decided that advertising and lead generation are less important to future success. On that basis, they decide to switch from their current nationally known advertising/PR firm to a much less expensive, good-enough local firm.
- A midsized medical equipment manufacturer had been using a sophisticated CRM solution that was capable of linking with its enterprise system. Unfortunately, the company's small IT staff continually had difficulties customizing the CRM to the needs and processes of the sales team. As a result, the company replaced its existing CRM with a simpler, cheaper, and more customizable CRM solution. Although the new CRM was not as sophisticated in terms of its enterprise-wide linkages and other functionality, it was good enough.

Being the low-cost leader is the mantra of the economy demand seller. While continuous improvement demand sellers hang their hats on sustaining new cycles of improved innovation, the economy demand proponent takes a different strategic path. Economy demand sellers understand that not all buyers appreciate the same value. Their foothold is gained by offering the most cost-efficient, good-enough alternative. "No-frills, lower costs" is their battle cry to customers. And, once a market beachhead is secured, these sellers work hard to stay lean and mean as a way to maintain their value leadership in this fourth and final demand type.

And the Cycle May Go On . . . And On . . . And On

The cycles of demand can be never-ending. A buyer invests in a new application to create one of four scenarios:

1. The buyer stays put. No more demand is created past the initial application. In effect, this one-time purchase sates demand completely. In this scenario, the cycle does not continue indefinitely.
2. The buyer purchases more of the same application (aggregate demand). The buyer is, in effect, content to purchase the same basic offering, most likely from the incumbent.
3. The buyer purchases an offering that improves the application (continuous improvement demand). This improvement may come in the form of added functionality, capability, new features, added seats, and so on.
4. The buyer decides the existing application overserves its needs. As a result, a decision is made to scale down to a more cost-effective version that is good enough.

Unless a certain job is altogether eliminated, the cycles will continue until another new application is introduced that replaces the old way of doing the job. The new application begins a whole new cycle of demand that will most likely end when a new, new application replaces it.

Two Broad Categories of Demand Cycles

To further organize the four cycles of demand, they fall under two broad categories. This division is notable.

Before explaining, how would you organize the four demand cycles? Can you see a common thread shared by some of them? Take a moment to think about it before continuing.

Aggregate, continuous improvement, and economy demand offerings share a commonality not possessed by new application demand.
These three demand types indicate that the buyer wants to continue
using some version of an existing category of application:

- *Aggregate demand offerings.* Exact same version of the *existing* application used by the buyer.
- *Continuous improvement demand offerings.* An improved version
  (bigger, faster, more features, etc.) of an *existing* category of application used by the buyer.
- *Economy demand offerings.* A scaled-down version (cheaper, more
  efficient, etc.) of an *existing* category of application used by the
  buyer.

In other words, all three of these demand types fall under the generally accepted or normal way the buyer is currently doing a job.
Therefore, with these demand types, the knowledge, infrastructure,
capability, systems, resources, and budgets are already in place to support the application . . . more or less. This method of doing things is
accepted and rarely questioned.

We label this first broad category of demand type offerings ***concurrent offerings.*** Again, the three demand types (aggregate, continuous
improvement, and economy) in this category all represent consistent or
parallel ways of doing an existing application.

Contrast *concurrent offerings* with *new application demand* offerings.
Whereas concurrent offerings represent a consistent (although possibly
somewhat varied) way of doing a job, new applications represent an
inconsistent or discontinuous way of doing a job already being done (or
perhaps a job not currently being done at all). Rather than parallel or
concurrent, new applications are divergent. Thus, the second broad category of demand type offerings, and the sole province of new application demand offerings, is called ***divergent offerings.***

With divergent offerings (essentially new application offerings), the
buyer does not possess the knowledge, infrastructure, capability, systems,
resources, or budget to support them. Therefore, from *both* the buyer's
and seller's perspective, divergent offerings and concurrent offerings
must be approached differently. This is a significant, fundamental lesson
repeated in this book.

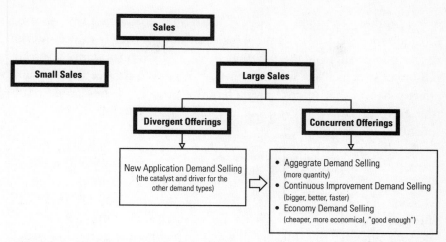

Figure 1.3 The four types of buyer demand fall under two broad categories of offerings: concurrent and divergent.

A new model for major account selling is taking shape. Figure 1.3 graphically illustrates the key points thus far.

Selling Tangible versus Intangible Offerings

Neil Rackham's book *SPIN Selling* is a landmark because it distinguishes large sales from small sales and claims they need to be treated uniquely. *Selling Is Dead* is a landmark because it distinguishes four types of large sales, which each needs to be treated uniquely. However, some people believe that tangible and intangible offerings need to be sold differently. Our question: Do you think best practices dictate that tangible offerings should be sold differently from intangible offerings, and vice versa?

It's an interesting question. Much has been written in sales training books about the difference in selling tangible offerings (hard products) versus intangible offerings (soft services). In fact, in terms of tangibility versus intangibility, we often hear salespeople comment that they are much better at selling one versus the other.

Yet our assessments of thousands of salespeople (using our behavioral assessment methodology) suggest there is little or no difference in the proper process used to sell an intangible versus a tangible product or service. Think of it from the perspective of the buyer: The buyer simply uses a product (tangible) or service (intangible) to accomplish a specific job and achieve a desired result. The buyer does not really care about the nature of the offering and whether it has a physical substance. Instead, the buyer's focus is on whether the job is getting done efficiently and effectively. In other words, buyers buy the concept of the desired result (the end), regardless of whether the offering is tangible or intangible (means to the end).

Interestingly, the sellers' instinct that some types of sales are fundamentally different from other types of sales is actually correct. However, these sellers are incorrect in their belief that these differences lie in whether the offering being sold is tangible or intangible. Rather, sales differ based on whether the sale is large or small and, with regard to large sales, on whether the offering is a divergent or a concurrent offering. Thus, there should be no separate model or selling approach for tangible and intangible offerings.

Demand Versatility

Salespeople know that they are in the business of creating and managing selling opportunities. Furthermore, they know that an opportunity can only come from one of three places:

- ◆ Existing customers
- ◆ Former customers
- ◆ Noncustomers

This is the *opportunity universe.*

Demand, on the other hand, can only originate from the buyer. Highly effective salespeople understand that demand manifests in one of four ways:

- ◆ New application demand
- ◆ Aggregate demand
- ◆ Continuous improvement demand
- ◆ Economy demand

This is the *demand universe.*

Ideally, an effective salesperson keeps a *balanced mix* across both the opportunity universe and demand universe. Salespeople who can navigate all four demand types effectively have tremendous value to their organization. They score high in demand versatility.

As an example, consider a top salesperson at an IT consulting firm. Let's call her Pat. Here are the selling opportunities she is currently working on:

- Create *new application demand* with a *noncustomer.* Pat is attempting to convince a mid-market prospect to outsource its IT department to her firm. Outsourcing is a new application for the buyer. In fact, it's a paradigm shift. This would be a huge IT project worth millions of dollars to Pat's company.
- Gain *aggregate demand* with an *existing customer.* This buyer is considering giving Pat's company expanded responsibilities in some other divisions of the company. The first project worked so well that they are considering more.
- Sell *continuous improvement demand* to a *former customer.* This buyer left Pat's company to do business with a competitor 3 years ago. The experience with Pat's competitor has been less than stellar in terms of service and technical competence. Pat is currently trying to win the account back by showing the former customer a higher quality outsourcing solution, which includes greater responsiveness and the ability to take on a greater breadth of projects.
- Propose *economy demand* to an *overserved prospect.* Pat has found that a buyer does not require all the manpower applied by its previous IT outsource on a recent systems integration process, or the complexity of the solution. Pat shows the buyer how to cut the fat from the offering and save almost 40 percent on an upcoming IT project.

Best-practice selling requires separate models and methodologies for each demand cycle. We already claimed there are large differences between selling divergent offerings (new application demand) and concurrent offerings (aggregate, continuous improvement, and economy demand). However, there are also nuances among selling the three types of concurrent offerings as well.

For now, though, let's focus on the uniqueness of selling divergent offerings versus concurrent offerings. Table 1.1 details how the principle challenges of selling these two broad categories differ from each

Table 1.1 The Differences in Selling Concurrent versus Divergent Offerings

Selling Challenge	Concurrent Offerings	Divergent Offerings
Decision Makers	Mid-tier personnel. Decisions are made by one or a few individuals within a given buying organization.	Mid- and upper-tier personnel. Consensus decision among a larger group of decision makers within a given buying organization.
Major Challenge on an Opportunity-by-Opportunity Basis	Convincing a smaller number of mid-tier buyers to purchase more of the same version (aggregate), a more robust version (continuous improvement), or cheaper version (economy) of an existing offering. Regardless, the way the job is done does not fundamentally change. Typically, the challenge represents getting the mid-tier decision base to switch to a new vendor for a comparable method of doing a job.	Convincing a larger group of buyers from mid and upper tiers within the buyer organization to fundamentally change the way a job is currently being done, or to begin doing a new job altogether (risky).
Marketing Challenge	Unearth qualified leads of buyers who have active needs.	Getting salespeople in front of buyers who do not yet have active needs so they can begin building the case for change.
Primary Competition	Competitive solutions.	The buyer's resistance to change (buyer inertia).
Budget	Existing budget is in place for this category of offerings, although it may have to be revised when the demand type is continuous improvement.	No budget is currently in place—or even on the horizon—for this type of offering.

46

Infrastructure for Offering	Original investment in infrastructure is already made, so at least some infrastructure is in place.	No infrastructure is in place. Significant investment in infrastructure is required.
Buyer Perspective	Low-to-moderate risk in and around the decision to buy/change.	High organizational, departmental, and personal risk to buy/change.
Typical Buyer Motivation to Change	Problem removal or problem prevention of day-to-day issues.	Typically, both of the following are required: ◆ Opportunity to help the buyer better achieve critical goals and objectives. ◆ Problem removal or problem prevention of day-to-day issues or constraints.
Proposals	Product/service-focused proposals or quotes.	Proposals that build and demonstrate the business case for change first and then present the offering a distant second.
Buyer's Understanding of How to Make, and Confidence in Making, a Purchasing Decision	Moderate-to-high competence and confidence.	Low-to-moderate competence and confidence.
Entry Dynamics into New Opportunities	Attempting to get into a buying organization at high levels is actually a strategic mistake. Higher-ups have little interest in this category because they see the value around change as marginal.	Entry can be either at mid or upper tiers. Contrary to conventional sales folklore, mid-tier entry can be quite effective as long as a selling process is in place that eventually engages both higher-ups and other mid-tier vertical department managers.

Table 1.1 (Continued)

Selling Challenge	Concurrent Offerings	Divergent Offerings
Buyer Behavior Subsequent to Decision to Change	Once a decision to change has been made, most buyers will proactively shop the category by evaluating other vendors (although the level of shopping can be to varying degrees). The common exception is when the existing category vendor is perceived by the decision base as critical.	Once a decision to change has been made, which is typically due to the catalystic efforts of a change-agent salesperson, a buyer will most commonly not shop the competition. Rather, the buyer will continue to progress with the existing seller, and the buyer's next driving psychology around decision making focuses on the buyer's desire to hedge its bets and reduce risk around the seller's new application offerings. Risk must be mitigated before a full rollout can be commenced.

other. You should begin to see from Table 1.1 how and why sellers must possess demand versatility.

The impact the cycles of demand can have on selling teams is often profound. Once understood, better paths can be built to new customers that work infinitely better for both buyer and seller.

Keep in mind that many companies sell a portfolio of offerings with varying degrees of maturity. Each new offering, if successful, will evolve over its useful life, satisfying new application demand, then aggregate demand, then continuous improvement demand after being enhanced, and, finally, economy demand after going down market to serve buyers who are overserved.

Case Study: One Salesperson's Difficult Adjustment to Selling Divergent Offerings

Selling divergent offerings is more difficult than selling concurrent offerings, and requires a separate set of models and strategies in order to be effective. Many sellers are effective at selling concurrent offerings (existing applications), but struggle to be consistently successful at selling divergent offerings (new applications). If you don't believe us, ask Laura Leggett.

Laura is a senior account executive for the RoviSys Company, a multi-faceted technology firm that provides tailored process automation and information systems for a diverse client base. Prior to joining RoviSys, Laura worked for a company that sold high-end phone systems to large and midsize companies. These phone systems almost exclusively represented existing applications, or concurrent offerings, to her customers.

At RoviSys, Laura's primary responsibility was selling a product called GrandView, a business software tool for organizations that operate in a multiple-project environment. It helps organizations (such as pharmaceutical companies, software developers, engineering firms, etc.) manage multiple projects by blending project management functionality, scheduling, automated communication tools, collaboration tools, library and project history functions, and much more in an online solution.

GrandView represented a divergent offering (new application) for the vast majority of Laura's prospects. These organizations usually managed their projects with much more narrow project management software such as Microsoft Project, or through unsophisticated combinations of Excel spreadsheets, e-mail, and Post-it notes. GrandView was a fundamental shift in how

(continued)

these organizations managed their multiple projects. It forced them to adopt an entirely new and more consistent project methodology. The ROI, though, is significant for organizations that make this leap to GrandView.

After attending one of our seminars that discussed the differences in selling divergent and concurrent offerings, Laura e-mailed us. She wrote, "The seminar was very helpful, and validating in terms of selling divergent offerings. I've been trying to figure out why it was much easier to sell $100,000 phone systems in my previous life than it's been to sell GrandView at a small fraction of that price. I never adjusted my approach to selling when I came to RoviSys and began selling GrandView. I realized what I was trying to do wasn't working, but I didn't know how to adjust my process until I saw your divergent offering models."

Although GrandView doesn't force organizations to incur high financial costs, it does make them incur high change costs. It forces them to work differently and communicate differently. Because GrandView was a divergent way of managing projects, buyers experience higher levels of risk in the decision process. Therefore, Laura will have to adjust to a divergent offering approach if she is to be successful selling GrandView.

A New World Order for Selling Teams

The theme of this book is that selling teams have not adjusted well to an economy in which demand cycles at an ever-dizzying pace. Very few teams know how to sell new application demand effectively. As a result, and considering that new application sales represent the economic driver for most companies, selling teams have become lower value-adding functions to their organizations.

The paradox is that organizations are increasingly more dependent on their sales and marketing teams than ever before. They rely on salespeople to sell innovation and create demand, because demand for new and innovative offerings is increasingly the lifeblood of a company (and source for more robust profit margins).

The cycles of demand approach to major account sales is based on our 17 years of work in sales productivity as well as formal research. Our premise is sixfold:

1. Selling strategy and skills change dramatically depending on whether the offering being sold represents a concurrent or divergent offering to the buyer.

2. The category of offering being sold determines the buyer's decision-making process; that is, buying behavior changes from concurrent to divergent offerings because buyer needs vary so significantly across the demand spectrum.

3. A salesperson's productivity will directly correlate with:
   a. The number of demand types one can successfully navigate (called *demand versatility*).
   b. The salesperson's ability to influence buyer demand throughout the buyer's decision making process (called *demand influence*).

4. Sales, as a profession, has been disrupted. This is causing sales teams to radically change the way they face their markets: they must adopt new roles and strategies. Also, salespeople's value to an organization is increasingly based on their ability to create all four types of demand with buyers where none existed before. Creating demand will be especially critical in new application selling where buyer contentedness (I'm satisfied), ignorance (I don't know what I don't know), or inertia (Why change?) are the real obstacles to sales success.

5. The large majority of salespeople lack the knowledge, expertise, and skills necessary to create buyer demand, especially when selling new applications. Although 90 percent of all salespeople describe their approach as consultative, few truly are. Our work in interviewing thousands of salespeople suggests that only a tiny percentage understand how to accomplish the most critical of all selling competencies—selling new applications and innovation.

6. Last, organizations will increasingly succeed or fail based on the market-facing ability of their sales team. A poor sales team will experience customer scarcity, while an effective sales team will experience customer abundance. Taking an identical business model, one sales team will see limited market opportunities. They will complain about buyer resistance, lack of leads, and limited brand awareness. Another sales team faced with the same challenges will experience endless opportunity because of its ability to create selling opportunities where none existed before. This opportunity creation is done not in a buyer's office, but in the only place possible—in the buyer's mind. *Buyer psychology is*

Salespeople play checkers (linear and tactical). Businesspeople who sell play chess (non-linear and strategic).

the new playing field for selling teams—where the real market battles will be won or lost.

Final Thoughts before Moving On

For too long, salespeople have been playing checkers where chess is the game necessary for success. The pervasive relationship and consultative selling methodology of yesteryear will not work for companies today—especially companies attempting to differentiate and succeed on the basis of innovation and new applications.

Selling Is Dead provides direction for creating and managing each type of demand. However, it primarily focuses on how to best sell divergent offerings. Of the four types of demand, selling innovative new applications, especially radical, nonmainstream offerings where buyer risk is high, is inarguably the most difficult.

This book is for people who want to go beyond consultative selling and become high-value-adding *businesspeople who sell*. Those who embrace the strategic principles of this book will see the world they sell in as one of opportunity and abundance. There will always be challenges and occasional frustrations, but these businesspeople who sell will be far better off than their dysfunctional counterparts who are plagued with self-inflicted sales productivity problems.

It's your choice. Which direction will you take?

A Preview of What's to Come, and What You Will Learn

We now want to provide a road map for where this book takes you. Here's a quick synopsis of what you'll learn in each section.

Section I: Building Your New Growth Engine

Your effort begins with the acceptance that the engine driving your sales growth may be inefficient or underpowered. The result is less than optimal sales performance. In Section I, you will learn the key components of a best-practice, high-performance growth engine.

Section I discusses the key concepts and models that are the basis for all of your sales strategies and selling activities. Much of this section focuses on *two buyer decision-making models.* The best salespeople are not only good businesspeople, but good psychologists as well. Understanding buyer psychology and buyer decision-making processes is critical because sales practices that are misaligned with how buyers think and make decisions create friction in the sales process. The sales process bogs down, and eventually breaks down, as a result of this friction. Sellers who enjoy the most success are always aware of the buyer's mind-set and stage in the decision process. This awareness enables top sellers to align their strategies and tactics accordingly.

Of the two buyer decision-making models, one is more traditional and one is less traditional. The more traditional model represents the decision process used by buyers of concurrent offerings. The new, non-traditional model represents the decision process used by buyers of divergent offerings. Buyers do not make decisions about divergent offerings in the same way they make decisions about concurrent offerings. Therefore, sellers must understand both buyer models and apply each in their strategic selling framework.

Section I also revisits the concept of a selling framework. Essentially, the architecture of a selling framework is the architecture of a new growth engine.

Section II: Igniting Your Growth Engine

Section II teaches the critical strategies, sales process steps, and competencies needed to become a best-practice, high-value-adding, major account businessperson who sells. This section begins by showing the tools and methodologies for selling divergent offerings, and ends with a similar discussion on selling concurrent offerings. Essentially, Section II equips you for managing all selling opportunities to "yes" decisions.

A key element of this section is a business process for creating buyer demand. *Demand creation* is the platinum competency of sellers faced with the large sale. For most organizations that sell large, expensive offerings that represent risky buying decisions for their market, the vast majority of their potential customers do not have active needs for their offerings at any given time. Regardless of your industry, 90 percent or more of your market has dormant or inactive needs for your offerings. In other words, less than 10 percent of your market has active needs for what you sell at any given time. The implication is that you and your sales team must adopt a business process for creating demand in order to optimize your market.

Another important discussion in Section II focuses on a new type of sales call. Traditionally, with most sales organizations, there have been two types of sales calls: *needs analysis* and *presentation of capabilities.* What these sellers are lacking, and what is described in Section II, is a third type of call that acts as a shock absorber between analyzing needs and presenting capabilities. We call this third category bridging sales calls.

Section III: Sustaining Your Growth Engine

Section III is a short section that concludes the book, and is written for executives and managers who must sustain the *growth engine* once it is built and ignited.

Selling opportunities must be created and managed in a manner that meets organizational objectives. Section III discusses how executives and managers responsible for their organizations' growth can tie together their sales frameworks and make them permanent fixtures within their organizations. These executives and managers need systems and tools for holding members of the sales organization accountable to the selling framework. Each member of the sales team must also learn the sales framework and become disciplined and proficient in its execution. Section III discusses how to teach your sales framework to your organization, how to hold people accountable to it, and how to ensure that your framework is being carried out with high degrees of competency.

Summary

In Chapter 1, the key points are:

- Think sales *framework*—not sales *training*. The five components of a sales framework are suppositions, strategies, steps to "yes," skills, and systems.
- There are four types of demand and two broad categories of offerings:
  - Divergent offerings satisfy new application demand.
  - Concurrent offerings satisfy aggregate, continuous improvement, or economy demand.
- Selling divergent new applications is the most challenging type of sale, but it is also a growth catalyst for your business because new application sales stimulate future cycles of demand.
- Sales organizations must gain high levels of competence in creating and managing each type of demand within their markets.

Notes

1. Wiersema, F. (1996). *Customer intimacy: Pick your partners, shape your culture, win together.* Santa Monica, CA: Knowledge Exchange.
2. Rackham, N. (1988). *SPIN selling.* New York, NY: McGraw-Hill.
3. Heiman, S.E., & Miller, R.B. (1985). *Strategic selling.* New York, NY: William Morrow and Company. Bosworth, M.T. (1995). *Solution selling: Creating buyers in difficult selling markets.* New York, NY: McGraw-Hill. Heiman, S.E., & Miller, R.B. (1987). *Conceptual selling.* Berkeley, CA: Miller-Heiman. Parinello, A. (Ed.) (1999). *Selling to vito: Increase your commissions by getting appointments with top decision makers today.* Holbrook, MA: Adams Media Corportion.
4. Christensen, C.M., & Raynor, M.E. (2003). *The innovators solution: Creating and sustaining successful growth.* Boston, MA: Harvard Business School Press.

2

Yesterday's Most Complete Buyer Psychology Model

Good work in Chapter 1. This chapter builds on some of its key concepts and further highlights the impact that the four types of demand have on sellers facing the large sale.

In this chapter, we lay a foundation for understanding how customers make major buying decisions. Essentially, this is a look at a buyer's psychology. Sellers must align their sales process to the decision process used by buyers. The result of misalignment between the seller's process and the buyer's process is friction, and this friction causes the sales process to break down. This point appears repeatedly in *Selling Is Dead* because it is very important.

In this chapter and the next, we present formal models for how buyers make large decisions. Before doing so, it's worthwhile to take a moment to discuss how and why buyer models were applied to sales theory.

The Customer Decision-Making Model—In a Vacuum

As we have just mentioned, the best sellers align their strategies with the process used by buyers to make buying decisions. Understanding how buyers get to "yes" is critical for formulating an effective selling strategy. One of the leading authors on this subject, Neil Rackham, outlined his buying model in his excellent book *Major Account Sales Strategy*.[1] His research indicated that when buyers make decisions involving moderate-to-high perceived risk, they engage in a logical and predictable decision-making process. Rackham credits John O'Shaughnessy, author of *Why People Buy,* for influencing his model on buying.[2]

Not surprisingly, Rackham's extensive research (a study of over 30,000 sales calls) found that the skills necessary for selling larger offerings and smaller offerings are inherently different. He also found that better selling teams who sell larger offerings use buying models to create superior selling strategies. For the purpose of *Selling Is Dead,* we modify Rackham's buying model to improve its accuracy and better reflect our philosophies. We give a great deal of credit, though, to Rackham for his pioneering work.

Remember, organizations are simply made of people, and people make decisions in a fairly predictable manner—especially bigger decisions where buying mistakes can have serious negative consequences. Although some buyers can be idiosyncratic, almost seeming to defy conventional wisdom, using a model of buying as the basis for a selling strategy is a powerful market-facing advantage. We are continually astonished by the nonuse of buyer model–based strategies with the vast majority of sales teams. Simply put, buying models help sellers align with buyer psychology, and alignment is one of the critical factors that lead to less buyer resistance and more successful outcomes.

The New Best Practices of Buyer Decision Theory

One of the major themes of *Selling Is Dead* is that a customer's decision-making process changes from one demand type to another. This is because the level of risk, potential impact (positive and negative), buyer sophistication, and buyer motivation all vary significantly across the spectrum of demand types. Such variations cause buyers to change their decision processes from demand type to demand type. Because there are multiple types of demand, there are multiple unique decision processes used by buyers. In other words, the decision process a buyer goes through depends on the specific type of demand an offering satisfies for the buyer.

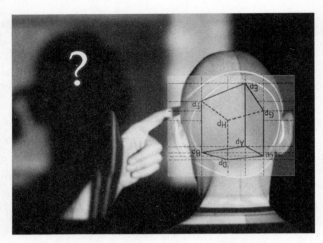

Buyers make large decisions in a rational, predictable manner that can be modeled. Better sellers use these decision models to create superior strategies.

Another major theme is that the best sales strategies are based on formal buyer models. Top sales organizations effectively utilize such models to develop strategy and sales processes. Because buyers have multiple decision processes, best practices dictate that sellers adopt multiple corresponding buyer models (you will see an example of a buyer model in a moment).

Neil Rackham's work produced a singular buyer model. Although it was a tremendously valuable model that advanced sales theory, such a single-model methodology is unfortunately based on the belief that buyers make all large buying decisions in the same manner. In other words, this single model makes no consideration for how a buyer's decision-making process changes based on whether an offering satisfies new application demand, aggregate demand, continuous improvement demand, or economy demand.

Rackham's model makes the assumption that, regardless of demand type, all buyer decisions follow the same protocol. Yet when one accurately categorizes large sales into different types, it becomes apparent that buyer decision processes change based on the type of demand in play.

Simply put, using a multiple-model methodology for large sales is now best practice. A one–size–fits–all mentality no longer suffices for sellers wishing to optimize all opportunities. However, a methodology that uses four models is too sophisticated and confusing for most sales organizations, which makes such a methodology unmanageable.

Fortunately, a four-model system that has a unique buyer model for each of the four types of demand is also unnecessary. Through research, we have developed a best-practice two-model system. This two-model system accounts for the existence of multiple decision processes used by buying organizations when making decisions about large, costly offerings. This system enables sellers to predict buyer decision behavior for all large sales scenarios and all demand types. The ability to use buyer models to predict behavior enables sellers to craft appropriate strategies that align with the buyer's psychology and behavior.

This superior two-model system is tied to the discussion in Chapter 1 on the differences between concurrent offerings and divergent offerings. Concurrent offerings satisfy either aggregate demand, continuous improvement demand, or economy demand. Generally speaking, from the buyer's perspective, new concurrent offerings represent an existing way of doing a certain job. In other words, concurrent offerings are the same as, or very similar to, the buyer's existing applications. Therefore, decisions concerning concurrent offerings represent only moderate risk because they don't fundamentally change how the buyer currently does a job. Moreover, the buyer already has the infrastructure and user sophistication to do the job in that manner.

Divergent offerings, conversely, satisfy new application demand. Therefore, divergent offerings represent a fundamentally new way of doing an existing job or a new job altogether. Decisions about divergent offerings are riskier because buyers have to undergo more change, they lack the infrastructure and user sophistication to support the offering, and they have not previously experienced direct results with the offering that would otherwise help them set expectations for how it will perform for their organization. Thus, the decision process buyers go through with divergent offerings varies significantly from the decision process buyers go through with concurrent offerings.

The two-model methodology we advocate has one buyer model for selling concurrent offerings and one model for selling divergent offerings. The concurrent offering buyer model should be used when selling all offerings that satisfy either aggregate demand (an additional quantity of what the buyer is already using), continuous improvement demand (an enhanced version of what the buyer is already using), or economy demand (a simplified, lower-cost, and/or more convenient version of what the buyer is already using). Buyers go through a similar decision-making process for all offerings that satisfy these three demand types because they all represent some form of an existing application. However, buyers go through a significantly different process when making decisions about divergent offerings, which represent a new application altogether and a greater amount of risk. Therefore, the divergent offering buyer model should be used when selling all offerings that satisfy new application demand.

The remainder of Chapter 2 focuses on the concurrent offering buyer model. Chapter 3 focuses on the divergent offering buyer model.

The Stages of Buying Concurrent Offerings

Neil Rackham's model serves as a good basis for the concurrent offering buyer model, although we have made some augmentations so that it is more appropriate and accurate. The model we have modified from Rackham's original model has four distinct stages. Your first thought will be that it's simple. Your last thought, which will occur later in the book, is that the model is profound. This base model, which is less sophisticated than what you will see in future chapters, is displayed graphically in Figure 2.1. Each stage is discussed in the following section.

This will be a conceptual exercise. Later, we will show how to apply effective, earthy strategies to these models.

Stage 1: Satisfaction Stage

Beneath it all, organizations make large purchases to remove problems. Those problems may either cause underperformance or jeopardize the achievement of important business objectives. Makes sense. Nothing new. With that being said, we introduce the first stage a buyer goes through along the way to making a large buying decision: the satisfaction stage.

Prospects in this stage are not yet ready to buy from you. They may have a few problems that your offering can solve, but they are not committed to taking action that will remove their problems. In other words,

The Concurrent Offering Buying Model

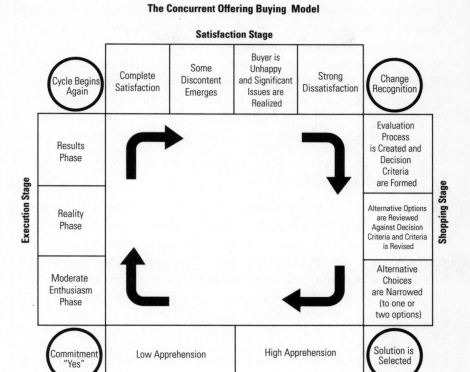

Figure 2.1 Buyers follow fairly predictable steps when purchasing large concurrent offerings.

their needs are dormant, and they don't feel that the problems are serious enough to warrant a change to one of the following:

- A new paradigm (new application demand)
- Additional quantity (aggregate demand)
- An improvement in the current products or services they procure (continuous improvement demand)
- A more cost-effective, good-enough version of what is already being used (economy demand)

Psychologically, buyers in this stage can run the gamut from being completely satisfied with their current situation to strongly discontented, although the common factor for all satisfaction stage buyers is that they are not yet ready to act. Figure 2.2 shows this psychological range of buyers who are in the satisfaction stage. Buyers who move to the next stage are first driven down this ladder.

What is the psychology of a buyer in the satisfaction stage? What are the predominant thoughts going through a satisfaction stage buyer's mind?

Buyers in the satisfaction stage ask themselves the following questions:

- Do I have a problem?
- How serious is my problem?
- Is my problem significant enough that I need to do something about it (change)?

Buyers in this stage are typically resistant to talk with sellers since they are not actively shopping for solutions. Why would a buyer who is in the satisfaction stage agree to meet with you, the seller, when there is no commitment to buying action? Generally speaking, the buyer could be curious about your offering, although not seriously considering a purchase at this time. Buyers also may agree to see you so that you can help them answer those questions previously listed. From their perspective, you can help identify the existence of problems, the severity of problems, the implications of those problems, whether action should

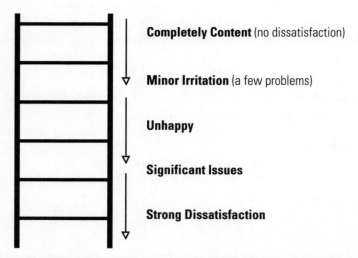

Figure 2.2 Buyer psychology in the satisfaction stage ranges from completely content to strongly dissatisfied.

be taken to address those problems, and whether that action fits with the overall strategic direction of the organization.

A sage observer once noted that life belongs to the discontented, for it is discontent that drives change. Without discontent, you have inertia. The status quo survives. To ensure that your prospects inherit "life" and break free from performance-stunting inertia, you must help them reach a sufficient level of discontent so

Satisfaction stage buyer psychology is "Do I have a problem, how serious is it, and do I need to act/change?"

they are willing to change. When the costs (financial, change, etc.) of a solution are high, discontent must be strong and serious for a buyer to commit to action. The buyer must accept that there is a problem, recognize the severity and implications of the problem, and understand that the costs of inaction are greater than the costs of action.

Relative to demand type, buyers can be dissatisfied for numerous reasons. Table 2.1 provides some examples.

Most buyers in the satisfaction stage are neither completely satisfied nor entirely dissatisfied with the situations you can solve with your offering. More than likely, prospects in this phase clearly have some challenges and issues you might be able to help with. Yet these prospects probably feel the problems are not worth the cost, time, and energy of removal.

Figure 2.3 represents the likely psychological categories of satisfaction stage prospects in your market at any given time. As depicted, the majority of your prospects in this stage recognize at least some problems and issues. Therefore, finding problems isn't the difficulty with these prospects. Instead, getting them to see the seriousness of their problems (as a basis for change) is often the bigger challenge.

Table 2.1

Aggregate Demand
Backlog: need more capacity
Slow turnaround in operations are leading to customer complaints: need additional equipment to speed up cycle times
Aging equipment causing high maintenance costs and downtime: replacement is necessary
Continuous Improvement Demand
Current system is overly labor intensive: need to upgrade to a better system
Existing vendor has dropped the ball too often: time for a change to a competitor
Current CRM software is inaccessible through the web, hard to customize, and has limited reporting functionality: need to adopt a better total solution
Economy Demand
Don't need all of this capacity in this department: using temporary staff to fill some positions would be good enough
We don't use 50 percent of the capabilities of our current project management software: let's switch to a more cost-effective version that isn't fancy, but that will get the job done
The flat-screen computer monitors we recently bought are nice, but the benefits haven't justified the added cost above traditional monitors

Here are a few additional notes about the satisfaction stage:

+ Until buyers reach a psychological stage of strong dissatisfaction, they will not move to the next phase—the shopping stage. In fact, the bigger the cost of change, the larger the dissatisfaction needs to be to create buyer momentum.
+ Usually, this psychological state of strong dissatisfaction must be reached in critical mass. That is, dissatisfaction must grow strong with a group of people in the organization who have power and influence in making this decision before the need for change becomes active.
+ Generating critical-mass consensus for a commitment to change is clearly one of the greatest challenges for major account sales-people. We would go so far as to say that the ability to create critical-mass demand for change is what ultimately separates the very best sellers from the rest. In essence, salespeople who are best at selling in this stage do two things extremely well:
  1. *Creative disruption.* They help buyers see problems that they may not have been aware even existed.

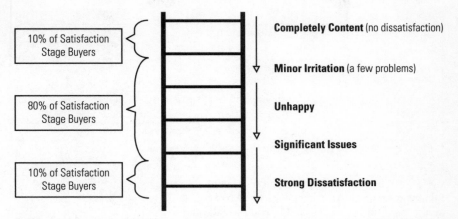

Figure 2.3 Most satisfaction stage buyers are aware of problems they are experiencing but do not yet have a high level of dissatisfaction that would cause them to seriously consider solutions.

2. *Consensus building.* They practice creating disruption among a group of people who eventually form a coalition toward change internally in the buyer organization. The individuals within this group may independently begin in different stages of the decision-making process and have varying psychologies and levels of dissatisfaction.

Stage 2: The Shopping Stage

Buyers who pass through the satisfaction stage enter the shopping stage. Buyers in the shopping stage clearly express active needs, or an intention to act. In other words, they are actively shopping for something that meets their needs and removes their problem(s). Essentially, your target shopping stage buyers are shopping for the type of offering you sell.

The driving psychological factor for buyers in this stage is, How do I make the best choice? and Which solution is best for my needs? They have already decided the problems are serious enough to warrant change.

Question: You are the salesperson. When in front of a buyer in the shopping stage, should you center your discussions on an in-depth analysis of the buyer's problems?

No. Absolutely not.

Instead, shopping stage buyers prefer discussions about the specific features, prices, service components, and differentiation of your product

Shopping stage buyer psychology is "Which solution is best for my needs and how do I make the right choice?"

or service. They're trying to make the best decision they can. Therefore, sellers who pick up on this clearly have an advantage.

A few notes on shopping stage buyers:

- If you, the salesperson, enter the customer decision-making process with a buyer in the shopping stage, do not be surprised if you are shoulder-to-shoulder with competitive salespeople. If the buyer called you, they more than likely called your competition, too. That makes the major shopping stage challenge a competitive selling one. The result is price pressure.

- Buyers want you to help differentiate your offerings from competitors. They want alternative offerings to have recognizable differences so they can rank them and choose among them.

- Buyers can be all over the board as well—from very unsophisticated about how to make a decision to extremely sophisticated (they know exactly what they want). However, Figure 2.4 shows a simple model of how a typical buyer moves through the shopping stage, beginning with no criteria (unsophisticated) and ending with criteria in place and prioritized (sophisticated).

After buyers have evaluated options, they narrow the field to one or two top picks. At this point, depending on the circumstances, they may or may not enter the third phase of decision making—the apprehension stage.

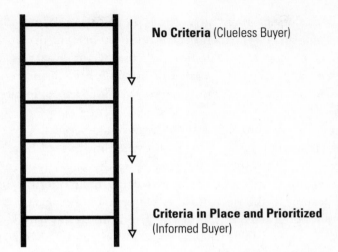

No Criteria (Clueless Buyer)

Criteria in Place and Prioritized
(Informed Buyer)

Figure 2.4 Shopping stage buyers are driven to become more sophisticated in terms of how to make the best decision for their needs.

Key Points about the Satisfaction and Shopping Stages of Buyer Behavior

Before moving on to the third stage of buyer behavior for concurrent offerings, let us share a few additional thoughts on the first two phases. We begin with two questions:

1. Now that you know the basics of the satisfaction stage and shopping stage, where is the majority of your market?
2. What percentage of your market is in the satisfaction stage (dormant needs), and what percentage of your market is in the shopping stage (active needs)?

Take a moment to formulate your answer before moving on.

Despite not knowing what industry you work in, we are very confident that the vast majority of your market, at any given point in time, is in the satisfaction stage. (We've worked in a lot of markets.) Across the spectrum of industries, typical ranges are from 80 to 99.5 percent of the market being in the satisfaction stage. If you were selling expensive capital equipment to steel foundries at any time from late 2000 through 2003, probably only 1 percent of your market was shopping for your category of offerings at any given time. If you were selling a hot new technology in the 1990s, then maybe up to 20 percent of your market was in the shopping stage. The few cases that we have witnessed where greater than 20 percent of a market is shopping have been the result of new regulations that forced those markets to adopt a specific category of offering.

Figure 2.5 represents the reality for most salespeople.

Most salespeople know what to do when in front of buyers in the shopping stage. Active needs are present, so the buyer is attentive and eager. Salespeople are comfortable presenting their offerings in a way that is appealing to the needs of these buyers. Unfortunately, there are very few shopping stage buyers at any given time, especially in a down economy. Moreover, the shopping stage is competitive. Most sales and marketing efforts are geared to buyers with active needs. Now that we have become well entrenched in the information age, buyers with active needs can easily find alternative solutions.

For most salespeople, the satisfaction stage is the most difficult phase in which to sell. Even when engaged, buyers are usually resistant to hear about solutions since they feel they have no active needs. Despite the fact that the best potential for sustainable sales growth lies with buyers in the satisfaction stage, most salespeople are ineffective at creating and managing satisfaction stage opportunities. Because most salespeople rely on inflexible, linear processes appropriate for buyers with active needs but not dormant needs, they are quickly dispatched by satisfaction stage buyers or strung out over a long selling cycle that ends in "no decision."

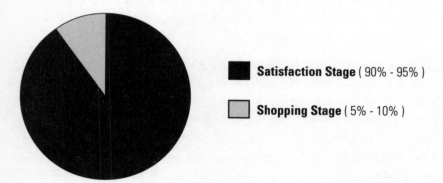

Figure 2.5 Regardless of industry, the vast majority of organizations in your market is likely to be in the satisfaction stage.

Selling IT in the New Economy

At the time this book was being written, corporate America emerged from a difficult recession. Stronger growth and profitability returned. Yet, instead of investing in IT, organizations largely made a strategic decision to sit on their proverbial hands and make due with existing IT resources. In fact, growth in IT expenditures for 2005 was projected at only 5 to 7 percent—much lower than the go-go spending years of the 1980s and 1990s.

Why has IT growth not returned to the pace of the 1980s and 1990s? Perhaps the answer lies in the lack of a driving force. The three former growth forces that spurred IT spending have now settled: the personal computer in the 1980s and 1990s, networks in the late 1980s and 1990s, and the Internet of the late 1990s and early 2000.

With the absence of a powerful driving force that could reshape the landscape of IT and create voracious demand for IT offerings, organizations that sell IT are even more dependent on their sales teams' ability to proactively create buyer demand.

Unfortunately, for the majority of IT sellers who have been spoiled by the excesses of the last two decades, demand creation has been an uneasy and difficult road. Clearly a small percentage of sellers today fail to become effective creators of demand due to their attitudinal refusal to accept this new role. But the real problem for the majority of IT sellers is they lack the knowledge, strategies, and competencies to create demand and advance buyers from the satisfaction stage into the shopping stage.

The paradox is clear. Today's salesperson is effective selling to the shopping stage universe, which is small, elusive, and competitive. Today's salesperson is equally ineffective at selling to the satisfaction stage universe, which is massive and noncompetitive.

Case in point: IT salespeople were wildly successful in the 1990s when demand was high and cash was streaming off corporate America. Large chunks of IT markets were consistently in the shopping stage (10 to 20 percent). Enter the recession of the new millennium. The number of shopping stage buyers in the market shrunk dramatically (to between 1 and 5 percent), and the same salespeople who were breaking records just months before were now sputtering and flopping. These highly paid professionals were excellent at servicing demand, but lacked the skills and methodologies necessary to create demand and advance buyers through the satisfaction stage and into the shopping stage.

Although the previous industry example and the next point are more appropriate for Chapter 3 on the divergent offering buyer model, companies that sell new and discontinuous innovations face a market that is uneducated. Therefore, no demand initially exists and all demand must be created. In other words, the entire buying universe is in the satisfaction stage for these new applications. Although innovators and early adopters will gradually learn about these new products or services and may drift into the shopping stage on their own cognizance, these selling companies must be able to execute proper satisfaction stage strategies in order to build a market and create customers.

Consider another interesting dynamic that demonstrates the value of learning best-practice satisfaction stage selling strategies. When you, the salesperson, enter a buyer's decision-making process while he is already in the shopping stage, you will most likely, and literally, get shopped. Competitors will be present, and they may have the advantage if they were there first because they can most easily assist the buyer in setting criteria that puts you at a disadvantage. However, when you enter a buyer's decision-making process while he is still in the satisfaction stage, you should not be shopped as the buyer moves into the shopping stage. If you manage the opportunity properly while the buyer is in the satisfaction stage and help him realize that change is necessary, you will earn tremendous credibility and be seen as uniquely able to remove his problem. The lack of competition preserves your margins. Moreover, even if the buyer does consider alternative solutions, you have the advantage of being able to help the buyer set and prioritize decision criteria favorable to your offering because you were there first.

Stage 3: The Apprehension Stage

In big decision scenarios surrounding concurrent offerings, especially ones where missteps will potentially have high negative consequences, buyers will more than likely enter this third stage once they have selected the option that best meets their needs. Although concurrent offering buying decisions are usually less risky than divergent offering buying decisions, there still can be significant perceived risk that causes members of the buying organization to experience apprehension.

In the apprehension stage, buyers have a tendency to become nervous about making a final commitment. Remember, this is an impor-

tant, high-stakes deci-
sion, so prospects can
be very cautious at
this point. Fear—of
failure, of mistakes—is
the driving emotion
for buyers in this stage.
Simply put, if fear or
apprehension is signif-
icant enough, buyers
will predictably lock
up, refusing to make
a "yes" decision until

Apprehension stage buyer psychology is "What are the consequences of making a mistake?"

their inner conflict (expressed or otherwise) is resolved. Buyers are especially conservative in their decision making when engulfed in politically
charged corporate environments or during a down economy, when the
threat of job loss is especially high.

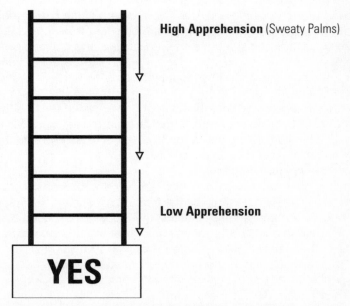

Figure 2.6 Buyers in the apprehension stage must reduce
their anxiety and perceived risk before formally committing to a
solution.

Buyers will not make a formal commitment until their apprehension is reduced. We previously established that the driving psychology of buyers in the apprehension stage is, "What if I make a
mistake?" As a visual representation, the buyer must move down the
apprehension ladder before a "yes" decision is made (Figure 2.6).

A certain amount of anxiety should be anticipated and managed.
However, some additional and unanticipated elevators of apprehension may be injected into the decision-making process. Perhaps
the buyer heard something negative about your offering or your company. For example, during the latter part of the shopping stage, she
might have talked to a customer of yours who expressed that the learning curve associated with your offering is very long. Alternatively, she

---

Case Study: Understanding Your Apprehension Stage Experiences

Have you experienced eleventh-hour failure where you felt a formal commitment was imminent but were never able to get a deal done? Most major
account salespeople have had such an experience.

Failure at the eleventh hour tends to follow a period of increased buyer
evasiveness and seemingly endless delayments. During this period, the
buyer is rethinking the use of scarce dollars on your offering, and attempting to calculate the return on investment that the offering can generate.
It's an emotional process for the buyer, wherein the buyer succumbs to
fear and apprehension and subsequently returns to either the shopping
stage or satisfaction stage.

If this has happened to you, think about one or two of those situations
for a moment. Did you miss any signs that the buyer was experiencing significant apprehension? What could you have done to address the buyer's
apprehension and lower it to an acceptable level?

These are difficult questions.

The most effective way to minimize a buyer's apprehension once he
has selected your offering is to prevent it from manifesting in the first place.
This can only be accomplished by building the proper value-based business
case, complete with an ROI determination, for your offering before the buyer
ever enters the apprehension stage. Building such a business case
requires constant alignment with the buyer and gaining an in-depth understanding of the buyer's situation, constraints, and goals. Once a business
case has been built effectively, the buyer's apprehension will remain low.

In summary, the best apprehension management strategy is apprehension prevention.

might have heard about a past customer who had mixed results with your solution. Sometimes, apprehension is elevated by an internal event on the part of the buyer. Other times, apprehension rises due to an external occurrence. Such an event may occur when the prospect's organization suddenly is rumored to be purchased by another company.

Regardless, even the slightest negative news can freeze buyers in the apprehension stage. For sellers facing mid-to-long selling cycles, random and unpredictable events can lead to frustrating delays toward gaining final commitment. Whereas the shopping stage is fun, the apprehension stage may become arduous if not managed appropriately by the seller. If anxiety and apprehension are managed properly, a final commitment will be attained.

Stage 4: The Execution Stage

After buyers finally get to "yes" for a concurrent offering—whether for an additional quantity, a better quality version, or a less costly version—they move into the final stage of the decision-making process. We call this the execution stage. In essence, you, the salesperson, have gotten the deal. Now, attention turns to implementation.

In this stage, buyers begin focusing on the details of the execution of your product or service. The driving psychological factor here is obvious: "Let's start generating the desired results ASAP and receive the expected ROI."

Again, buyers in this stage vary across wide ranges. Some buyers are unrealistic, having expectations quite lacking in fairness—which might be your fault if you didn't manage expectations properly earlier in their decision process. Other buyers, especially more reasonable, experienced, or sophisticated ones, expect bumps and bruises along the way during implementation.

Also, it should be noted that the demand type being sold will largely influence a buyer's attitude during the execution stage. Aggregate demand is usually the easiest of the three concurrent demand types to implement because it assumes buyers already have infrastructure for the specific application. Thus, little education or support is probably required. Continuous improvement demand buyers typically lie at the top of the frustration continuum for concurrent offerings. That's because buyers will probably have to make some adjustments to your company and offering in order to get an optimal ROI. However, adjustments should not be so severe as to warrant the type of buyer angst found in new applications. The infrastructure supporting the existing application should be fairly consistent with the adjusted infrastructure needed to support the continuously improved application. With economy demand, frustration during the execution stage is typically low. Although the solution does change from the previous solution, existing infrastructure should be consistent. *(Note: The implementation of divergent offerings is typically much more frustrating than the implementation of concurrent offerings. Buyers have no direct experience to help them set realistic expectations for the implementation of new applications.)*

With most large purchases, the execution stage has three, sequential subphases as depicted in Figure 2.7.

As the illustration shows, the frustration associated with the implementation process tends to follow a *moderate enthusiasm phase.* The moderate enthusiasm phase is the first phase, which typically occurs directly after a decision to proceed has been reached. Both the buyer and seller are excited about the union and the realization of the promised results.

Unfortunately, even with concurrent offerings, few solutions are truly plug 'n' play. This is especially true when the offering is a continu-

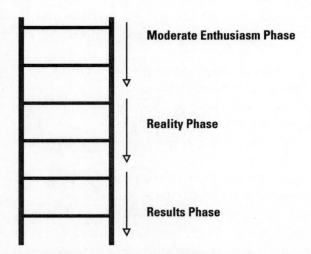

Figure 2.7 Buyers of concurrent offerings go through three predictable phases in the executing stage when they are implementing the solutions they buy.

ous improvement of an existing application. As a result, the enthusiasm is typically diminished as buyers realize it will require effort and learning to generate the ROI expected with the purchase. We call this period the *reality phase* of the execution stage. Good sellers anticipate buyers becoming a little frustrated during this phase of learning and *trial and error.*

As time passes, results begin to be analyzed (*results phase*) in order to determine the relative success or failure of the purchase. Once again, the seller is responsible for setting the buyer's expectations regarding what constitutes a reasonable period of time necessary to achieve the intended ROI.

Round and Round She Goes

After buyers settle in and begin getting returns on your offerings, they move to the satisfaction stage once again. The whole buying process starts over.

Even irrational buyers seem to fit well in the customer decision-making process models in *Selling Is Dead.* This predictability makes the buyer models described in Chapters 2 and 3 highly useful tools for creating effective sales strategy.

As we mentioned earlier, for unexplainable reasons, we have seen only a small minority of selling organizations using buyer models as a basis for strategy. We think this is a huge oversight, for the models force sellers to constantly stay flexible to the psychological needs of the buyer. As you will see over and over in this book, process must be adjusted to psychology, and psychology adjusts to demand type. Any selling team that uses a step-by-step, linear model in market facing (blindly following the same steps over and over) will not optimize their opportunities.

The purpose of this book, though, is not to present the preceding concurrent offering buying model. Instead, our focus is to build on Rackham's previous work and this model to show how the buying model deviates significantly from concurrent offerings to divergent offerings. The model for divergent offerings is the true innovation for sales organizations.

Last, a recent trend of sales training books use the philosophical essence of Rackham's customer decision-making model, yet take ownership of the concept itself. We urge those authors and companies to give credit where credit is due—to Neil Rackham. His research and ideas have paved the way for a better model of market facing—one based on a rigorous, scientific, proven approach versus guesswork, showmanship, and manipulation.

Summary

In Chapter 2, the key points are:

- ◆ Research has proven that buyers go through a formal and sequential decision-making process when the decision is about a major purchase.
- ◆ Best-practice sales strategies are based on buyer models. In other words, all sales strategies and tactics should be based on the buyer's psychological decision-making process, and where the buyer is in that process.
- ◆ Best practices dictate the use of two buyer models: the concurrent offering buyer model and the divergent offering buyer model.
- ◆ The concurrent offering buyer model has four stages, which sequentially are the satisfaction stage, shopping stage, apprehension stage, and execution stage.
- ◆ Top salespeople focus on buyers in the satisfaction stage as a means to prevent competitive selling situations, and because the vast majority of their opportunities are with buyers in the satisfaction stage.

Notes

1. Rackham, N. (1989). *Major account sales strategy.* New York, NY: McGraw-Hill.
2. O'Shaughnessy, J. (1987). *Why people buy.* New York, NY: Oxford Press.

3

Diverging from Tradition:
Understanding How Organizations Buy
Your High-Risk Innovations

Two chapters down. If you apply yourself for one more conceptual chapter, we'll reward you in Chapter 4 with some practical ideas and strategies that you can begin implementing immediately. This chapter is a turning point on your path to the new best practices of selling. Keep going.

For sales teams who must create demand for their new application offerings, here is the proverbial good and bad news:

The bad news. The concurrent offering buyer decision model you just learned in Chapter 2 doesn't quite fit for organizations acquiring higher-risk divergent offerings. Although the four-stage buyer model from Chapter 2 is needed to most effectively manage selling opportunities for concurrent offerings, it must undergo some changes when dealing with the sale of divergent offerings (which represent new applications for buyers). A buyer's decision-making process changes dramatically when considering the adoption of a new application. The more disruptive the new application, the more dramatic is this shift in buying behavior. *Those of you who have a great deal of experience selling new applications may have felt that the model in the previous chapter was a bit awkward relative to your selling realities.*

The good news. Buyers of divergent, new application offerings still engage in a rational decision-making process. The divergent offering decision process just differs from the concurrent offering decision process, and has a unique set of principles and rules that guide a buyer to "yes." In this chapter, we explain the divergent offering buyer decision-making process. Once you've learned this buying model, Chapter 4 introduces strategies based on it that will yield greater and more consistent performance when selling new applications.

In Chapter 1, you learned there are four different types of demand that buyers have: new application demand, aggregate demand, continuous improvement demand, and economy demand. You also learned there are two types of offerings (concurrent and divergent), each posing unique challenges relative to selling strategy. In Chapter 2, you learned that buyers go through a rational and predictable buying process when considering the purchase of a higher-risk offering. Good sellers understand buyer decision processes and create buyer models to guide them in aligning sales strategy with buyer strategy.

You also learned in Chapter 2 that the decision-making process of a buyer changes based on demand type. A buyer with new application demand goes through a different decision-making process from a buyer with aggregate demand, continuous improvement demand, or economy demand. In other words, the buyer's decision process for a divergent offering is different from her decision process for a concurrent offering.

Because buyers go through multiple decision-making processes depending on the type of demand at play, *no longer is it sufficient for sellers to create strategy based on a single buyer model.* The need for multiple buyer models will be a surprising revelation to even the most forward-thinking major account sales organizations. Best-practice sellers must understand and use multiple buyer decision-making models.

We showed you the concurrent offering buyer model in Chapter 2, and this chapter presents a second buyer model: the divergent offering buyer model.

The concurrent offering buyer model is a best-practice buyer

The concurrent model is appropriate when selling offerings that represent existing applications to buyers. The divergent model, however, is the unique model that must be applied when selling offerings that satisfy new application demand for buyers.

model that should be used when selling offerings that satisfy aggregate, continuous improvement, or economy demand. The decision processes used by buyers with these three types of demand are similar and can be adequately represented by a single buyer model. The decision processes corresponding to each of these three demand types are similar because these three demand types are all satisfied by offerings that represent *existing applications* to the buyer. The *divergent offering buyer model,* however, is unique and should only be used when selling offerings that satisfy new application demand.

The fact that buyer decision behavior changes *significantly* based on the type of demand has major implications for sellers. It means that one set of selling strategies won't work with every buyer. Buyers who possess different demand types will display disparate behavior—which would disrupt a single set of selling strategies. Sporadically, that single set of selling strategies may work. More often, though, that single set of strategies is not appropriate and fails.

Fortunately, having a comprehensive set of buyer models with multiple sets of selling strategies in place enables sellers to predict buyer behavior as long as the appropriate buyer model can be matched to each buyer. Therefore, sellers must be aware of the type of demand at play with each individual buyer so they can correctly choose either the concurrent offering buyer model or the divergent offering buyer model (see Figure 3.1). Once the correct model is selected, the seller can predict the decision process used by the buyer and craft selling strategies that tightly align with the buyer's decision process.

Sellers who lack buyer models and the ability to correctly identify each buyer's demand type are destined to fail in the large sale for one

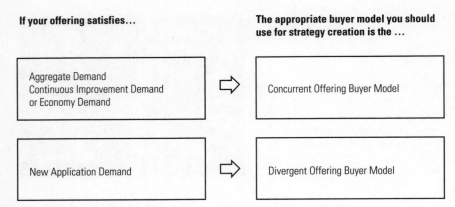

Figure 3.1   Effective sellers use different buying models to create superior strategy.

reason: strategic misalignment. In other words, unless sellers are using an appropriate model that matches the buyer's decision process, sales strategy will be inconsistent with the way a buyer wants to make buying decisions, and the sales strategy will be rejected by the buyer.

The remainder of this chapter focuses on the divergent offering buyer decision model. Mastering the divergent model and becoming highly effective with selling divergent offerings is especially important for several additional reasons:

- *New applications represent the greatest risk to buyers, which makes the sale of new applications the greatest challenge to sellers.* However, this challenge must be overcome because new applications must be sold to launch a new cycle of demand. After a new application has been sold to a buyer, most organizations have an opportunity to subsequently sell additional quantities of the application, continuously improved versions of the application, or scaled-down versions of the application.

- *Very few prospective buyers of a specific new application are in the shopping stage at any given point in time.* Very few. Because of the scarcity of low-hanging fruit, sellers must be disciplined in how they create and manage selling opportunities for their divergent offerings. Scarcity of buyers who already possess active needs is especially problematic for highly innovative discontinuous offerings, where a great deal of education is needed for buyers to fully understand the offerings, and the value and implementation of those offerings. In addition, very few prospective buyers are in the shopping stage for a given new application in soft or slow-to-rebound economic periods where fewer discretionary dollars are available for new applications. New applications are almost always discretionary, except when new regulations impose them on industries. Remember, organizations and departments are able to function prior to the introduction of a new application. This makes the status quo difficult to supplant. During sluggish economic periods, organizations are more willing to renew existing applications than adopt new ones.

Note: It is acceptable to use the words *divergent offerings* and *new applications* interchangeably. Divergent offerings are always new applications, and vice versa.

Divergence and the Death of Sales

Selling isn't really dead, as our sensationalistic title implies. However, the traditional sales roles, strategies, and skills that organizations have relied on have become ineffective when selling divergence. The best of these traditional mechanisms, though, continue to produce some respectable (yet underoptimized) results when selling concurrent offerings.

Therefore, when we proclaim selling to be dead, one thing we mean is that professional, strategically rooted, and skillful selling is missing on the divergent, front edge of the economy where true growth originates. Of course, many organizations are able to make divergent sales of new applications . . . but not in an acceptably fast, predictable, or controlled manner. Success is left to chance. Sales teams challenged with selling divergent offerings are typically too loose, too unsophisticated, too misguided, and too ineffective.

Because most organizations have difficulty selling divergent offerings, we spend a great deal of time from Chapters 3 to 7 teaching how to breathe life back into sales where it is needed most—the divergent beginning of new product and service categories. We'll now start by expanding our discussion of why and how divergent offerings come to be.

In broad terms, there are two sources for future divergent, new application offerings. The first and more obvious source is from market disruption. As mentioned in Chapter 1, multiple types of market disruption can stimulate new applications. Adams Capital Management, previously referenced, identifies four types of disruption: *technical* (discontinuous innovation of technologies), *regulatory* (new regulations triggering new products and service categories), *standard* (broadening acceptance of new platforms such as Wi-Fi), and *distribution* (new distribution methods and mechanisms enabling the creation of new product and service offerings; or enabling existing products and services to be delivered to new and previously unexposed markets).

Each type of disruption can be a powerful source of new applications. However, the most celebrated and publicized disruption is probably technical, which entails new and discontinuous innovations that produce new-to-the-world categories of products and services. We see significant investment in the biomedical/health, technology, and advanced materials sectors (to name a few) that will yield discontinuous new application offerings and even give birth to new industry segments altogether.

This first source of new applications—market disruption—can be broken into two categories:

1. *Vertical new applications.* New offerings that affect a single business domain (a single function or department within an organization).
2. *Horizontal new applications.* New offerings that affect multiple business domains.

Clearly, the more departments or business domains that would be affected by the introduction of the new application (or the more horizontal an offering is), the more difficult the sales challenge. An Enterprise Resource Planning (ERP) software platform is a good example of a horizontal application that replaces islands of software found in vertical department silos.

Although the market disruptors discussed previously will always be a powerful and constant source of meaningful new applications, more people reading this book will be affected by the second source of new applications: integration and bundling of value.

As you have likely experienced firsthand, the Internet, globalization of competition, and shorter times-to-market of new offerings have ravaged both the uniqueness and profitability of organizations in most industries.

Unfortunately, most companies don't have the ability to innovate into superior market positions. Most organizations also can't depend on market disruptors to create cracks in their markets, or entirely new markets in which they can uniquely seize and exploit opportunity for an extended period of time.

Therefore, many companies choose to integrate and bundle products and services in order to create total solutions that are unmatched by competitors. In other words, rather than continuing to sell individual and largely undifferentiated products and services (which their competition can also sell, and possibly at a lower price point), they bundle combinations of related products and services to effectively create a new value proposition altogether. These organizations create a new and less competitive playing field out of existing applications.

Such bundling can occur organically or through strategic acquisitions. Acquisitions enable organizations to quickly acquire new and related competencies that enhance the total bundled value. The best integrated bundles typically form a total outsourced solution for customers—a one-stop shop, if you will.

Examples of integrated and bundled value solutions include:

◆ A company that previously sold only surgical instruments moves toward an integrated business model that offers a total surgical instruments solution. Such a solution might include selling, organizing, cleaning, and disposing of the instruments as well as consulting on and planning the instrument needs for a surgery center.

◆ A company that previously sold only document management software and hardware (such as high-volume scanners) moves toward an integrated total document management solution model. Such a solution might include a total outsource for scanning or filming documents, data entry, archiving documents, data storage, and data management as well as consulting on document management needs.

Integrated and bundled solutions often represent divergent new applications to buyers. Although the individual components of the bundled solution are not new applications or necessarily even unique, *the combined offering represents a total and integrated solution that is divergent and unprecedented for buying organizations.*

Organizations that choose the path of selling tailored, mass-customized, and integrated value solutions (as a means to reestablish higher margins, differentiation, and competitive advantage) encounter a divergent selling challenge. Most struggle with this adjustment because their traditional concurrent offering selling systems are ill-equipped for producing consistent success in divergent environments. In other words, the skills, strategies, and process steps that generated desirable outcomes for the former concurrent model do not correlate to success in the new divergent environment.

The integrated and bundled value source of new applications can also produce vertical new applications (affect a single business domain within buyer organizations) or horizontal new applications (affect multiple business domains). Again, the more domains or departments affected by a new application, the more difficult the selling challenge.

In summary, regardless of the source of new applications, all companies must eventually turn to divergent offerings for long-term revenue and profit growth. Before they can leverage their divergent offerings into profitable and sustainable growth, however, they must adopt an appropriate selling framework that is conducive to a divergent selling environment. If this adjustment is not made, the new application will fail. Sellers and marketers will blame poor engineering, functionality, or cost of the new value proposition, but the real culprit will be poor market facing.

The Divergent Offering Buyer Decision-Making Model

The buyer decision-making process for divergent offerings differs in five primary ways from the concurrent offering process model in Chapter 2. We begin by briefly introducing these five critical shifts (Figure 3.2). Later, we discuss each stage of the divergent offering buyer decision-making process model in detail.

1. *The divide.* The first significant change is the introduction of a divide into the model. The divide represents the buyer's steep psychological resistance to new applications. This resistance is caused by the high costs of change associated with successfully implementing a divergent, new application. Remember, new applications are scary to most buyers. This fear factor prevents most buyers from ever committing to change.

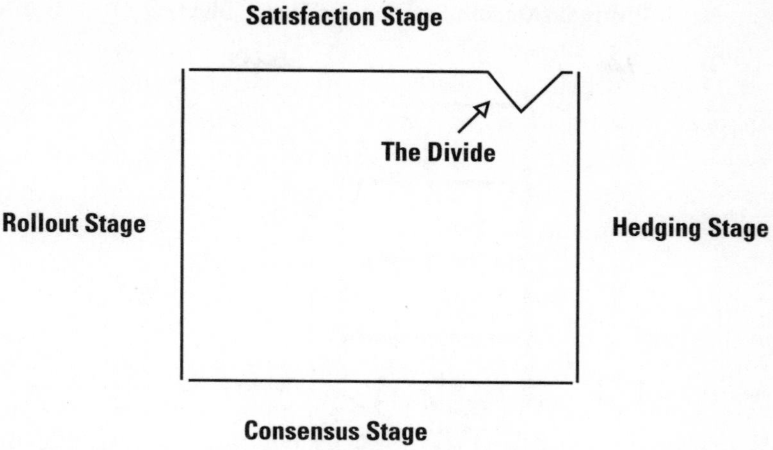

Satisfaction Stage

Consensus Stage

Figure 3.2 The divergent offering buyer model differs from the concurrent model in several ways, including the existence of a psychological divide that causes many selling opportunities to be lost.

The divide is a satisfaction stage dynamic that we'll get into in more detail soon. It is illustrated in Figure 3.3. On one side of the divide lies *curiosity* to change; on the other side, *commitment* to change. Between the two extremes lies the leap of faith sellers expect buyers to take for the new application. Unfortunately, most buyers never take the leap, preferring the safety of the status quo.

We'll spend more time on the divide later in this chapter. For now, understand that this dynamic is unique to selling new applications in major account environments.

2. *The hedging stage.* Another significant change from the model in Chapter 2 is the introduction of a hedging stage of buyer behavior. *Hedging* is a term to describe the risk-reduction and prove-it-to-me mentality buyers will predictably move into once the salesperson has successfully built a case for change. A rule of thumb: The more intense the buyer risk, the more pronounced the hedging stage strategy.

3. *The consensus stage.* A third key difference is that the apprehension stage is replaced by the consensus stage. In this consensus stage, the buyer seeks to attain, or reattain, organizational consensus to

Divergent Model's Satisfaction Stage "Divide"

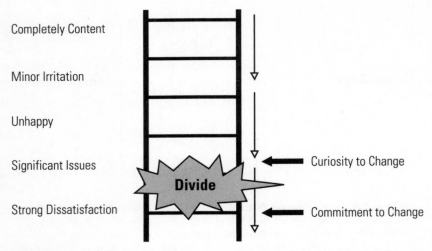

Figure 3.3 The divide represents the psychological gap between a buyer's curiosity and commitment to change.

move forward with a full rollout of the new application. In essence, once the hedging stage has been successfully navigated, the buyer goes back into the organization to make sure that all the key players in the decision base are on board.

4. *The rollout stage.* The fourth shift is in the name of the decision model's final stage. The execution stage becomes the rollout stage, a name that better reflects the final implementation process of a new application. You will learn the subtle differences between the execution and rollout stages.

5. *The entry point determines the buying model.* The fifth significant change is that, in new application selling scenarios, the buyer decision-making model shifts based on the *entry point* of the salesperson. This is very complex.

   You should recognize that when a seller first engages a buyer, the buyer is always somewhere in a decision process for the seller's offering. Practically speaking, the seller enters the buyer's decision-making process with the buyer either being in the satisfaction stage (not shopping) or the shopping stage. In other words, the seller engages the buyer in the first dialogue (probably an initial phone contact) while the buyer is either in the satisfaction stage or the shopping stage.

Again, the constant reality is that the vast majority of the buyer population is in the satisfaction stage (Figure 3.4). Therefore, with many selling opportunities, sellers of new applications enter the buyer's decision process when the buyer is not yet convinced of the need for either change or the specific new application.

Okay, so we have two possible scenarios:

1. The buyer is in the satisfaction stage when first engaged by a seller.
2. The buyer is in the shopping stage when first engaged by a seller.

It is critical to note that the buyer decision-making process differs significantly under these two scenarios.

For example, consider a new application salesperson who calls on two different buyers. Buyer A is in the satisfaction stage for the salesperson's offering. Buyer B is in the shopping stage. Buyer A will have a different, yet predictable, decision-making process from Buyer B. The reason: Buyer A and Buyer B are in different psychological states when first engaged by the salesperson.

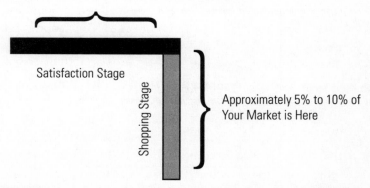

Approximately 90% to 95% of Your Market is Here

Satisfaction Stage

Shopping Stage

Approximately 5% to 10% of Your Market is Here

Figure 3.4 The vast majority of a market resides not in the shopping stage but in the satisfaction stage.

Let's explore this change briefly.

From time to time, a buying organization will realize active needs for a costly and disruptive new application on its own. This is usually when the buyer contacts the seller—a likely sign the buyer is in the shopping stage. For most major account salespeople, these situations are more the exception than the rule. In these shopping stage situations, the seller becomes engaged with a buyer who is already evaluating alternatives, shopping competition, looking at options, and developing buying criteria. In such a scenario, the buyer's decision-making process looks like Figure 3.5.

Alternatively, and with many new application selling opportunities, the seller enters the buyer decision process with the buyer still in the satisfaction stage. When this is true, assuming the seller manages the opportunity properly, the buyer never enters the shopping stage and goes directly from the satisfaction stage to the hedging stage (discussed later). The decision model now morphs as shown in Figure 3.6.

Confused? It's understandable if you are. Let us summarize what you have just read.

As we established, the major sales challenge faced by new application demand sellers is not, "How do I convince a shopping stage buyer to choose me?" Rather, the major sales challenge faced by the selling

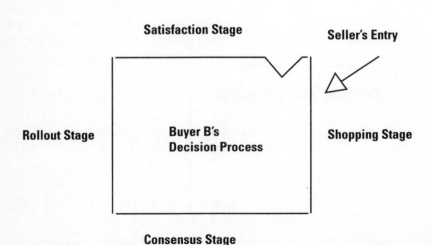

Figure 3.5 In the divergent sale, sellers typically only engage buyers in the shopping stage if the buyer realized the need to change independently.

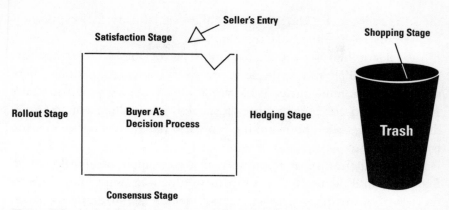

Figure 3.6 In the divergent sale, sellers engaging buyers initially in the satisfaction stage tend to prevent buyers from shopping, causing them to move instead to a hedging mentality.

team revolves around, "How do I create buyer demand for my new application offering?" This demand creation challenge must typically be accomplished with buyers who, upon initial contact, may be curious about the new application, but are a very long way from being committed to adoption.

Again, in most instances, new application sellers engage buyers who are still in the satisfaction stage. The seller, then, is typically involved in helping the buyer realize active needs for the new application offering.

A curious reality of the buyer decision-making process in new application demand scenarios is that most buyers never enter into the shopping stage when the seller enters their decision-making process in the satisfaction stage. This goes completely against the grain of conventional sales wisdom that indicates buyers spend a great deal of time evaluating alternatives, shopping competition, looking at options, and developing buying criteria. In fact, very little of this ever happens with a large percentage of new application buyers.

This is due to one simple reason: Satisfaction stage buyers who have been shown a better way by a businessperson who sells will rarely shop that salesperson once they develop an intention to act or buy. What they will do, however, is move into a hedging phase wherein the buyer attempts to mitigate risk of a full rollout of the new application offering.

Alternatively, if the buyer determined the better way on her own (realized active needs on her own) without the influence of a salesperson, then she will enter a shopping stage and evaluate alternative offerings before moving into the hedging stage.

We'll stop here for a moment. Some of you may sell new applications and routinely find yourself in competitive selling situations where the buyer is shopping around. However, effective new application sales strategy should yield many more satisfaction stage selling opportunities than shopping stage opportunities. How can this be when the opposite is true for you?

Good question. Our response is that new application sellers who frequently find themselves in competitive situations don't know how to recognize and manage satisfaction stage selling opportunities. It's not that satisfaction stage opportunities don't exist in large quantities. Rather, it's just that new application sellers are burning through them and only getting traction with shopping stage opportunities, which are easier to manage when they are found. Put another way, these new application sellers are well equipped to fish in a pond full of buyers with active needs, but ill-equipped to fish in the great sea of buyers with dormant needs.

So, where do we go from here?

We know that the large majority of selling opportunities for new application salespeople are with buyers still in the satisfaction stage. These buyers need to be engaged. Selling to satisfaction stage buyers represents the greatest potential for growth. Therefore, we will focus on the buyer decision-making model with the buyer initially being in the satisfaction stage and set aside the buyer decision-making process used when buyers are engaged by sellers when they are in the shopping stage.

With that said, we focus your attention to Figure 3.7. The buyer model it represents must be mastered by new application sellers. This is the divergent offering

Most salespeople are ill-equipped to fish for buyers with dormant needs.

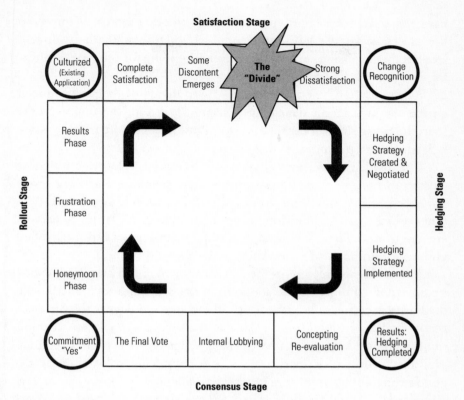

Figure 3.7 The divergent offering buyer decision model should be used by sellers of new applications and innovations to craft strategy.

buyer decision model. All strategies, tactics, and methodologies used by these new application sellers should be based on this model, which depicts how buyers decide to purchase high-risk, and potentially disruptive, new applications.

Stage 1: Satisfaction Stage with the Divide

Just as the buyer model in Chapter 2 begins with the satisfaction stage, the new application buyer decision model also begins with the satisfaction stage. Buyers in the satisfaction stage range from having no dissatisfaction to high dissatisfaction *with their current situation.* The common link with all satisfaction stage buyers, however, is that they do not yet have active needs for your type of offering. In other words, *all* buyers in the satisfaction stage lack sufficient dissatisfaction with their current realities to seek change and begin actively shopping for the type of offering you sell.

As you can see, the previously discussed divide has been introduced within the satisfaction stage from Chapter 2. Again, the divide represents the psychological distance a buyer must travel before making a significant first-step commitment to change (Figure 3.8).

The divide is a necessary element of this model. Why? Because most satisfaction stage selling opportunities never survive the satisfaction stage—especially those opportunities dealing with new applications. In other words, new application sellers have difficulty getting buyers to emerge from the satisfaction stage into the next stage of buyer behavior with a commitment to act on their problems.

The divide also represents the extreme uncertainty a buyer will experience when considering the adoption of a new application. The higher the buyer associates risk with change, the wider and deeper the divide.

As discussed earlier, on one side of the divide is *curiosity* to change. On the other side is *commitment* to change. Between the two extremes is the valley of lost sales opportunities, a graveyard where many perfectly good selling opportunities are lost. *Although this vernacular may sound corny,*

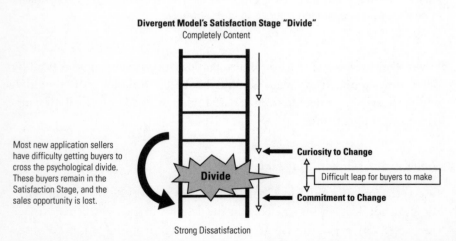

Divergent Model's Satisfaction Stage "Divide"
Completely Content

Most new application sellers have difficulty getting buyers to cross the psychological divide. These buyers remain in the Satisfaction Stage, and the sales opportunity is lost.

Divide

Curiosity to Change

Difficult leap for buyers to make

Commitment to Change

Strong Dissatisfaction

Figure 3.8 Failure to bridge the buyer's psychological divide causes divergent sales opportunities to be lost to no decision rather than to competition.

the concept is not. In fact, this is the key failure point in more than 80 percent of new application opportunities that are engaged with satisfaction stage buyers.

The divide graphically illustrates why it is so difficult for salespeople to create demand for new applications. New applications are simply a leap of faith most buyers are reluctant to take. These buyers have never implemented your type of offering in their organization, so they have no first-hand evidence that it will generate the desired result. Most people are risk averse, and organizations consist of people. Those mainstream buyers prefer the safe harbor of the status quo to the rough, uncertain waters that swirl around new applications.

As a result, most new application opportunities are not lost to the competition, but to the real enemy of new application sellers—*buyer inaction.*

For many buyers considering the adoption of a new application, the question is not, "Do I have a problem(s) that can be solved by this new application?" As shown on the bell curve of satisfaction stage buyers (revisited from Chapter 2), most buyers readily admit to some problems that the new application could help ease or remove. This minor discontent is typically what fuels any initial buyer curiosity. Yet, most buyers

Case Study: Losing Prospects to the Depths of the Divide

Many IT executives were very curious about the concept of software reuse and Axcellerant's innovative reuse offering discussed in Chapter 1. Most of these IT executives admitted to having problems that could be solved by Axcellerant's new application. One such problem was redundancy in programming activity, which caused costly inefficiencies and unnecessary bottlenecks in their programming departments. Programmers had to write similar lines of code over and over for different projects when one code could have been used for all of them. This redundancy problem was viewed by IT executives to be significant enough to warrant a discussion with Axcellerant's sellers.

Nonetheless, after seeing demonstrations of Axcellerant's reuse software, the vast majority of IT executives chose to do nothing—preferring the status quo to change. With most of these satisfaction stage opportunities, Axcellerant sellers routinely lost prospects to the depths of the divide. They lacked the understanding and strategies to get buyers safely across the divide, where they would arrive committed to change.

rarely get beyond just that—curiosity. Few commit to take action that will reduce or eliminate their discontent. The majority prefer the safety of the known to the risk of change despite the presence of lingering problems.

As a good example of this dynamic, let's revisit our Axcellerant case study from Chapter 1.

As we shall learn, best-practice new application selling teams are masters at *building bridges* that help buyers cross this psychological divide. They do this by executing one or all of the following broadly defined *bridging methods:*

- *Using analytic tools that explore the* total sum *of problems.* These tools investigate the scale and scope of problems and their implications. Remember, once the cost of the problem outweighs the total cost of the solution (including nonfinancial change costs), the buyer will be ready to change.
- *Introducing* process mechanisms *that create and grow critical-mass dissatisfaction among the decision base of the targeted organization.* Less experienced salespeople see finding and growing dissatisfaction as an event. More experienced new application sellers know it is a process. Process mechanisms are powerful bridge-building mechanisms we observed better-practice salespeople using time and time again in their new application selling endeavors.
- *Documenting, via a satisfaction stage breed of value-based proposals, how the offering enables the furtherance of strategic objectives of the company.* Buyers will be more apt to move across the bridge toward change if the offering helps accomplish a critical departmental or organizational goal. All sellers understand this, but few understand the process of proper documentation to achieve this alignment with buyer objectives. As you will learn, a proper value-based, or change-document, proposal has little to do with a product or service offering, yet everything to do with building a business case for change. In these documents, sellers must align their business case with buyer objectives.
- *Meeting, via key progression steps,* diverse vertical department personnel. Another unique reality for new application demand sellers is that, many times, multiple department buy-in is necessary before a final "yes" can occur. This multi-silo challenge has frustrated many account sellers who were successful at influencing

one department to change, but not the sufficient *critical mass.* In essence, getting a diverse group of vertical managers to agree on a new application has a unique complexity unto itself. Often, it takes an enterprise—or collective—"yes" for the initiative to move forward. Best-practice new application sellers successfully access these varied people and channels. In addition, they are effective at strategically persuading many of these influencers to be champions of the change process.

In essence, these bridges are not typical proposals, quotes, or demonstrations. Rather, they are mechanisms intended to help a key group of decision makers and influencers *see the need for change first,* and *the need for the seller's offering second.* We discuss bridging steps in greater detail later in this book.

Building a logical case for change that helps buyers bridge their steep psychological divide can be a tricky endeavor. Yet, it is an essential competency for any new application seller whose best market opportunities are with satisfaction stage buyers.

Stage 2: The Hedging Stage

After a salesperson has convinced a buyer of the need for change (by building a logical business case), the buyer predictably enters the second stage of divergent offering buyer behavior—the hedging stage.

It is important to note that the hedging stage is predictable for buyers who have emerged from the satisfaction stage as a result of the catalystic effort of the salesperson. In effect, expect new application buyers to move into the hedging stage when the salesperson has convinced the buyer that the costs of not doing anything are greater than the price of change.

Buyers who have entered the hedging stage are committed to taking action in the way of the seller's specific solution. However, in this stage, they seek to take action in a low-risk way. Therefore, the buyer's psychology changes from "Do I need to act?" to "How do I reduce the risk of taking this specific action?"

As mentioned previously, when the salesperson has properly managed a satisfaction stage opportunity and has been the catalyst behind the buyer's intention to change, the shopping stage is averted. It never comes into play.

Avoiding the entrance of the shopping stage is a good thing. Sometimes a great thing. Buyer shopping opens the door to competition, whether from direct competitors or alternative solution providers. The seller loses leverage and typically experiences diminishing margins upon being competitively shopped around.

Avoiding the shopping stage requires salespeople to be consultative businesspeople

The psychology of a buyer in the hedging stage is "How do I reduce the risk of taking this specific action?"

who sell. Transactional salespeople will unlikely advance buyers from the satisfaction stage. Most of their satisfaction stage opportunities will end at the bottom of the divide. These transactional sellers are not able to avoid the shopping stage and will spend their days in the precarious and limiting position of hunting for buyers with active needs and already in the shopping stage.

Again, this observation seems to go completely against the grain of conventional wisdom. Many selling teams we talk to actually refuse to engage with anyone other than a "qualified" buyer who has a predefined and active need (shopping stage buyers). These selling teams often lose out on the greatest opportunity in their marketplace—satisfaction stage buyers who need help, but just don't know it yet. What salespeople lack is a process to psychologically move these buyers along the path of change.

Why would a satisfaction stage buyer who has been convinced of the need for change by a seller *not* enter into the shopping stage and formally evaluate alternative solutions (enter the hedging stage) instead? Consider the following:

- *Loyalty.* A buyer who has been educated by the consultative businessperson who sells about the reasons for change feels strong loyalty to the seller. The buyer will be reluctant to shop the seller.

Are You a Consultative Salesperson?

Our firm, Sogistics, assesses thousands of people annually for compatibility to sales positions. Often, companies use us as a checkpoint before they make a final hiring decision. We've found it to be the perfect tandem research vehicle for critical sales productivity issues. In these assessments, we've learned that almost all salespeople describe themselves as consultative. Yet, one of the primary roles of a best-practice consultant is to help buyers see the need for change in areas where the client did not see it before the engagement. By this definition, our research shows very few salespeople to be consultative at all—those few who can create demand with satisfaction stage buyers. More often, salespeople are only effective with shopping stage buyers, which is a lower-value-adding role to both the buying and selling organizations.

This rings true even in this day and age when the definition of loyalty is the absence of a better price. Loyalty still matters. It is a trait ingrained in us as children, and serves as a powerful motivator that holds buyers accountable to do the right thing.

◆ *Expertise.* A satisfaction stage buyer convinced of the need for change by the seller sees that seller as an expert within the product or service domain. With new applications, buyers are unsophisticated, making them dependent on the expertise of the seller.

◆ *Relationship.* Multiple relationships have now been built between the seller and diverse people within the buyer organization. Often, these relationships are across vertical boundaries, in different departmental silos. The members of the buying team *trust* the seller. It would be risky for the decision maker of the organization to shift allegiances at this point. At minimum, it would probably be politically sensitive. In addition, the extended sales process that has culminated in the buyer developing active needs has necessitated an extensive flow of information. Both the buyer and seller have developed the necessary intimate understanding of each other's organizations. Forging such a relationship with a new supplier would require another significant investment of time and trust.

The Two Phases of the Hedging Stage

Once a buyer emerges from the satisfaction stage, he moves into two pre-dictable phases within the hedging stage. Remember, the buyer may have been working with the salesperson for weeks, months, or possibly even a year or more. The satisfaction stage divide has been bridged by the seller and crossed by the buyer. In other words, the critical mass of the buying organization has become convinced of the need for change primarily as a result of the diligent efforts of the salesperson. The end of the satisfac-tion stage is typified by a change recognition meeting, which happens internally within the buying organization and occurs independently of the salesperson. At this meeting, the decision makers and influencers make a final decision about whether they want to commit to action. This may be a rubber stamp at this point, or a strongly debated event.

At this internal meeting, the decision base gets to its first critical milestone of the change process (see the top right corner of the diver-gent offering buyer model in Figure 3.7). Change recognition is the critical-mass shift in buyer behavior at this point. Again, the buyer's emphasis turns from the driving satisfaction stage mentality of "should we change?" to the driving hedging stage mentality of "how can we *reduce risk* around this change?"

Large account, new application buying decisions are accompanied by major risk. Forgive us for continuously harping on that point. Because of this significant risk to the buying organization, most buyers won't go directly from the satisfaction stage to a full rollout of your offering.

Buyers advancing from the satisfaction stage have committed to action that reduces or eliminates their problems. If you have managed the opportunity properly, your offering is the course of action that will be taken by the buying organization. However, the buying organization will not yet be prepared to sign off on a full rollout until the members of the decision base have explored, or even exhausted, options for reducing risk of a full rollout of your offering. As you know, a full roll-out represents high financial and change costs to the buyer.

This results in the existence of the hedging stage of buyer behavior. This stage may be very brief and informal or very lengthy and formal.

In summary, the buyer's psychological switch in the form of change recognition is a pivotal point in the process of an eventual full rollout of the divergent offering. *Please note, however, that the sales process is far from over as the buyer enters the hedging stage.* The buyer's commitment to change should not be viewed as a signal that a full rollout of your offering is inevitable. At this point, any number of things can happen, although all revolve around the broad buyer intent to reduce risk. We now introduce the first of two phases in the hedging stage.

PHASE 1: HEDGING STRATEGY CREATION AND NEGOTIATION

In this initial phase, buyers consider various methods for reducing risk of a full rollout. Buyers believe that a full rollout will be necessary to help them remove their problem(s) and achieve their objectives, but first want some verification that they are making the proper decision to proceed with your offering.

In this hedging strategy creation and negotiation phase, the buyer brainstorms how to taste your offering in a smaller, less threatening way than a full rollout. In other words, the buyer wants more proof that your offering will deliver the expected results. The buyer may also look to the seller to contribute risk-reduction options. Assuming there is no time pressure urging the buyer to enact your new application offering, the eventual risk-reduction strategy employed by the buyer may take a few different forms. The selected method may be as informal as reference checking or as formal as one of the following hedging options (not a comprehensive list):

- ◆ *Trial or beta.* The buyer may prefer a casual or formal trial of your product or service. This may be some simulated endeavor aimed at allowing the buyer to experience your offering in a low-risk way.
- ◆ *Demonstration.* The buyer may want to see your offering produce results for the buyer's specific application.
- ◆ *Implementation of solution analysis.* Dollars may be budgeted to study the best way to integrate your solution in the buyer's organization. The psychology here is not "should we do it?" but "what is the best way to integrate the solution we've selected?"
- ◆ *Visitations.* Site visits to your location or visits with your existing clients who have similar applications for your offerings can serve to reduce a buyer's perceived risk.

Many effective hedging stage progressions give the buyer the ability to test drive the concept and prove that it works.

♦ *Modeling.* Creating accurate and elaborate models that can simulate the effects of the new application on the buying organization, using data or scenarios that precisely represent the actual buying organization.

Remember, at this point, the buyer is convinced of the need for change. The actions and intentions are now, "How do we reduce risk around the solution itself?" Overall, the hedging strategy creation and negotiation phase is about coming up with a way for the buyer to experience the validity of your offering without the time commitments, risk, or expense of a full rollout.

Most effective new application sellers fully expect buyers to enter this phase. They view it as a key advancement in the buyer's process before a full rollout can occur. Best-practice new application sellers understand that organizational skepticism is the dominant behavior in this stage. In other words, fear of making a mistake becomes the overriding buyer motivation.

As a result, savvy new application sellers get well ahead of this hedging curve. These sellers accommodate buyers and actually suggest meaningful risk-reduction strategies prior to full rollout that are quickly agreed to by buyers eager to begin testing the waters of change.

The key to proper hedging strategies is to propose options for mitigating risk that *emotionally* and *financially* commit a buyer to rollout—in a gradual manner. The best way to achieve this is by asking buyers to make minor and gradual financial investments during the hedging stage. One example of this can be found in the accompanying case study.

> ### Case Study: Valuable Lessons about Hedging Strategies from a Best-Practice Organization
>
> A client of ours, Physicians Imaging Solutions, sells multimillion dollar partnerships to large group physicians' practices. The partnerships involve implementing new, high-end diagnostic imaging capabilities on-site, which is certainly a high-risk venture from the perspective of the physicians' groups. More often than not, Physicians Imaging must create demand for their offering. Predictably, they must eventually deal with a group practice that has psychologically shifted from the satisfaction stage ("Should we change?") to the hedge stage ("How do we reduce risk around this initiative?").
>
> Without going into great detail, Physicians Imaging proposes a multiple-step risk-mitigation plan that helps these hedge stage buyers experience some early successes with the proposed initiative—before having to make a very large commitment of a final full rollout decision. Yet, the buyer must financially ante up from small to progressively larger phased-in increments in order to experience these victories that prove the merit of the new application.
>
> The buyer can walk away at any time during the hedging stage. But, should this occur and the buyer has already made some financial commitments in the execution of hedging strategies to reduce the risk of a full rollout, they forfeit the investment to date. By applying this risk-mitigation strategy, Physicians Imaging Solutions has successfully introduced progression steps that build the type of emotional and financial commitment that leads buyers down the path to the "yes" that counts most: "yes" to full rollout.

A common mistake by sellers of high-risk new applications or disruptive innovations is to offer the hedge for free. In effect, they allow the buyer to taste the offering without any financial commitment. More often than not, the buyer tries the offering in a half-hearted manner because she has nothing to lose. Because of the lack of effort and attention, the hedge goes poorly by the seller's standards, and the buyer subsequently returns to the satisfaction stage or refuses to undertake a full rollout. Once the buyer puts money on the table, it heightens attention, motivates the buyer to achieve a successful outcome, and demonstrates resolve to solve problem(s) and undergo change. Remember, a good hedging strategy results in gradually higher buyer commitment on two very important levels: financial and emotional.

It's possible to predict a buyer's behavior within the hedging stage based on the level of both financial and emotional commitment the buyer has made. Consider Figure 3.9, which can be used to anticipate a buyer's hedging stage behavior.

During the hedging stage, if a buyer has strong emotional commitment to move forward but has not financially put skin on the table, the buyer's resolve to move forward may be tested by unforeseen events (Quadrant 1). Random events such as management turnover, management distraction by the latest fire that needs to be put out, or other industry disruptions may be enough to prevent the buyer from moving forward. However, should no such events disrupt the sales process, the buying organization most likely will proceed.

If a buyer in the hedging stage has little emotional commitment to move forward with the seller's specific solution, and has made little or no financial commitment to the seller's solution because the seller offered a hedge for free, the probability that the buyer will walk away is elevated (Quadrant 2). In such a case, the buyer may return to the satisfaction stage or begin looking for an alternative solution to remove a problem or achieve an objective.

Quadrant 3 represents a hedging stage scenario in which the buyer has made a significant financial investment in the hedge, but has little

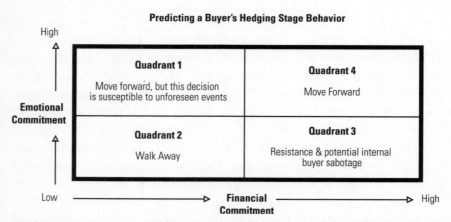

Figure 3.9 Once in the hedging stage, buyer behavior is contingent upon the organization's critical mass level of both financial and emotional commitment to the divergent offering.

emotional commitment across the entire decision base to move forward. Because commitment may not be high or wide enough, the initiative has the potential to be sabotaged by those who have not emotionally bought in. Yet, since the buyer has already made a notable financial commitment, the buyer will be willing to continue the dialogue and entertain the seller's efforts to rebuild both a business case for the offering and the buyer's emotional commitment to it.

Quadrant 4 is the most favorable hedging stage scenario. It represents the outcome of an effective divergent offering sales process. In Quadrant 4, the buyer has put significant skin on the table financially for the hedge. The buyer also has a deep and wide level of emotional commitment across the decision base for a rollout of the seller's offering. With a high level of commitment in both dimensions, the buyer will likely move forward even if significant and disruptive events occur.

Let us now turn away from the commitment matrix, and return to a more general discussion on hedging stage strategy.

Once again, effective sellers do not resist the hedging process. Moreover, they do not view the hedging process as manipulation or a stall tactic by the buyer. Sellers should realize that, unless the buyer is able to reduce risk to a satisfactory level, the buyer will either return to the satisfaction stage or begin shopping for another solution. Either scenario would represent a major setback for a seller who has likely invested a significant amount of time, resources, and effort convincing the buyer of a need for change.

Establishing agreement about the hedge to be used can be a source of derision between the buyer and seller. Both parties may arrive at disparate ideas for hedging risk. The buyer is motivated to reduce risk in the direction of zero, while the seller wants to speedily advance the sale toward full commitment. Occasionally, the buyer's desired hedging path is unreasonable, and a lengthy and dangerous negotiation process ensues. Ideally, as the buyer initially enters the hedging stage, the seller suggests a preconceived risk-reduction option that is sufficient for the buyer's needs, and little or no negotiation is necessary.

PHASE 2: HEDGING STRATEGY IMPLEMENTATION

The second and final phase of the hedging stage is implementation. At this point, a hedging strategy has been created and negotiated. Now, the implementation of the risk-reduction strategy begins in earnest. Again, this may take the form of an elaborate beta, a formal trial, a brief simulation, a casual site visit at a customer's location, or one of many other possibilities.

The higher the buyer's costs of change, the more elaborate the hedge often must be to suit the buyer's risk-mitigation needs. Most mainstream buyers at executive levels (where budgets are created for new applications) are neither mavericks nor late adopters. Rather, they are calculated risk takers who are willing to gamble to further their strategic objectives, but not bet the house on an all-or-nothing proposition.

The hedge becomes a test—one that must be passed by the seller's offering before a full rollout may be awarded by the buyer. New application sellers must gain an understanding of what constitutes a passed test, and what is considered failure by the buyer. In other words, hedging implementation success or failure should be clearly defined by both parties and appropriately documented prior to the execution of the hedge. The seller should manage the buyer's expectations for results while the seller will also need to learn the buyer's evaluation criteria for the results. Hard, nonsubjective timetables, guidelines, and parameters should be agreed upon before commencing the hedging implementation phase to avoid long processes and ambiguous conclusions. Results must be jointly analyzed.

Fortunately, buyers and sellers share the same objectives in the hedging stage. Buyers recognize that they have a problem and hope the sellers can remove it with their offerings.

Too many sellers feel the new application sale has been completed when they've convinced a satisfaction stage buyer of the need for change. Nothing could be further from the truth. More experienced new application sellers understand that the hedging stage is where the *real work* begins. At this point, if full rollout is to be realized, it's time to ramp up effort, thoroughness, diligence, and communication if the buyer is to emerge from the hedging stage to the next stage of buyer behavior—the consensus stage.

To wrap up our discussion of the hedging stage in this chapter, please understand that when buyers recognize a need to change and their solution represents a major new application for them, they will look for ways to reduce risk. Sellers must provide these risk-averse buyers with some method of alleviating their fears; otherwise, the buyers will either return to the status quo or begin searching for safer alternatives.

Stage 3: The Consensus Stage

After a buyer has gone through the hedging stage, she moves into the third stage of divergent offering buying behavior, which is the consensus stage. In this stage, the buyer's primary motivation is confirming, securing, or regaining organizational consensus. In other words, the activities in this stage are focused on critical-mass agreement and buy-in to a full and final rollout of your solution.

Perhaps no single element typifies the changes in organizational behavior over the last two decades as much as the decision by consensus. Yesterday's organization was driven by dictation and mandate. Today, even Patton-type leaders understand the importance of decisions made *with* others, versus *for* others. Smart leaders know that consensus is the difference between cooperation and compliance. Cooperation means successful implementation of a decision or agenda. Compliance means potential politics, bickering, mistrust, sabotage, and eventual failure. Employees now expect a voice in how things get done. And with talent being the critical component to sustainable competitive advantage today, the smart leader makes sure opinions are heard—and debated—before a final decision is reached.

The underlying driver of the consensus stage is a different type of risk reduction. In the hedging stage, the motivation of buyers is to reduce the risk that the offering will not work and fail to remove their specific problems or fail to help the organization achieve its objectives.

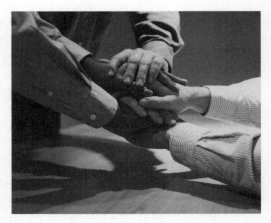

Consensus stage buyer psychology is as follows: "Am I sure that the right people have bought in? Let's double-check before we commit to a full rollout."

It is more of a *functional* risk-reduction motivation ("Will the offering perform?"). Those fears, though, are reduced through the hedging process.

In the consensus stage, the risk experienced by buyers is more *personal*. The psychological driver of this stage is centered on reducing personal and political vulnerability. Individuals supporting the acquisition of the new application offering will want others to publicly support a "yes" decision as well. Remember, new applications don't just represent high financial costs, but also the additional burden and distraction of disruption and change. Even a successful introduction of the new application often trails a long, frustrating implementation process. Smart decision makers will want a final buy-in from others in the power structure so there is a greater likelihood of a successful outcome. In the end, they also do not want to be singled out as being solely responsible for bringing about the often painful burdens of change.

Remember, big decisions are politically risky. A wrong decision can mean significant losses: financial, job security, status in the organization, lost time, and so on. There is no bigger decision than a "yes" to a full rollout of the new application you've proposed. More experienced sellers understand this, and anticipate that buyers will predictably pull into the consensus stage before a final go-ahead can be secured.

The Initial Phase of Consensus: Concept Reevaluation
Assume the buyer has emerged from the hedging stage with a stronger belief that your offering will function as advertised. Skepticism has now been reduced via some form of hedge (beta, trial, etc.) that has proven— beyond a reasonable doubt—your offering will deliver on its functional promise. At this point, the buyer will leave the hedging stage and move into this initial phase of the consensus stage—the concept reevaluation phase.

Concept reevaluation occurs when the decision base predictably looks at the concept to make sure that it still fits within the context of the current organizational situation. Whereby the driving question in the hedging stage is, "How can we test the water and hedge our bets before jumping in?" the psychology in this early reevaluation phase is, "Let's make sure the concept still applies." Remember, organizations today are constantly being disrupted. These disruptions are increasingly sharp and more frequent. Economic volatility, competitive shifts, leadership turnover, and merger and acquisition are just a few variables that force buyers to retake their pulse on your offering before committing to a full rollout.

Phase 2: Internal Lobbying Phase

Assuming that your concept is still seen as a resource priority, the buying team will move into the next phase of the consensus stage, the internal lobbying phase. This is where the champion of your offering makes sure that the offering has the final blessing of the people with political power and influence. Jim Holden, in his excellent book *Power Base Selling,* discusses the *who* aspect of how major decisions are made.[1] His contention that decisions are made less by organizational chart hierarchy and more by political influence has strong merit.

Leaders and managers know that the unemployment line is typically only one bad and unpopular decision away. As a result, internal lobbying for final decision support prior to rollout spreads the risk for the champions of your offering. Champions know that a group decision to go forward with a rollout—should that rollout go awry—gives them a position of defense concerning job security and protects their power and title status.

From a purely performance perspective, supporters of the offering know that having the decision base solidly on board before a final "yes" will ensure commitment to a proper implementation. After all, implementing the new application offering will predictably lead to a few rough waters. Smart champions know that it's a lot wiser to rally for political consensus in the beginning than to do so later when pockets of forest fires may crop up.

Phase 3: Final Vote Phase

Finally, the last phase of the consensus stage is the final vote. This may be a formal meeting among the leadership or an informal rubber stamp by a particularly powerful decision maker. Either way, this is the final roadblock to full rollout. If the stage has been set properly, it is rarely a big event that requires an elaborate closing strategy. Note that the Columbo close, the alternative choice close, the puppy dog close, or any other closing technique you may have read about over the years will have little positive effect at this point. In other words, you and the buyer are both ready to do business. Final consummation is already assumed by both parties. Closing is just a detail, and you don't want over-aggressiveness to get in the way of a final commitment at this late stage.

Length and Intensity of the Consensus Stage

In some selling situations, the consensus stage can be very drawn out, and fierce debating in the buying organization emerges about whether to adopt the new application. In other selling situations, the consensus stage is passed through almost imperceptibly and with a great deal of haste.

We have found that the length and intensity of the consensus stage is positively correlated to two primary variables: *the political level of the buying organization and the risk to the buying organization associated with the full rollout of the new application.* As you might guess, the more highly charged an organization is politically, the more time and effort is typically put into the consensus-building process by the internal champions of the new application. Similarly, the more inherent risk associated with the new application, the longer the consensus stage extends. This is because more risk means that either (or both) there is an increased probability of a full rollout going poorly or delivering lackluster results, or that the effects of a poor rollout will be more severe for the buying organization. In either case, the internal champions of the new application are personally exposed to possible negative consequences, and will be more diligent and thorough in their efforts to build consensus.

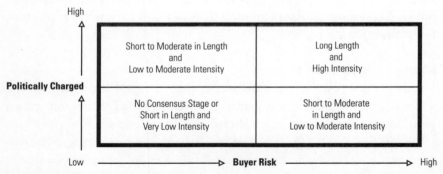

Figure 3.10 The length and intensity of the buyer's consensus stage depends on the organization's perceived risk and internal political climate.

The matrix in Figure 3.10 should help you determine how long the consensus stage will be relative to your new application selling opportunities.

Stage 4: The Rollout Stage

After a decision to "yes" has been reached, the buyer moves into the final stage of decision making—rollout. Although there are more than a few subtle differences between rollout execution in divergent offering scenarios and execution in concurrent offering scenarios, we see no need to go into great detail at this point. The main difference between the rollout stage in the divergent model and the execution stage in the concurrent model is that emotions are amplified in the rollout stage.

The first phase of the rollout stage is called the honeymoon phase. After a "yes" decision has been formally made, buyers and sellers are both initially excited about getting started and extracting the results expected from the offering and the relationship between the two organizations. However, when rolling out divergent, new application offerings, the honeymoon phase will draw to a predictable, and sometimes abrupt, conclusion.

We have already indicated that the implementation of new applications can be particularly frustrating and difficult for buyers because they often initially lack the knowledge, experience, and infrastructure necessary to support the new application. Therefore, we call this frustrating, or intense, phase the effort phase. A great deal of effort is expended by both the buying and selling organizations during this phase to ensure a successful implementation.

The final phase of the rollout stage is called the results phase. The new application offering has been implemented, and results are beginning to be generated. Buyers will almost certainly measure performance. Good sellers will also monitor performance and gather results. If the seller has done a good job at managing expectations, the results phase should be a rewarding period for both the buyer and seller.

With a successful rollout stage, the buyer will return to the satisfaction stage, and the cycle will begin again. Eventually, the application will be perceived as inadequate or incapable of helping the organization achieve its objectives. At this point, the buying organization will commit

Case Study: Expecting the Unexpected

Trimble, a California-based firm that is the leader in construction and land survey instrumentation (among other things), is very familiar with the effort phase of the rollout stage. Trimble continuously applies new technologies such as Global Positioning Systems (GPS) and computerization to change the way work is performed by such organizations as road construction companies and survey firms. These new technology-driven solutions dramatically increase productivity for its customers.

One Trimble application puts GPS systems on bulldozers, which essentially controls the blade of the bulldozer. The blade moves automatically as the operator simply steers the bulldozer. Earth is moved by the automated blade to meet the engineering specifications to a very high rate of accuracy. This automated system leads to less rework, reduced operating costs, reduced materials costs, and significantly faster work.

When Trimble initially installs its new technology onto bulldozers and other earth-moving equipment, their clients are excited to have this new capability. "This will change our business" or "This will really speed up our turnaround time on jobs" are common customer thoughts immediately after successful installation.

Predictably, reality sets in soon thereafter. The Trimble installers and trainers have left, and buyers must operate the new technology. Many buyers, especially unsophisticated ones, quickly grow frustrated at the predictable hiccups and challenges that occur in this early phase of rollout.

Fortunately, Trimble anticipates buyer complaints, frantic calls, and so on, during this tenuous timeframe. By preparing for this natural buyer reaction during the rollout of a divergent offering, Trimble has implemented creative strategies to quickly help buyers who are struggling with their new equipment before frustration reaches high levels.

Eventually, buyers learn to independently operate the new technology and they experience the gains they originally expected from the new application. Both parties are satisfied.

This is all accomplished less painfully for buyers as a result of Trimble's effort phase strategies that reassure and comfort divergent offering buyers during a predictable period of tumult.

to change in the form of an identical replacement (or addition), a continuously improved version, an economy version, or a new application.

This is the end of our discussion on the rollout stage for now. Because the major challenge of new application sellers revolves around creating demand from satisfaction stage buyers (as opposed to proper implementation), this is what Chapter 4 discusses next.

Congratulations! You now have a solid understanding of how buyers buy both concurrent offerings and divergent offerings. It's time to roll up your sleeves and get down to business. We're going to learn the specific strategies, competencies, skills, and mechanisms that best-practice new application sellers employ to move satisfied buyers to "yes" in a way that is straightforward, nonmanipulative, and value-adding.

Summary

In Chapter 3, the key points are:

- Buyers of major account new applications go through a unique decision-making process. The steps of this process are contingent upon where the buyer is in this process when the seller engages the buyer.
- Sellers who engage buyers while they are still in the satisfaction stage are able to prevent competitive selling situations, and simultaneously protect margins.
- Effective salespeople anticipate that buyers will need to reduce the risk associated with a full rollout of a new application. Therefore, sellers develop and offer hedging options that allow buyers to experience success with the new application and that increase the buyer's financial and emotional commitment to the offering.

Notes

1. Holden, J. (1990). *Power base selling.* New York, NY: John Wiley & Sons.

4

From Entry to Closure: Models and Frameworks for Creating and Managing New Selling Opportunities

Chapter 4 teaches you how to think like a best-practice, market-optimizing businessperson who sells.

_____

This chapter resumes a discussion from Chapter 1 about sales frameworks. It also begins to explain how you can effectively sell *new applications* to buyers in your market. Furthermore, over the course of this and the next four chapters, a complete strategic framework for selling new applications and managing buyers through their new application decision-making process unfolds.

Let's pause for a moment to once again explain what we mean by *strategic sales framework*. To be effective on a consistent and sustainable basis, salespeople must utilize a framework that properly guides all of their decisions: which strategies to execute, which steps to take in the sales process, and which actions or processes to employ within each step. A framework ultimately defines, dictates, and drives the manner in

The 5 "S's" of a Proper Sales Framework

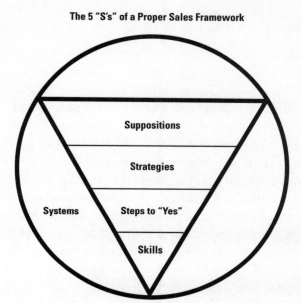

Figure 4.1 A disciplined framework ultimately defines, drives, and dictates selling behavior.

which new selling opportunities are created and managed. As introduced in Chapter 1, an effective strategic sales framework can be diagrammed as in Figure 4.1.

We need to break down this model into its components. As we do so, you will gain an understanding of how complex the decision process is for new application salespeople. Getting them to understand and routinely operate within this best-practice strategic framework requires repetition and disciplined sales management. However, the end result of a sales organization executing this framework is rapid and controlled revenue growth. The A players on your team will raise the bar to new heights when indoctrinated in such a sales framework. Fortunately, the less-talented B players can also learn this system despite its inherent complexity. The system will actually compensate for their lesser talent and help them achieve significant productivity gains. As for the C players, they will likely not be able to execute this framework.

Suppositions

Beginning at the top of the diagram, *suppositions* are the guiding beliefs that dictate how an organization uniformly decides to face its market. Good belief systems are a prerequisite for sales optimization and they should be deliberately spread throughout an organization. Sellers will think, act, and behave in a manner consistent with their beliefs. Executives must proactively program each member of their sales organizations with good and appropriate beliefs as they relate to their sales environment in order to get them to exhibit desired behaviors. Without such a proactive effort to manage perspective, individuals will acquire and hold incorrect or inappropriate assumptions that can be very detrimental and self-limiting with regard to sales performance. If you ignore beliefs in your selling system, you do so at your own peril. Remember, beliefs are viral and will spread throughout your team if left uncontrolled.

Table 4.1 lists some common self-limiting beliefs about selling along with the beliefs that more closely correlate with high sales productivity.

Our assessments of thousands of salespeople suggest there are several additional erroneous beliefs held by many salespeople. For example, a common self-limiting belief is that no budget equals no sale. Most salespeople believe that if a budget is not in place and available for their product or service, it is not possible to get a sale. That's not true. Other sellers believe that if budgets are not available for their products or services, budgets can be created if the seller has properly engaged a member of the buying organization who possesses high levels of authority and political power. This is also typically not possible. If money isn't available for a new budget, it simply isn't available. Period.

The proper belief relative to budgets and selling is that, although budgets *can't* be created, funds *can* be shifted within existing budgets. If you, the seller, fully understand the buyer's business, challenges, and objectives on organizational, departmental, and personal levels, you should have some opportunity to tie your offering to one or more existing budgets. Again, although it is generally very, very difficult to get new budgets created, it is much more likely to get funds shifted within and around existing budgets. Some examples follow on page 116.

Table 4.1 Selling Is About . . .

Productivity-Limiting Suppositions	Productivity-Enhancing Suppositions
. . . being a salesperson.	. . . being a businessperson who sells.
. . . relationships.	. . . adding business value (if you add business value, the relationship will grow strong).
. . . more activity equals more sales.	. . . strategic activity equals more sales.
. . . competition (playing a game within a field of competitors).	. . . sur/petition (playing a new game . . . with new rules . . . where the real competition is buyer inertia).[1]
. . . problem solving.	. . . helping buyers achieve their strategic initiatives and capitalize on their best opportunities as much as it is about solving problems.
. . . winning.	. . . positively impacting buyers.
. . . closing the deal.	. . . not striking out (i.e., keeping the opportunity alive with a series of meaningful progressions until a case for change has been made).
. . . selling more of my products and services through selling techniques and influence strategies.	. . . selling more of my offerings by ultimately helping my buyers sell more of *their* products or services (showing them how to differentiate, grow revenues, reduce costs, and gain competitive advantage).
. . . being in front of qualified buyers at the right time, when they have active needs.	. . . optimizing each opportunity, whether it is with buyers who have active or dormant needs. The greatest source of opportunities and growth, however, is with buyers who need (dormant need) what we have, but just don't know it yet (and having a process for creating and managing these types of opportunities).
. . . needs analysis and presenting capabilities.	. . . bridging the gap between buyer needs and your capabilities, which requires building a compelling business case.
. . . checkers (step-by-step, linear approach).	. . . chess (flexible and dynamic approach based on buyer decision psychology).

- One of our clients sells sophisticated, interactive websites to colleges and universities. These specialized websites essentially stimulate more financial contributions and participation from alumni members. If the alumni office at these schools has no budget available for such an online initiative, then our client can look to have funds shifted from other budgets controlled by the office of development, the school's marketing budget, or the school's budget for the general school website (or a little from each).

- Another client that we have already discussed—Trimble—sells high-end construction and surveying instrumentation. This instrumentation is sold to construction contractors, mining companies, engineering or survey firms, and state and municipal road or highway departments. When a construction contractor has no funds available in its capital equipment budgets, the funds for such equipment often come from operating budgets associated with one or multiple specific construction projects.

Keep in mind that budget shifting becomes much easier if the salesperson can demonstrate a clear ROI. If you don't currently possess a model for calculating a buyer-specific ROI from investing in your offerings, create one. Chapter 5 discusses the first steps for building an ROI case.

Let's look at another supposition area: How high up the organizational chart should you target for entry? Such beliefs determine who sellers target for a passageway into a buying organization. Considering that entry is the front edge of the sales process, improper beliefs in this area can completely stall selling efforts.

Some sellers and sales managers believe they should focus initial access portals as high as possible: The C level is a common starting point. Realistically, these high-level individuals typically don't own the specific problems you can solve, although they commonly do have the authority and political power to make economic decisions.

Other sellers believe they are condemned to engaging lower-level individuals within buyer organizations as an entry point. Their world is full of purchasing agents and bottom-tier tactical staffers and managers.

So, where is the correct point of entry for major account sellers? We'll answer this question very specifically, but the general answer is that mid-level managers and executives who actually have the problem you can solve or the opportunity you can help them realize are the best point of entry. Getting in very high as a means to increase the probability of eventual sales success has never been validated by research . . . at least to our knowledge. Our experience is that strategies of exclusively attempting to get in very high with buying organizations are products of sales folklore and often diminish sales productivity. The lesson: Focus on the *problem channel* early on for an access point.

Chapter 1 briefly touched on entry channels. We said that the proper point of entry hinges on whether the offering you are selling is a concurrent offering or a divergent offering. Beginning with concurrent offerings, the buying organization is already doing a job in a consistent manner to how your offering would enable them to do the job. Generally speaking, smaller changes make smaller impacts. Therefore, a change to your concurrent offering could logically generate only a moderate return (moderate from an organizational perspective, although potentially significant from a departmental perspective). Because concurrent offerings represent an existing category of offering and there is marginal perceived value-add from changing to your offering, higher-level executives would have little interest and would therefore be a poor point of entry. Mid-tier managers who possess problems you can solve are the better entry point for concurrent offerings. These mid-tier managers often make the final decisions about concurrent offerings as well.

Divergent offerings represent a fundamental shift in how a job is performed, or a new job altogether. Divergent offerings, therefore, have the potential for a significantly higher payoff. Top-tier executives may have interest in these offerings and can represent a viable point of entry for the salesperson. At the end of the day, top-tier executives are typically the economic decision makers for expensive divergent offerings.

Although top-tier executives often represent a viable initial entry point for sellers of divergent offerings, our experience suggests that mid-level executives are often an excellent entry point. *The appropriateness of this strategy is contingent on the seller having some process in place for eventually engaging higher-ups and other mid-tier or departmental managers.* These mid-tier managers have the problems to be solved or the opportunities to be achieved, which commonly makes them more receptive to sellers. However, they often cannot make formal decisions relative to divergent offerings because they carry high risk, require greater investment in infrastructure, and are disruptive to multiple departments/verticals within the buyer organization. Therefore, if entry is with mid-tier managers, top-tier executives

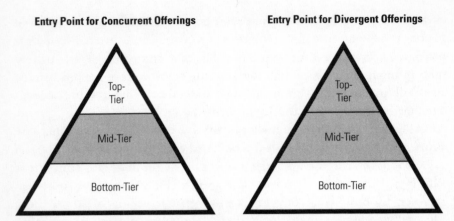

Figure 4.2 The proper entry strategy differs depending on whether the sale is of concurrent or divergent offerings.

must be subsequently engaged if there will be any chance of a "yes" decision because only top-tier executives have a broad view of each vertical.

Consider the diagram in Figure 4.2 of proper entry points for selling concurrent and divergent offerings.

Final Thoughts on Suppositions

Beliefs about proper entry points are a good example of how suppositions can either self-limit or enhance a selling team. Therefore, in a larger context, sales managers must identify and choose proper beliefs to be part of their organization's sales framework. Subsequently, they must clearly and continually communicate these beliefs to their sales team until these suppositions are ingrained in the culture.

In addition, sales managers must frequently gauge the beliefs held by members of the sales team. A salesperson's beliefs can be uncovered during strategic coaching exercises that ask the seller to explain the reasons behind their past successes and failures. By probing for beliefs about these past

Because beliefs drive actions and actions drive results, it is important that salespeople hold beliefs that are consistent with high productivity.

events, patterns and suppositions emerge. Explanations given by salespeople for their past actions unveil the actual beliefs they hold. When hiring new members of your sales organization, you will benefit from incorporating this technique in your interviewing process. Learning about the sales candidate's belief system provides some additional evidence of whether he or she is a demand creator or just someone else's current or former sales baggage. Remember, *beliefs* drive *actions,* and *actions* drive *results.* Good sales managers understand this well.

Strategies

Sales *strategies* are the overall *plans* for achieving the *goal* of moving buyers closer and closer to a *final commitment* (full rollout of the new application). As we have discussed, sales strategies must be based on the psychology of the buyer. The psychology of the buyer, in turn, is dependent upon where the buyer is in the customer decision-making process (Figure 4.3).

Keep in mind that as the buyer predictably moves from stage to stage in the decision process, the buyer's psychology also changes. This necessitates that the salesperson's strategy must also change with each leap from decision stage to decision stage by the buyer. Therefore, because there are four stages in the buyer decision process, the buyer's psychology during the sales process can change four times. If this is the case, the seller's strategy must change four times to ensure constant alignment with the buyer's psychology.

Be careful. In Chapter 3, you learned that the buyer decision-making process for *new applications* can have two different sets of four stages. The set that applies depends on where the buyer is in their decision process when first engaged by the salesperson. Consider Figure 4.4.

You will recall that most buyers are in the satisfaction stage at any

Figure 4.3 Selling strategy should always be driven by the buyer's stage in their decision-making process.

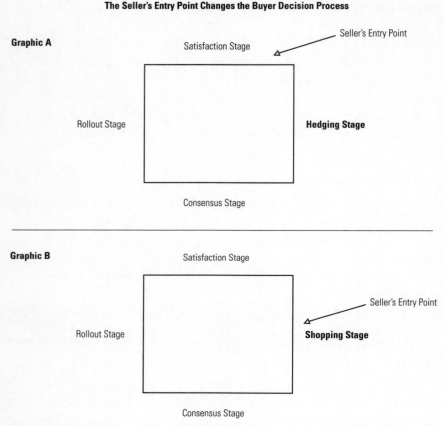

Figure 4.4 The initial entry point of the salesperson influences the buyer decision-making process.

given time, so Graphic A represents the most common decision-making process buyers go through regarding new applications. Selling to buyers in the satisfaction stage requires sophisticated demand creation strategies. Graphic B, with the seller engaging a buyer already in the shopping stage for a new application, should represent a less frequent occurrence. Demand has already been created internally at the buying organization, and the seller's opportunity is probably a competitive opportunity.

We will discuss the appropriate strategy for each buyer decision stage in the chapters ahead.

Steps to "Yes"

The third component of the model—*steps to "yes"*—refers to the major steps in the sales process that salespeople employ to move selling opportunities toward final commitment. Salespeople must have a portfolio of predeveloped steps that can be executed situationally—not linearly. Traditional steps to "yes" include demonstrations and proposals. Keep in mind that the specific steps that you lead the buyer to take should be determined based on the specific strategy you are trying to execute. In other words, look at the steps you, the seller, encourage the buyer to take as the *tactics* that lead to the accomplishment of the strategy at hand (steps = tactics). This chapter, as well as the next three, discusses several critical steps to "yes."

Skills

The fourth component of the strategic framework model is *skills.* A skill, or competency, is something that is performed at a quantifiable level to achieve a desired outcome. Each step to "yes" has a separate but consistent set of sales skills or competencies that the salesperson must possess *and* execute for that specific step to be successful. As we discuss the various steps to "yes" in this chapter and the following three chapters, we also spend time discussing the skills necessary to support each specific step and make each step successful.

Knowing how to perform a competency and actually performing a competency are two very different things. In other words, there is a gap between knowing and doing that we see in many salespeople. Sales managers who don't spend much time in the field with their team are often convinced their salespeople are executing properly in the field because they can articulate the theory and process behind what they are trying to do. At practice in the field, though, these same salespeople are often poor at executing those skills.

Note there are two types of skills and competencies:[2]

1. *Threshold competencies.* Those skills that lead to an acceptable level of performance (B level sales results).
2. *Differentiating competencies.* Those skills that lead to top-tier performance (A level sales results).

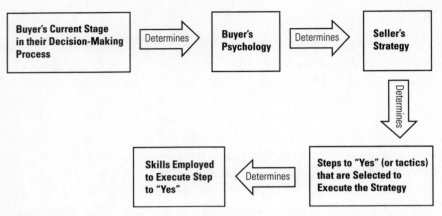

Figure 4.5 All of the execution components of the sales process should be derived from buyer psychology.

Throughout the course of this book, we'll flag the key differentiating competencies that separate the best salespeople from the rest of the pack.

Strategies, steps to "yes," and skills round out the execution portion of the sales framework model. These components of the sales framework can be summarized visually as in Figure 4.5.

Systems

Systems are the mechanisms that must be in place to hold the sales framework together. Once again, we will defer the bulk of the dialogue on systems to the end of the book. For now, though, here are some examples of systems:

- ◆ Coaching systems, which include formal skill and strategic coaching. Both can be conducted in the field or in simulated environments.
- ◆ Appropriate CRM systems that not only collect vital information, but, more important, also help strategically guide salespeople to choose the proper steps to "yes."
- ◆ Reporting and management systems that yield the type of information that can verify sales representatives are executing properly in the field.

Without such systems, individual members of the sales team lose discipline and stray into negative suppositions, strategic misalignments, poor step selection, and poor skill execution. Investment in and dedication to such systems is necessary. However, this investment should come after the development of the rest of the sales framework to ensure systems are appropriately selected, deployed, and tailored.

One final point on systems: The systems employed by most sales organizations are solely dedicated to the insurance of call activity (i.e., effort). Better-practice sales management uses systems that move beyond the measurement of call activity and efficiency. In other words, benchmark selling teams also have measures in place around *selling effectiveness,* which is the most critical set of metrics when determining sales success in the large sale.

Additional Thoughts on Sales Frameworks

Developing a disciplined sales framework has paid tremendous dividends to organizations who have instituted them. Without such a disciplined and universal framework, salespeople fall prey to inconsistency and chance, inevitably resulting in lost selling opportunities. Our clients view their frameworks not only as a competitive weapon and source of greater sales productivity, but in many cases, as a source of value for potential strategic merger partners or strategic buyers of their organizations. To buyers and partners, such a sales framework represents a disciplined and scalable system for growing revenue and protecting their investments.

The sales framework we are exposing you to can also be viewed as a social science, such as economics or psychology. Again, it should guide thinking in a disciplined manner. It's a framework for thinking; a thought model.

This sales framework represents a disciplined and scalable system for growing revenues.

Exercise: What Would You Do?

You should now know the importance of a strategic sales frame-work, as well as the general components of such a framework. You also have been exposed to the various stages in the buyer decision-making process for new applications. Let us now begin to put your understanding of these concepts to the test with a quick exercise.

The Scenario

You are about to meet with Joe Flynn, a VP with authority in your domain at Questar Corporation. The appointment was set as a result of a referral that you proactively generated. Questar represents a large account potential for you.

You are now in the lobby, but you previously had a phone conversation with Joe. From that conversation, you learned that your offering represents a new application for Questar. Joe was only moderately interested, but still agreed to the appointment. Also of importance, Joe seems to be one of the people at Questar who has significant power and influence in decisions about your type of offering.

Your Challenge: Answer These Questions

1. Where is Joe in the decision-making process?
2. What should be your strategy for this call?
3. Using the boxes in Figure 4.6, write down the sequence of steps in the sales process you should take on the way to "yes." *You do not have to use all six boxes.*

The Answers

Let us provide you with the correct answers, one question at a time. The answer to the first question is that the buyer appears to be in the sat-isfaction stage of the new application buyer model. The buyer, Joe Flynn, seemed to be only moderately interested. The buyer agreed to the appointment on the basis of a referral, and there were no apparent signs that Joe, or Questar, had active needs for your offering. Because

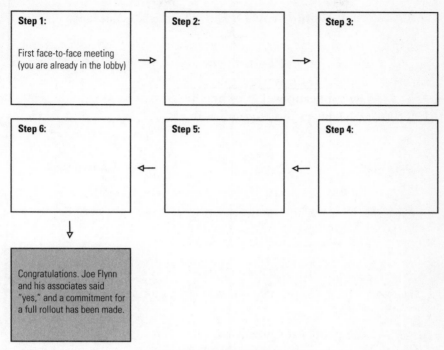

Figure 4.6 What are the steps to "yes" post-discovery?

you have entered Joe's decision-making process while he is in the satis-faction stage, and because your offering represents a new application for Joe and Questar, the appropriate buyer model is in Figure 4.7.

The second question asked you to determine the appropriate strat-egy to execute with Joe. As discussed, the strategy employed is to be based on the psychology of the buyer. The psychology of buyers in the satisfaction stage is that they are asking themselves the following ques-tions:

- ◆ Do I have a problem?
- ◆ How significant is my problem?
- ◆ Is my problem significant enough that I must act to remove it?
- ◆ Does this fit with our strategic objectives?

As buyers advance through the satisfaction stage, their level of dis-satisfaction becomes more severe. Visually, the effect can be shown as moving down a satisfaction ladder as in Figure 4.8.

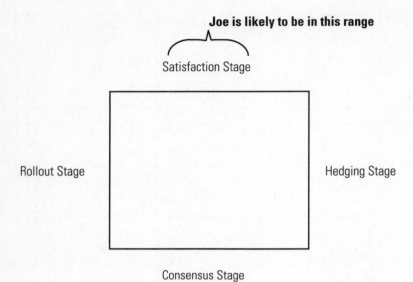

Figure 4.7 The divergent offering buyer model is the appropriate model for this scenario.

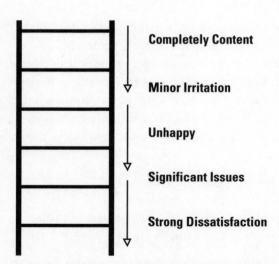

Figure 4.8 Sellers must drive buyers down the satisfaction stage ladder by creating and growing dissatisfaction.

As a seller dealing with a buyer such as Joe, who is in the satisfaction stage, you must drive them down this ladder. Once they are driven down the ladder, dissatisfaction will be strong and serious, and they will commit to action. In effect, after they reach the bottom of the ladder, they will commit to change and move into the next stage of the new application buyer model: the hedging stage.

The strategy then for buyers like Joe who are in the satisfaction stage is to *find* dissatisfaction, *grow* dissatisfaction, and *create* dissatisfaction, as well as identify key *objectives* Joe and Questar are trying to accomplish. As dissatisfaction is found, grown, and created, the buyer will move down the ladder toward a commitment to change and the hedging stage. Sellers must also identify buyer objectives so that:

- They can be certain that their recommendations and offerings are aligned with the desired direction of the overall buying organization, the specific department, or the individual people in the role of buyer.
- They can take advantage of the other side of organizational motivation, which is the *desire for gain*.

Don't forget that there is typically a *divide* in the satisfaction stage of the buyer's decision-making process. This divide separates curiosity to change and commitment to change. This is visually depicted in Figure 4.9.

When dealing with a large, new application buying decision, the buyer will not always be able to psychologically cross the divide between *curiosity* to change and *commitment* to change if the seller is *only able to solve the buyer's problems*. Often, with the large sale, the buyer will not commit to change until the seller adds more value than the removal of problems. This value must come from the ability of the seller to help the buyer capture an opportunity or achieve some objective that the buyer cannot achieve without the seller's offering. This is why the seller must gain an understanding of the buyer's critical objectives during the early phases of the sales process.

Another point is that in major account, new application selling scenarios, buyers cannot often be moved through the satisfaction stage with one step. Typically, multiple steps are involved. One reason: Dissatisfaction must be grown until it is greater than the total sum of the costs of change.

Divergent Model's Satisfaction Stage "Divide"

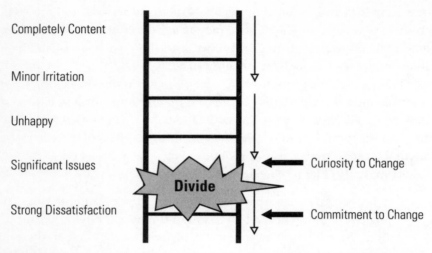

Figure 4.9 The psychological divide must be bridged by both growing buyer dissatisfaction and aligning solutions with buyer objectives and opportunities.

The costs of change, which can be both financial and nonfinancial, are often tremendous when the change is to a new application product or service offering. Therefore, with the Joe Flynn/Questar example, you will likely need to conduct several steps in the sales process to execute the strategy of finding, growing, and creating enough dissatisfaction to get Joe to commit to change and tip over into the hedging stage.

A second reason why multiple steps are required: The new application seller must often meet multiple members of the buyer decision team to uncover their personal and departmental objectives, which may require multiple meetings. The seller needs to get the full range of buyer objectives that can impact the decision. As you will recall, one element of the buyer's satisfaction stage psychology when dealing with a new application is, "Does this fit with our strategic objectives?" If the answer is "no" because the seller failed to demonstrate alignment between the new application and the buyer's objectives, then the selling opportunity will be scuffled at the bottom of the divide. No commitment to change will occur.

While your buyer remains in the satisfaction stage, each step in the sales process that you take with the buyer must serve to identify and grow the buyer's dissatisfaction with their current realities . . . in a *non-manipulative, results-oriented fashion*. Consider Figure 4.10.

Now that you understand the strategy for satisfaction stage buyers, we need to turn our attention to the best-practice steps to find, grow, and create dissatisfaction in a nonmanipulative, results–oriented manner. Unfortunately, there is no linear set of steps to execute sequentially for each and every sales opportunity. As you will learn later, you must develop a portfolio of steps to use situationally based on where the buyer is in their decision process. Please remember, though, that each step selected with a satisfaction stage buyer must be consistent with satisfaction stage strategy.

Applying the proper step, or progression, at the right time to the right situation can be a formidable challenge for sellers. Even worse, many sellers and entire sales teams simply and completely lack the proper progression steps. In effect, these salespeople and sales teams essentially lose selling opportunities, not because of the sales steps they

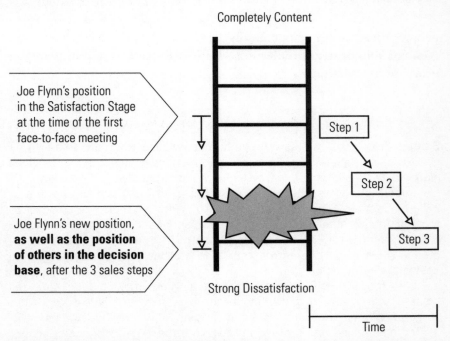

Figure 4.10 Advancing the buyer down the satisfaction stage ladder and bridging the buyer's divide typically takes multiple steps in the sales process.

Sellers often lose quality opportunities because they lack awareness of effective progression steps.

take, but because they are *unaware* of the proper steps that they should be taking in those situations. We'll add to your awareness of excellent progression steps in the coming chapters.

Returning to the Joe Flynn exercise, the third question asked you to identify the series of steps that should be taken to reach a "yes" decision. Because there is no universal, linear set of steps to be dogmatically executed by salespeople, the answer emphatically is . . . *it depends.* Many different combinations of steps may lead to "yes." That may be frustrating to you now, but bear with us.

Creating and Growing Dissatisfaction Sounds Manipulative. Is It?

Some would say that it is inherently manipulative to create and grow a need or a dissatisfaction. This is a good example of a supposition that clearly acts as an impediment to higher sales productivity. Here's why.

In selling, always return to the psychology of the buyer for answers to selling questions. Research has shown that the psychology of a buyer in the satisfaction stage is, "Do I have a problem and, if 'yes,' how significant is it and should I act to remove or reduce it?" If that is correct, *and it is,* then a seller is only being responsive to the buyer by helping the buyer answer those questions.

With that in mind, we are not suggesting any manipulation when we instruct sellers to find, grow, and create dissatisfaction with satisfaction stage buyers. What we are suggesting is that sellers develop and use various competencies and tools to help explore the existence, scale, scope, and implications of buyer problems and issues. This book will identify some of these competencies and mechanisms.

Best-practice sellers, who must be consultants and businesspeople rather than peddlers, should be able to help buyers identify real problems that the buyers were unaware of in many occasions. Sellers also must be adept at measuring and quantifying problems, as well as linking problems to their various implications so that buyers gain a better understanding of the true and collective costs of their problems. When done appropriately by the seller, the buyer will be grateful. Often, it is difficult for buyers to understand and link their problems and implications on their own.

So, does creating and growing dissatisfaction imply manipulation? No, absolutely not. Those who profess it does just don't grasp or have awareness of the best-practice set of selling tools and skills for selling major account offerings.

Outcomes of a Sales Step

Before introducing you to the first best-practice step to "yes," let's discuss the potential outcomes to each step of the sales process. In doing so, we'll add to a common sales vernacular.

Simplistically, there are two possible outcomes from a sales call: a positive outcome or a negative outcome. Taking it a little further, a negative outcome may take one of two forms:

- A straightforward and clear "*no.*"
- A *delayment,* when the buyer delays a commitment to move forward to a positive next step in the sales process. A delayment is typically a masked "no" and hides the buyer's intent to *not* move forward. Examples of delayments include a buyer telling you that he will "call in a few weeks" or that she will "think it over while you see purchasing first." Delayments are typically less desirable for the seller than a clear "no."

The two potential positive outcomes of a step in the sales process include:

- A final and committed "*yes*" for a full rollout.
- A specific *progression* toward "yes." A progression is a minor buyer commitment to advance to the next step in the sales process. A progression from a first face-to-face meeting may be to set a specific time to meet again for the purpose of discussing options or to meet with other individuals who will impact the buying decision.

Prior to every step in the sales process, a salesperson must know where the buyer is in the decision model, what the strategy is for that step, and the objective for that step. The objective for each step in the sales process is *either* to achieve a "yes" (final commitment) *or* to achieve a specific, predetermined progression (minor commitment to move forward). For a sales step to be considered a success, the objective must be achieved. If a salesperson fails to achieve this predefined objective, the step should be viewed as unsuccessful.

Summary

In Chapter 4, the key points are:

- An effective strategic sales framework consists of suppositions, strategies, steps to "yes," disciplined skills within each step, and systems for sustaining the framework.
- Suppositions, or beliefs, are what drive and influence the strategies you employ and the tactics you execute. Suppositions can either be productivity limiting or productivity enhancing. Suppositions should be carefully selected, and ingrained in the sales team.
- All selling strategies and tactics should reflect the buyer's psychology, which is contingent on location in the decision-making model.
- When selling divergent offerings to buyers in the satisfaction stage of buyer behavior, the proper strategy is to find, grow, and create dissatisfaction while also identifying key buyer objectives. Remember, a buying organization will not cross the *divide* between *curiosity* to change and *commitment* to change unless dissatisfaction is strong and serious, and unless your offering is aligned with the attainment of the buying organization's strategic objectives.

Notes

1. De Bono, E. (1992). *SUR/PETITION: Creating value monopolies when everyone else is merely competing.* New York, NY: HarperBusiness.
2. Spencer, L.M., & Spencer, S.M. (1993). *Competence at work: Models for superior performance.* New York, NY: John Wiley & Sons.

II

Igniting Your Growth Engine

5

FOCAS: The Language of a Businessperson Who Sells

The hard, conceptual work is now mostly behind you. Now, let's begin to apply practical strategies and competencies to what you have just learned.

The Discovery Step

When selling divergent offerings, or new applications, to buyers in the satisfaction stage, the strategy is twofold:

1. To find, create, and grow dissatisfaction until the level of dissatisfaction exceeds the collective costs of adopting the new application.
2. To uncover strategic organizational and departmental objectives that might serve as a basis for a future relationship.

The first *step to "yes"* that we will discuss, one that contributes to the accomplishment of satisfaction stage strategy, is called a *FOCAS discovery*. A FOCAS discovery can be defined as the first significant meeting between a buyer and seller at the beginning of a sales process. There are two types of discoveries: a FOCAS discovery and a REAP discovery. A FOCAS discovery is conducted with satisfaction stage buyers, and a REAP discovery is conducted with shopping stage buyers. We'll discuss additional distinctions of each in Chapter 8. For now, our focus is on the FOCAS type of discovery.

Discoveries may take place in person (face to face), over the phone, or digitally via a web-based or video-conferencing platform.

During the FOCAS discovery step, the seller must identify a basis of a relationship with the buyer and begin to uncover key goals or initiatives and find, grow, and create dissatisfaction. As with all steps in the sales process, the seller should create a clear objective for each discovery. That objective, for a major account selling situation with a satisfaction stage buyer, is almost certainly to achieve a commitment for a specific progression because there is almost no possibility of achieving a formal and final "yes" during this early step in the process.

There are four components of a proper FOCAS discovery, and experienced and effective sellers eventually learn to execute the components with a certain rhythm and timing. These components, and a broad estimate for the amount of time it takes a seller to complete each during a discovery, are listed in Table 5.1.

These four components are generally completed in the order listed in Table 5.1. Please recognize that each component is actually a *skill* that must be executed properly for the *discovery step* to be successful. We now discuss each of these components separately.

FOCAS Discovery Component 1: The Approach

The first component of a FOCAS discovery is the approach. The approach should be executed when it is time to get down to business.

Table 5.1

Discovery Component	Estimated Time
Approach	90 seconds
Questions	30–90 minutes
Summary	1 minute
Commitment: Progression or Close	30 seconds

The approach is the positioning component of the call. Sellers position their organization, the reason for the sales call itself, and themselves personally during the approach. Although this initial element is very brief, it is very important to execute well.

The approach is a tailored monologue performed by sellers in which they answer the following questions for the buyer (which the buyer is probably asking). Read these questions as if you are the buyer:

- Who are you (the seller)? What organization do you represent?
- What does your organization do, or what business are you in? What type of value do you offer?
- What kinds of companies do you work with?
- What is the purpose of your visit?

This structure is based on Larry Wilson's approach from his *Counselor Selling* material and coursework.[1] This approach still resonates today in a FOCAS discovery situation where the unknown is the common factor for both parties.

Keep in mind that your discovery appointment may have been set days, weeks, or months in advance. Therefore, the buyer needs you to identify exactly who you are and what the purpose is for your visit or call. The buyer will also be curious about who your organization has worked with in the past and what you were able to do for those organizations.

The absolute key to delivering an effective approach is in how you answer the question, "What business are you in?" When describing your business, talk about the highest level value you might be able to deliver to the buyer's organization. Too often, salespeople position their organizations as transactional ones instead of high-value-adding organizations who can remove problems and add innovation.

Remember, satisfaction stage buyers are *not* in the market for your products and services. Thus, a transactional positioning statement focusing on your products and services is a surefire strategy for failure. A better positioning strategy that satisfaction stage buyers will be receptive to revolves around the language of results.

For example, consider the right and wrong way to position our firm, Sogistics Corporation. We offer a variety of customizable services, but predominantly we offer sales training frameworks and sales assessment services. The assessment services are for companies who need to evaluate existing or prospective members of their sales teams. An example of a transactional way of describing our business, and one that would get us grouped in with the many, many sales training firms and outsourced HR providers, would be: "We are a sales consulting firm that offers major account sales training and sales assessment services, such as testing, behaviorally based interviewing, and turnkey sales hiring services." Such a description would fail to differentiate Sogistics in a buyer's mind, and it would possibly disengage the buyer for the remainder of the discovery call.

A much better *value positioning statement* for our firm, Sogistics, would be: "We are in the sales productivity improvement business. We work with our clients to remove a wide range of sales constraints as a means to accelerate revenue growth (results). A lot of our work focuses on making our clients much more effective in several areas of creating, not just new customers, but the types of new customers that represent significant new revenue and profit." Such a value positioning statement is easily understood and makes it difficult for the buyer to pigeonhole us in a transactional, commoditized cluster. It also communicates that we are a broad and significant provider of bottom-line value.

In creating your personal value positioning statement for your approach, remember that you are in the results business. Better yet, the *impact business.* Using results and impact language is especially critical when in front of buyers in the satisfaction stage who do not possess active needs. These buyers are not ready to entertain solutions. Using transactional language is only sometimes acceptable if the buyer is in the shopping stage and has active needs for your type of products and services. Such a buyer is looking for solutions.

In addition to using transactional positioning statements, other common mistakes that sellers make with their overall approaches include:

- Spending too much time delivering overly elaborate and long-winded explanations of the company and its products or services.
- Coming across as presumptuous or overly assertive. For example, a salesperson may mistakenly ask, "Is it alright if I ask you some questions to see *how* we can help you?" The proper wording is *if* we can help.
- Sounding rehearsed.
- Failing to tailor the approach to the buyer's title, industry, and so on.

FOCAS Discovery Component 2: The FOCAS Questioning Model

If your energy, alertness, or attention span is running low, grab some coffee before continuing. This is a critical section of the book.

An obvious element of an initial sales call with a buyer is a *needs analysis.* The seller must gain an understanding of the buyer's situation. The FOCAS questioning model is a sophisticated, best-practice method of conducting a robust needs analysis. The FOCAS model is also a platinum competence . . . a giant of a competence. *FOCAS is the most important discovery step skill.* It must be mastered. With it, you will be able to uncover a basis for a relationship with buyers and begin to achieve your satisfaction stage strategy of finding, growing, and creating the buyer's dissatisfaction. Moreover, it is a skill that can be woven into other demand creation sales process steps, as well as into other facets of your life in which you seek to lead change in other people or organizations.

What is a *questioning model?* A questioning model is a disciplined structure of questioning in which specific types of questions are asked in a deliberate sequence that satisfies the mutual needs of the buyer and seller.

As you probably have guessed, FOCAS is an acronym with each letter signifying a unique type of question. Each type of question is unique in its intent and function, but not in its form. Broken into its components, the FOCAS questioning model is:

Fact questions
Objective questions
Concern questions
Anchor questions
Solution questions

We'll elaborate on each type of FOCAS question momentarily. Before we do, however, let us make a brief comparison between FOCAS and an older acronym-based questioning model: Neil Rackham and Huthwaite's SPIN model. The SPIN model was a breakthrough in effective questioning strategy at the time of its release in the mid-1980s. FOCAS is SPIN on steroids—without the long-term negative consequences. FOCAS has an element of innovation not possessed by its elegant, yet aging, predecessor. FOCAS is more strategic. More potent.

Moreover, the components of FOCAS are easier to remember than those of SPIN. We'll highlight the relative advantage of FOCAS in a little while.

As you will learn, FOCAS is a very Socratic method of helping buyers uncover, understand, and define their issues, problems, and unrealized opportunities for advancement. Each type of question within the FOCAS model has a unique strategic significance, all related to the strategy of finding, growing, and creating dissatisfaction—and uncovering critical strategic objectives.

Be careful. The complexity of FOCAS is typically unappreciated by people at the time of their initial exposure. The complexity lies in the subtle nuances of the model. Moreover, a salesperson's conceptual understanding of the model does not quickly translate into an ability to execute the model at a high level in the fast-paced environment of the field. The point is that you should be prepared to practice this questioning model in a disciplined manner before you can execute it to an expert degree in your real-life discovery sales calls.

We explain each type of FOCAS question and provide some examples in the following.

Fact Questions
Fact questions are the easiest type of questions in the FOCAS model. As is clearly implied in the name, fact questions are used to collect data, facts, and information about the buyer's *current situation*. In other words, these questions are used to investigate the buyer's realities.

Fact questions are simply information-gathering warm-ups that get the strategic ball rolling. The puzzle that is pieced together with fact questions represents where the buyer is today. You will learn to ask the specific fact questions that will yield the information necessary for you to identify the starting point for an investigation into a possible basis of a relationship with the buyer. Again, a basis for a relationship is usually grounded in problems or issues the buyer is experiencing, or in an opportunity to innovate and reach a new higher ground.

A good rule of thumb is to begin the questioning part of a discovery by asking some fact questions aimed at understanding the buyer's general business. Next, ask fact questions that are more specific to understanding the key information (personnel, processes, infrastructure, knowledge, etc.) necessary for you to understand the applicability of your offering and how your offering would be implemented should a "yes" decision eventually be made.

Examples of general business fact questions include:

- What are your annual revenues?
- How do you segment your market?
- How is your organization structured?

Although product- or service-specific fact questions vary significantly by industry, examples include:

- A question that an IT consulting firm sales rep would ask an IT executive: "How many programmers do you have in your development group?"

Fact Questions take a snapshot of the buyer's current situation. They gather key data and facts.

- A question that a logistics firm sales rep would ask the owner of a midsize trucking company: "How do you track and monitor your truck fleet?"
- A question that an advertising firm sales rep would ask a marketing executive: "Are you currently working with another ad firm right now?"

Fact questions are necessary to capture vital information that you are unable to acquire through pre-call research. Unfortunately, though, fact questions are low-payoff questions from both the buyer's and the seller's perspective because they don't deal with buyer objectives or problems. Therefore, they should be limited. High-level buyers will turn off mentally if asked too many fact questions, and possibly escort the seller downstairs because it is not their job to educate the seller. Be aware of how many fact questions you ask (5 to 10 minutes at most) and move to higher-value types of questions that you and the buyer find more rewarding.

Although they are low-payoff questions from the buyer's perspective, don't discount the importance of fact questions. They accomplish two feats:

1. They effectively relax the buyer through soft and easy questions that are neither problem nor goal focused. It is valuable to relax the buyer before delving into more sensitive areas that require a greater degree of candor.
2. They fill in the blanks of the factual context of the situation, which is a necessary element in any needs analysis process.

Objective Questions

Objective questions are used to identify and investigate the buyer's objectives, goals, aspirations, and visions. Because objective questions deal in goal-driven psychology, they are much more impactful than fact questions. Objective questions might include, "Could you tell me some of the things you are trying to accomplish over the next 12 months in your department?" or "How do you see yourself evolving in the company over the next few years?"

Objective questions are especially interesting to senior executives who have a high *locus of control*. This is a psychological term that behaviorists use to describe people who believe they control their destiny. This is a common trait of executives who, because they believe they can accomplish whatever they put their minds to, have a tendency to be more proactive and goal driven—especially with the implementation of new applications.

We typically teach salespeople to look for buyer objectives at three broad levels:

Objective Questions help the seller understand where buyers want to go and how they plan to get there.

1. *Organizational objectives.* Big-picture, strategic goals often considered mission critical to the organization or a division of a large organization. Examples: reduce cost structure by 5 percent, implement strategic quality programs, or grow through acquisitions.

2. *Departmental objectives.* Smaller-picture, typically more departmental in nature. For example, every IT department in a company has two or three important objectives to accomplish annually. This is the second layer of goals that are critical to achieve.

3. *Personal objectives.* At times, it can be helpful to learn the personal goals of the individuals you're dealing with. These goals are best learned casually during a walk down the hallway. For instance, you might ask, "Pat, where do you see yourself heading within the company over the next two to three years?" Such personal questions become easier and more appropriate to ask as the relationship with the buyer develops.

Whereas fact questions uncover where the buyer is now, objective questions get the buyer to explain where she, her organization, and her department is trying to go: the destination. The separation between where the buyer is going and where the buyer is currently represents a fertile ground of dissatisfaction. Essentially, this separation is a *gap of accomplishment* that must be crossed for goals to be reached. Crossing this gap can be problematic or unsettling to the buyer. Figure 5.1 depicts the gap of accomplishment.

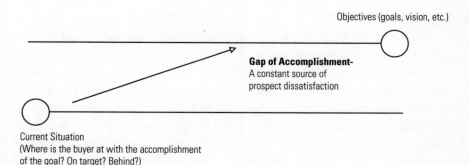

Objectives (goals, vision, etc.)

Gap of Accomplishment-
A constant source of
prospect dissatisfaction

Current Situation
(Where is the buyer at with the accomplishment
of the goal? On target? Behind?)

Figure 5.1 The gap of accomplishment is the separation between current realities and the attainment of the buyer's desired objectives.

Why else are objective questions so important? It's obviously very difficult to get new budgets created, especially if you are selling highly expensive products or services. If no funds exist that can be used to create a new budget, they simply don't exist regardless of how high you are in the organization. If a new budget cannot be created on the spot, your offering is shelved until a new round of budgeting begins. Therefore, trying to get new budgets created in the near term for your offering is often a mistake. It is much better to identify existing budgets and initiatives that you can tie your offering to as tightly as possible.

Objective questions are necessary to identify strategic initiatives and the budgets that are supporting them. You must understand the buyer's objectives and initiatives and align yourself and your offerings within the context of these initiatives. Later in the selling cycle, you must be able to demonstrate that your offering can assist the buyer in achieving or exceeding key, strategic objectives . . . and hopefully in an accelerated manner. If you fail to align your offering with key objectives, no sale can be made. Therefore, the strategic intent behind objective questions is twofold:

1. Identify and create avenues of alignment with buyers and their objectives.
2. Identify gaps of accomplishment that will represent a starting point to look for dissatisfactions and problems.

Objective questions are the key differentiator of FOCAS in comparison to the SPIN model. SPIN does not incorporate objective-type questions, which are powerful tipping-point questions in a major account, new application selling environment. In other words, without understanding and documenting key buyer objectives, the probability of selling divergent offerings is very low.

Moreover, the SPIN model only seeks to find, grow, and gauge dissatisfaction (as you will soon see, the C, A, and S questions of FOCAS are also used to find, grow, and gauge dissatisfaction). Problems and dissatisfactions that the seller can remove are only one basis of a relationship between the buyer and seller. SPIN limits the seller to identifying this single basis. However, the seller's ability to add an innovation to the buying organization and capitalize on an already good situation is a second potential basis of a relationship between the buyer and seller. This second basis is unaccounted for in the SPIN model.

Often, sellers cannot find, grow, or create sufficient buyer dissatisfaction for the buyer to grant a "yes" decision. Objective questions in the FOCAS model enable the seller to look beyond problems and dissatisfactions to the other side of the value equation via the buyer's opportunities and goals. *The forward-looking element of objective questions enables sellers to explore this second basis of a relationship: the potential for the addition of an innovation that will carry the buying organization toward the accomplishment of its objectives and the fulfillment of its best opportunities.*

Case Study: How Buyer Objections Appeal to the Other Side of Buyer Motivation

Does asking objective questions correlate to sales success? Our research would suggest *yes*—especially when selling high-risk, divergent offerings at the senior levels of a buyer organization.

Medcore Systems is a leader in the niche of selling laboratory and blood-testing equipment to hospitals and other healthcare institutions. Medcore Systems, a fictitious name for a real company (loosely based), has traditionally sold to mid-level hospital personnel such as nurses, lab managers, technicians, and purchasing. This niche has served Medcore well, evidenced by its strong growth over the last two decades.

Recently, though, the company has seen signs of commoditization in its marketplace. As the number of competitors has increased, margins have tightened. As a result, the company's leadership implemented a new growth strategy around a different and higher-level value proposition—one that more significantly impacts the economics of its hospital clients.

No longer will Medcore only sell laboratory and testing equipment. In simple terms, the new business model also entails the outsourcing of lab technicians to Medcore to run hospital labs, rent certain types of equipment, maintenance and repair of equipment, and the disposal or remarketing of underutilized or consumed equipment. Medcore has become a total solution provider of lab and blood-testing equipment for its hospital clients.

After the transition, Medcore salespeople initially contacted their existing contacts to discuss the new integrated value concept. Not surprisingly, these mid-level personnel did not appreciate the new value proposition. Mid-level nurses, department heads, and procurement personnel were most concerned with day-to-day issues, such as poor equipment functionality, service problems, and patient dissatisfaction.

As a result, Medcore quickly adjusted. Salespeople began engaging VP and above executives of hospitals, where Medcore's strategic value proposition would be fully valued.

(continued)

Unfortunately, gaining intellectual traction with higher-level executives was difficult for Medcore salespeople. The questioning strategies that had served them well in past mid-level sales calls seemed less effective with the senior executives they were now calling on. For instance, asking questions about functional department problems worked well at the mid-level of a hospital's organizational chart, but not so well with the upper tier. Presenting the concept of a total integrated solution to executives might also raise some initial enthusiasm, but nothing sustainable. In the end, too many of these new sales calls at higher levels were ending in a "no" decision.

Although the new value proposition could save hospitals hundreds of thousands to millions of dollars, the sales team was producing disappointing results. The good news, though, was that a few Medcore salespeople were making significant inroads at hospitals with the new concept. One salesperson who quickly began to advance some selling opportunities was Ed Wetzel, a relatively new salesperson for the company.

Ed's questioning strategies had a different focus when engaged with senior executives. For instance, Ed spent a lot more time asking questions focused on opportunities rather than focusing only on problems and constraints. Ed's questions delved into such areas as the hospital's best opportunities for growth, key goals, important initiatives, and critical strategies. What was the reasoning for these opportunity and goal questions that moved beyond "pain"? Ed was searching for whether Medcore could play a role in helping the hospital better achieve its most important aspirations and initiatives.

For example, Ed conducted a discovery with a VP of Operations at an internationally renowned hospital. The new Medcore value proposition of an integrated lab and equipment solution represented a divergent offering to the hospital. During the discovery, he asked a wide variety of questions to the VP. By asking *objective questions,* he learned some of the following mission-critical goals for the hospital:

- ◆ To leverage technology in a way that would help the hospital maintain their top-tier national ranking.
- ◆ To gain better alignment internally between senior management and department level management as a means to better execute initiatives.
- ◆ To become more strategically efficient in their use of capital (especially with medical equipment) in order to free up capital for expansion initiatives.

Medcore's new value proposition could play a significant role in helping the hospital accomplish these goals.

(continued)

Ed also found some problem areas at the senior level. For example, the hospital had recently made some poor large equipment decisions in the laboratory and blood-testing area. The hospital also was experiencing a faster degree of equipment obsolescence in certain areas than they had originally anticipated. Medcore was also capable of removing these issues in the lab and blood-testing equipment domain.

When it was time for Ed to present capability, he appealed to both sides of buyer motivation: the desire for gain and the removal of problems. However, Ed noticed that the senior executives involved in the decision were more energized by the discussion of gain than the discussion of problems. The executives were very interested in learning how Medcore might play a role in helping the hospital achieve its objectives. Even when problems and constraints were discussed, the executives spoke about them in reference to how the problems would impact goal and opportunity attainment.

In the end, the hospital bought into the concept of a total solution approach, and entered into a partnership with Medcore. As a learning organization, Medcore transferred Ed's experiences, and similar experiences of other salespeople, to the rest of the sales team.

The lesson is that, when selling divergent offerings, sellers must often call on senior executives. When doing so, objective questions are essential if one is to align their divergent offering with the future direction of the buying organization.

Concern Questions

Concern questions explore the dissatisfactions, difficulties, concerns, and problems that your prospect may be experiencing. Therefore, the strategic intent of concern questions is to *find* buyer dissatisfaction. Most salespeople understand that they are ultimately in the business of removing constraints, but, before they can remove a problem, they first have to find a problem. Some examples of concern questions are, "Can you tell me about any challenges you might be having in the area of inventory management?" or "Have you had any issues with losing market share to overseas competition?"

The good news with concern questions is that they are an excellent foundation on which to begin the process of growing and creating dissatisfaction. The bad news, however, is that although concern questions are typically asked by average salespeople, these questions are not by themselves enough to get prospects to bridge the divide between curiosity and commitment to change. Our interviews of thousands of salespeople clearly indicate that better sales-people ask more and better concern questions than average salespeople. Furthermore, they ask these questions fairly early in the conversation.

Concern Questions uncover both strategic and tacti-cal problems, issues, and constraints that sellers can solve with their offerings.

Last, when selling new applications, it is best to think of your offering as a problem-removing vehicle. Even thinking of the features of your offering as *constraint removers* is an effective way to formulate qual-ity concern questions. Once you have an understanding of all of the problems your offering solves, organize these problems into broader problem buckets, such as productivity issues, cost issues, market issues, labor issues, or production issues. During a discovery call, explore each broad problem bucket with concern questions in your search to find problems you can solve with your offering.

Finding buyer discontent through good concern questions is impor-tant. However, as we mentioned a moment ago, finding this discontent won't be enough to bridge the divide and get commitment from the buyer to undergo change. Remember, prospects won't want to explore your offering (past a general curiosity level) unless their problems are perceived as strong and serious. Even more important, a buyer will not want to move to the next step unless a more intense level of discontent is quickly attained.

Concern questions will not help you, or the buyer, realize this type of necessary fervor. The next type of question in the FOCAS sequence will.

Anchor Questions

Anchor questions enable salespeople and buyers to explore the serious-ness of problems that are identified. Anchor questions investigate the effects and consequences of problems and dissatisfaction areas. Anchor questions are extremely high payoff because they help buyers see the true implications of a problem they are experiencing.

Problems rarely exist in a vacuum or silo. Rather, problems usually create other negative implications in a chain reaction. As a simple example, consider how late incoming shipments of materials or components affect a production organization. The problem is a late incoming shipment (or series of late shipments), and it causes a stoppage in the production flow (implication #1), which causes unproductive and costly downtime on the production floor (implication #2), which causes overtime to catch up and fulfill the order on time (implication #3), which causes costs

Good sellers "drop anchor" on found problem areas (with Anchor Questions) in order to explore implications and grow dissatisfaction.

to inflate (implication #4), which adversely affects profitability on the order (implication #5), which leads to frustration and pressure from the plant manager (implication #6), and so on. All of these implications must be included in a discussion of the true cost and weight of a problem: in this case, late incoming shipments. Buyers often don't calculate all of these implicated costs to their problems, leaving them unaware of the seriousness and gravity of their problems. True consultative salespeople help buyers understand the full impact of their problems by using anchor questions to tie together all of the associated implications and consequences.

Buyers appreciate the exploration of implications, which makes anchor questions an opportunity for the salesperson to add value beyond the products or services being sold. Often, buyers don't have the time, knowledge, experience, or energy to proactively try to comprehend and sum up the associated costs of problems on their own. Keep in mind the psychology of buyers in the satisfaction stage:

- ◆ "Do I have a problem?"
- ◆ "How serious is my problem and do I need to act to remove it?"

Anchor questions assume a problem has been found. Although the initial reaction of salespeople may be to jump in with solutions, savvy salespeople know it is time to *drop an anchor*. The strategic intent of anchor questions is to *grow* dissatisfaction. Remember, buyers will not commit to change until their dissatisfaction is strong, serious, and more weighty than the associated costs of change. If solutions are introduced too early, before dissatisfaction with current realities is equal to or greater than the costs of change, then buyers will object to the introduction of solutions. Objections are friction and will reduce the likelihood of an eventual sale.

The sequence that you should begin practicing is:

1. Use concern questions to find problems and dissatisfaction areas.
2. Avoid the impulse to immediately solve the buyer's problems or remove the dissatisfaction areas.
3. Then, use anchor questions to grow problems and dissatisfaction areas.

Review Table 5.2 to see some common examples of anchor questions and how they should be employed.

Here is what we know about anchor questions:

- They are extremely high payoff. They correlate strongly to sales success.
- Most salespeople ask few, if any, anchor questions. As a result, they fail to get to the next step in the chain. Thus, anchor questions should be viewed as a differentiator between top and average salespeople.
- Anchor questions get problems off the back burner ("We can live with this") to the temporary front burner ("Perhaps this problem is serious enough to consider action").

We see it over and over, so we'll say it one more time: Average salespeople continually jump in with solutions when they find "pain." Better salespeople, instead, grow dissatisfaction by moving to anchor questions. Be a change master by dropping an anchor question on the next prospect problem you find.

One final note before moving on: Truly consultative salespeople, or customer productivity improvement experts, are able to use a series of

Table 5.2

Concern Questions to Find Problems and Dissatisfactions	Buyer's Response Indicating the Presence of a Problem	Anchor Questions to Explore the Implications of the Found Problem
Have you had any difficulties keeping costs down in that area?	Yes, costs are an issue and we are having difficulty with managing them.	How significantly are those costs impacting profitability? Are you experiencing any pressure from the CFO to better contain those costs?
Do you find that there is some redundancy of effort?	Yes, some processes and activities are done multiple times.	How much unnecessary cost is incurred due to this duplication of effort? What is not getting done that could be completed by the same personnel if this redundancy was not occurring?
Are you satisfied with your time-to-market of new products and services?	Not really. We've been consistently beaten to market by our competitors with new features and technologies.	How much in lost revenues has been incurred? Are you concerned that being a "me too" entrant with new features and technologies will erode your brand preference?

insightful concern and anchor questions to identify problems and implications the buyer was not previously aware of. This is what we mean
when we say creating dissatisfaction. Although there are other more
powerful methods for creating dissatisfaction that we'll discuss in
upcoming chapters, good concern and anchor question combinations
are an excellent start to accomplishing this high-level strategy.

Solution Questions

The last type of questions in the FOCAS questioning model are solution questions. Solution questions develop the buyer's recognition of
the value or usefulness of your solution.

One strategic intent behind solution questions is to *measure* buyer
dissatisfaction. In other words, these questions take the pulse of the
prospect's current dissatisfaction levels by asking things such as, "How
much of a savings would that mean annually?" or "In what other ways
might that help you?" Solutions questions generate responses from the
buyer that indicate where the buyer is in the customer decision-making
model—satisfaction stage or beyond.

Solution questions are value based. In effect, this begins the inquiry
about whether the prospect sees value in the removal of problems. For
that reason, they are a bit more
optimistic in tone, unlike the dissatisfaction focus of concern and
anchor questions. Solution questions get the buyer to think about
potential solutions and determine whether their problems
or dissatisfactions are serious
enough to justify action. On the
flip side of buyer motivation,
they also help the buyer see your
potential role in the achievement
of objectives and opportunities.

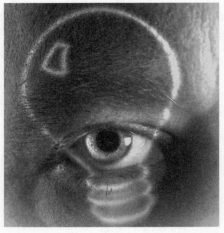

We've always felt that in a
discovery call, a salesperson is
buying as much as selling. By

Solution Questions open the buyer's
eyes to the true value and benefit of your
solution.

this, we mean a salesperson is evaluating the opportunity and deciding if it's worthwhile to invest more time and resources into it. Solution questions are a nice way to get buyer feedback on the value of removing problems or the value of innovation from the buyer's perspective.

Not only can solution questions gauge the buyer's perception of your solution's value, they can extend value in the buyer's mind as well (i.e., "Are there any other ways this might help you?"). Solution ques-

The Value of FOCAS to Buyers

Do buyers derive actual value from a FOCAS dialogue? It's a good question, especially in this age when buyers have limited time and less reliance on salespeople due to easily accessible information through the Internet.

Over the years, we have done a great deal of field coaching with salespeople. During these exercises, we have occasionally taken time to debrief buyers in these real-world situations. We used these opportunities to get the buyer's perspective on their interaction with the sellers.

When sellers had effectively executed a FOCAS dialogue with buyers, the buyers commonly mentioned during the debrief sessions that they *valued* the seller's ability, through their questioning process, to crystallize priorities and problems in a way that went well beyond traditional consultative selling. Here are some paraphrased examples of buyer comments we've heard after an effective FOCAS discussion:

- ◆ "I'm not saying that we're going to do business with this person for certain, but she is the type of person we're looking to partner with— someone who spends the necessary time learning about our organization, our goals, and our unique challenges. I'm not sure where we're heading exactly, but for now, she's got my attention."
- ◆ "Actually, this person didn't seem like a salesperson at all. I didn't feel pressured. It felt like he was working for me, and not working on me. I found our conversation to be collaborative and engaging. I think maybe he can help us."
- ◆ "Excellent listener. Some of the questions really made me think. I didn't have answers to a few of the more important questions he asked. I'm going to make it a point to get those answers for my own purposes, because they are important."

tions may also be used to clarify buyer needs (i.e., "Why is that important to you?").

Best-practice salespeople use more solution questions than average salespeople. Solution questions are nonmanipulative and are not to be confused with trial closes. However, we see many salespeople misuse solution questions. The key with solution questions, like good comedy, is timing. Only use them after you've *uncovered* and *grown* a problem through concern and anchor questions, and before you introduce solutions.

Summary of FOCAS questions

The FOCAS model is a skill within the discovery step that enables the seller to generate buyer momentum and find, create, and grow buyer dissatisfaction. The effect of FOCAS on a buyer should be moving closer to having demand for your category of solutions. Therefore, view FOCAS as a demand creation tool.

FOCAS, again, is also a method of conducting a value-adding needs analysis. Hopefully, this questioning process will begin to uncover a potential basis of a relationship between the buyer and seller. But to understand the multiple bases of a relationship, you must first understand why people change.

So, why do companies and people change? In other words, what stimulates individuals and organizations to buy new applications, especially risky ones where the cost of failure can be high? There are two general reasons (Figure 5.2).

In both cases, the buyer must be strongly discontented with the current situation to commit to change, even though this is actually a less risky alternative than staying with the status quo.

One of the measures of an effective salesperson is the ability to add significant amounts of value to the buyer environment. The highest value-adding scenario would be a combination, depicted in Figure 5.3.

The value gap partly explains what Jeffrey Immelt, CEO of GE, meant by "These days, my [salespeople] must be customer productivity experts."[2] His observation that "selling is dead" was meant to bury the old paradigm of salespeople as walking brochures who deliver little value

1) Removal or Prevention of a Problem(s):

Removal of a Problem:

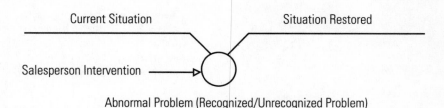

Current Situation   Situation Restored

Salesperson Intervention ⟶

Abnormal Problem (Recognized/Unrecognized Problem)

Prevention of a Problem:

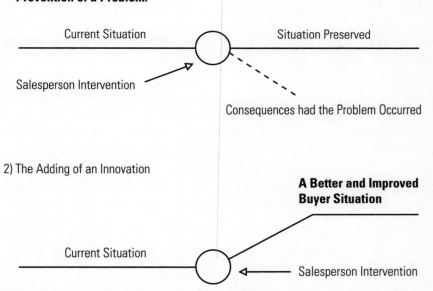

Current Situation   Situation Preserved

Salesperson Intervention

Consequences had the Problem Occurred

2) The Adding of an Innovation

A Better and Improved Buyer Situation

Current Situation

Salesperson Intervention

Figure 5.2 The basis of a relationship, and the reason buyers change, is typically one or a combination of the following: problem removal, problem prevention, addition of innovation.

beyond explaining the features and benefits of a product/service line. Immelt understands that buyers who require product specifications and service explanations can simply access the Internet.

The value gap clearly illustrates what the new breed of salesperson attempts to deliver—impact value. The bigger the gap, the higher the

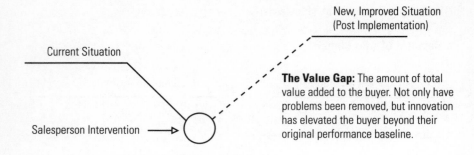

Figure 5.3 The value gap represents the total value a seller delivers to the buyer.

buyer value. Equally important, the more extreme the value delivered, the higher the price the buyer is willing to pay.

FOCAS Discovery Component 3: The Verbal Summary

The verbal summary is a technique for bridging from your FOCAS questions to your pursuit of a buyer commitment. The commitment you will be seeking is essentially an agreement to undertake a specific action.

The verbal summary is simply reporting key information uncovered during the discussion. A good verbal summary includes:

- The most significant problems, issues, and concerns that you heard.
- The critical goals, aspirations, and objectives that were discovered.

We did not tell you to reiterate all of the problems, objectives, and factual information. Rather, just the most important problems and objectives, which will later serve as the basis of a relationship with the buyer.

There are numerous associated benefits to the seller who is able to deliver an effective verbal summary. Summarizing shows you have listened well and understand what is important. Good summaries demonstrate to the prospect that you are focused on helping them remove their problems and achieve their objectives—not just shoehorning your offerings.

Moreover, sorting information quickly for your summary is a clear sign to the prospect that you are intelligent.

Delivering good summaries requires being able to recall key information. You will need a system for organizing and tracking key concerns and objectives during the course of a discovery. You will need some method of flagging this critical information to assist you when delivering verbal summaries at the end of your FOCAS questioning. Some effective salespeople leave columns in their notepads so they can put clearly visible checks next to the problems and objectives they want to revisit in their summaries. Others simply put large *P*'s next to important problems and large *O*'s next to significant objectives so they can quickly sift through their notes at the end of the discovery call and target these large letters.

Upon completing your verbal summaries, it is worthwhile to request buyers to add to the list if they feel it's necessary, and then rank and prioritize both the critical problems and goals. Such a ranking will assist you in making recommendations at a later time.

FOCAS Discovery Component 4: The Commitment

An effective discovery call is concluded by getting the buyer to make a clear and specific commitment. A commitment can be either a close (final "yes"), which is rare in major account selling, or a specific progression (advancement in the sales process). We will begin discussing high-impact progression steps in Chapter 6. For now, however, it is important to mention that the progression you pursue should be consistent with your strategy, and that strategy is dependent upon where the buyer is in the buyer decision-making model. For example, if at the end of the discovery step the buyer continues to remain in the satisfaction stage, then the progression selected should be one that helps accomplish the satisfaction stage strategy of identifying objectives and finding, growing, and creating dissatisfaction.

Understanding and Gauging Buyer Needs

We conclude this chapter with a summary on buyer needs. Remember, at a basic level, there are two types of buyer needs:

1. *Dormant needs* exist when a buyer has expressed problems or dissatisfactions with their current situation, but has no commitment to take action to remove those problems or dissatisfactions.
2. *Active needs* exist when a buyer has expressed problems or dissatisfactions with their current situation, and the buyer expresses a desire or intention to take action to remove those problems or dissatisfactions. Active needs can be recognized when the seller uses language that implies an intention to act (i.e., "I need to do something . . ." or "We are going to do something . . ." or "We are currently doing something . . .").

Buyers with dormant needs are in the satisfaction stage. Buyers with active needs have advanced out of the satisfaction stage and into either the hedging stage or shopping stage. FOCAS is an effective tool for growing buyer needs and beginning the process of tipping dormant needs over and making them active needs. Anchor questions serve this purpose.

At the beginning and end of each sales step, the seller must gauge the buyer's needs and determine which stage of the decision-making model the buyer is in. The seller's strategy hinges on the buyer's stage. Therefore, if at the end of the sales step the buyer appears to have dormant needs and resides in the satisfaction stage, the progression the seller should seek commitment for must be a demand creation progression. However, if the buyer's needs are active and the buyer is in the hedging stage, the progression pursued by the seller should be a risk-mitigation progression. Alternatively, if the buyer's needs are active and the buyer has entered the shopping stage, the progression pursued by the seller should be a demand-servicing progression.

As you are probably realizing, the seller's ability to quickly and accurately gauge the buyer's needs and location in the decision-making model is essential. As you have learned in this chapter, solution questions are an effective gauge mechanism. They can be used to determine if the buyer's needs are active or dormant and where the buyer is in the decision-making process. Consider the following solution questions and how they gauge buyer needs:

"Do you need to address this issue right now?"
"Do you feel that you need to be looking at different alternatives right now?"

"As an organization, are you committed to implementing something like this?"

"Is this something you personally think should happen, but others may not be on board yet?"

Once you have identified the buyer's type of needs and decision-making stage, you can select the appropriate progression step that aligns with the buyer's psychology. This is how best-practice sellers advance the sales process and eventually get formal and final "yes" decisions.

Summary

In Chapter 5, the key points are:

- *Discovery* is perhaps the most critical sales process step. The discovery is used to begin identifying a potential future basis of a relationship, and it has four components that assist the seller in executing an effective satisfaction stage strategy. Each component is a unique *skill*. These components are listed in Table 5.3.
- There is a specific strategic intent behind each type of FOCAS question. The intent behind each type of question is as follows:
  - *Fact questions.* Gain an understanding of where the buyer is today.
  - *Objective questions.* Gain an understanding of where the buyer wants to go organizationally, departmentally, and personally. The distance between where the buyer is now and where he wants to go represents a challenge or problem. Once the seller knows the objectives that the buyer wants to obtain, the seller is able to build a business case around the buyer's desire for gain as well.

Table 5.3

Discovery Component	Estimated Time
Approach	90 seconds
FOCAS questions	30–90 minutes
Summary	1 minute
Commitment: progression or close	30 seconds

- *Concern questions.* Used to *find* dissatisfaction.
- *Anchor questions.* Used to *grow* dissatisfaction.
- *Solution questions.* Used to *gauge* dissatisfaction, and determine where the buyer is in the buyer decision model.

    Demand can begin to be *created* via combinations of objective, concern, and anchor questions.

- A basis of a relationship can be problem removal, problem prevention, or the addition of an innovation that better enables the attainment of a desired business result.

Notes

1. *Counselor Selling* was a sales training program taught by Wilson Learning. Some of this work culminated in the following book written by Larry Wilson: Wilson, L., and Wilson, H. (1987). *Changing the game: The new way to sell.* New York, NY: Simon & Schuster.
2. Wiersema, F. (1996). *Customer intimacy: Pick your partners, shape your culture, win together.* Santa Monica, CA: Knowledge Exchange.

6

Bridging the Divide

Better-practice sellers understand that there is always a reason for a failed sales outcome. This is an essential supposition or belief if adjustments are to be made to increase the probability of future success. Hopefully, this chapter gives you some ideas about why you have lost quality selling opportunities in the past—either to a "no" decision or to the competition.

This chapter is about creating and maintaining positive momentum once a FOCAS discovery has been completed. More specifically, this chapter introduces key progression steps that are highly effective at advancing the selling cycle forward in a nonthreatening, value-adding way. As you will learn, best-practice sellers and sales organizations develop a portfolio of progression steps that they can deploy situationally. To illustrate, let's return to our overall story from Chapter 5.

Congratulations! You've nearly completed an effective discovery with a buyer in the satisfaction stage for your divergent, new application offering. You've delivered an effective approach that not only differentiated your organization and yourself, but also clearly articulated the intriguing value proposition you are capable of delivering. Next, you used the

FOCAS questioning model to find, create, and grow dissatisfaction with the buyer, as well as identify key buyer objectives at organizational, departmental, and, possibly, personal levels. After asking your questions, you quickly scanned your notes and then executed a concise summary of the buyer's most significant problems and concerns, as well as objectives and goals.

Although you've managed to find, create, and grow buyer dissatisfaction, you sense that the buyer's needs are still dormant. Answers to your solution questions signaled the buyer's recognition of problems and concerns. However, the buyer gave no indication of a commitment to action to remove the problems. You have given the buyer a lot to think about, and the buyer is clearly trying to process the conversation.

Now you're faced with a key decision: With a full buyer commitment not a realistic option, what minor commitment (or *progression*) should you ask the buyer to make?

To help you decide on an appropriate progression step to suggest, return to your strategic selling framework from the previous chapters. Your thought process should be as follows:

1. The buyer is in the satisfaction stage (Figure 6.1), and . . .
2. The buyer has progressed along the satisfaction stage at least to the point of acknowledging some problems and issues, so . . .
3. The buyer's psychology is, "Yes, I have a problem. But how significant is my problem? Is it significant enough to warrant action? And, does this seller seem to be taking me down a path that is consistent with my strategic objectives?" Therefore . . .
4. The appropriate strategy is to continue to find, create, and grow dissatisfaction, and continue to identify objectives held by members of the decision base (the individuals who will be involved in making the final decision). This strategy must be implemented in a manner consistent with the buyer's psychology, which means helping the buyer answer, "How significant are my problems?" Thus . . .
5. The proper progression, or next step, that executes satisfaction stage strategy and helps the buyer advance through the satisfaction stage and into subsequent buyer decision-making process stages on the way to "yes" is . . .

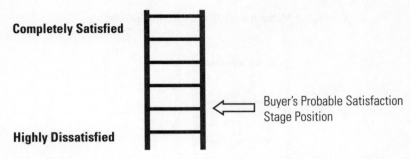

Figure 6.1   The buyer is in the satisfaction stage and is experiencing some significant problems and frustration.

We'll keep you in suspense and finish that thought in a moment. In the meantime, here's a related question: *How does one shorten a long selling cycle?* It's an important question for a few reasons. First, the more efficient the sales process, the more time available to sell. Increased selling time equals higher and faster sales growth. Second, the more productive the seller can be, the lower the cost-per-sale for the seller's organization. Last, the answer gives light to selecting the proper progression step in our scenario.

So, how do you shorten a long selling cycle? Think about it for a moment. Don't cheat yourself by reading ahead.

The answer is: You shorten a long selling cycle by making it longer . . . *on the front end*. Sure, it's a paradox, but it is also reality. Let's explain.

Sellers who rush to final solutions foster resistance with the buyer. Remember, discovery essentially is a needs analysis. It looks at where the buyer is currently, where the buyer is trying to go, and what obstacles stand in the way of reaching that destination. Typically, at the end of a discovery, the buyer contemplates the scope and severity of problems— but is unsure about whether to pursue solutions. This is especially true in *your* major account sales environment, where the solutions can be a literal shock to buyers due to the high financial and change costs. Shock is counterproductive and can snuff out the sales process. That resistance extends the selling cycle.

To illustrate the peril of introducing solutions too quickly, let's return to the key concept of the *divide*. There is a psychological distance between curiosity to change and commitment to change (Figure 6.2).

Divergent Model's Satisfaction Stage "Divide"

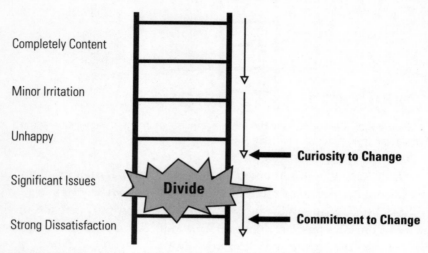

Figure 6.2   The major enemy of divergent sellers is the divide.

If the buyer hasn't crossed this psychological divide by the end of the discovery, then introducing solutions as a next step would be premature. The end solution is likely to be very costly, and a buyer not yet fully committed to change would likely be unprepared for the financial and time commitments necessary to implement the solution. The sales process would break down or be set back significantly if end solutions were presented.

Instead, if the divide has not been crossed by the end of a discovery, the seller must select a progression step that will help *bridge* the divide for the buyer. Once the divide has been crossed, the seller can introduce solutions more safely.

General Recommendations

So, in our scenario from before, the next progression step shouldn't focus on final solutions. Doing so would cause the selling cycle to bog down, or even lead to it being lost in the buyer's psychological divide. The next progression step should be a combination of further needs analysis and a *shock absorber* between needs analysis and the presentation of solutions.

We simply term this hybrid progression step *general recommendations.* As you will see, general recommendations progressions enable the seller to further explore the buyer's objectives. This step also helps buyers gain more clarity on the problems and issues that may be related—*or unrelated*—to the accomplishment of those objectives.

General recommendations is the first step in laying out a solution path in a nonthreatening manner. This is necessary because the buyer needs to generally understand what the seller is building or leading to in the sales process. Please be clear: A crit-

General recommendations is a key step to bridging the psychological divide between curiosity and commitment to change.

ical function of general recommendations is to communicate a solution path for the buying organization, but not focus on very specific, end solutions.

Most important, general recommendations is the step that begins to construct a case for change that bridges the buyer's psychological divide. In other words, general recommendations is a business argument for why a buying organization should commit to change. The basis of this change will be to either remove a problem(s), prevent a problem(s) from occurring, or to achieve some objective(s) more quickly and assuredly. However, it is important to note again that commitment to change does not necessarily mean commitment to a specific product or service solution.

You're probably wondering, "Exactly what is the general recommendations progression step?"

General recommendations is an actual document you prepare and then walk through with the buyer in a page-by-page manner. *The process of delivering the document is as important as its content, and the delivery should become a disciplined skill.* This page-by-page delivery process can be done either in person, through the web (using an online meeting platform such as Microsoft Live Meeting), or, as a last resort, over the phone. We'll discuss proper delivery in detail a bit later.

A general recommendation document is a new form of value-based proposal. It is simple in form, and buyers find it logical and straightforward. Its impact, though, is great. A well-constructed general recommendations document consists of five parts:

1. Situation summary
2. Goals and objectives
3. Constraints, issues, and challenges
4. Options (from which the buyer can choose)
5. Value of each option

We will also discuss each of these sections later in this chapter. This discussion shows you how and why general recommendations is a powerful selling tool when dealing with buyers in the satisfaction stage.

Yet, general recommendations is not always the ideal next step with a satisfaction stage buyer. The key here is that your next step always depends on where the buyer falls on the ladder of decision making *as an organization* (Figure 6.3). An organization whose collective psychology falls in the middle of the satisfaction stage (a few problems are realized) should be treated differently from one that admits strong dissatisfaction (bottom of the ladder). That being said, we are well aware that most buyers, especially those of new applications, fall more to the middle of the ladder (a few issues, but not strong enough dissatisfaction to warrant change).

General recommendations is most appropriate for buyers in the middle group of the satisfaction stage ladder. About 70 percent of buyers are in the middle group. Buyers in the top group (15 percent), who possess little dissatisfaction and are quite content, will not yet be ready for even general options. This is because they believe their problems are not significant enough to entertain the idea of taking action. General recommendations also is sometimes inappropriate for buyers in the bottom group (15 percent), who possess strong and well-defined

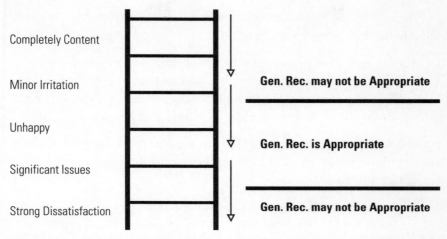

Completely Content

Minor Irritation   **Gen. Rec. may not be Appropriate**

Unhappy   **Gen. Rec. is Appropriate**

Significant Issues

Strong Dissatisfaction   **Gen. Rec. may not be Appropriate**

Figure 6.3 The appropriateness of all progression steps, including general recommendations, depends on the buyer's psychology.

dissatisfaction. They do not want general recommendations, but rather more specific recommendations and clear direction.

Let's go back in time to the selling scenario from Chapter 5. You're at the end of a discovery call with a buyer. Assuming that the buyer is in the middle group of the satisfaction stage ladder, let's explore how an effective salesperson might bridge to the next step—general recommendations. You've just asked your FOCAS questions. Your verbal summary to wrap up this call might sound something like this:

> Karen, thanks for your time and being so open about your situation. Let me take a moment to feed back what I just heard. I'm hearing that you want to finish your ISO quality program within 12 months (objective). You also want to grow revenue in your core markets 15 percent over the next 18 months (objective). Unfortunately, you've experienced a few problems in the area of selling your new high-margin products (key problem). Last, margins have been slowly, yet steadily, decreasing (key problem). This has put a lot of pressure on cash flow (key implication), forcing you to reduce inventory (key implication). As a result, you've received some complaints from customers who are frustrated at having to wait too long for their orders (key implication). Is that about right?

Assuming you have successfully summarized and reached conceptual agreement with your buyer, here's what you might suggest next.

Karen, instead of me suggesting casual solutions to some obviously complex problems, I'd like to give your situation more thought, and perhaps come back with some ideas and options as to how you might best solve some of those problems. Would that be okay with you?

Assuming you've done your job to this point, the buyer will gladly set a time with you in the future to hear your ideas and options. Two important points:

1. Set the specific date and time for the next appointment (general recommendation step) at the end of the discovery call. About 2 to 3 weeks is usually appropriate. Remember, needs aren't active, so urgency isn't a factor yet.
2. Suggest that another *specific* buying influence from the decision base be at the next meeting. This is another individual who has ownership of one or some of the problems you discussed. Most important, this person will clearly have some influence in the future decision. By pulling one or two additional individuals into the next meeting, you're laying the groundwork for finding and growing more critical-mass dissatisfaction with your buyer. Scheduling the general recommendations meeting in 2 to 3 weeks increases the likelihood that these other decision influencers and decision makers will be available to attend this next meeting.

Okay, the table is set. The buyer agrees to the general recommendations meeting. Buyers rarely resist moving to this step, as the risk is low while the potential payoff is high. Put another way, the buyer has little to lose and a lot to gain by agreeing to this next meeting. Consequently, you'll almost invariably succeed in progressing the opportunity forward. Now you're ready to prepare your general recommendations document and then execute a general recommendations call.

Once again, general recommendations is the ideal next step for buyers who admit they have some problems that they are concerned about, but who are not dissatisfied to the point where they actively wish to look at specific solutions and commit to change. With such buyers, general

General recommendations is an ideal mechanism to gain access to other influencers in the decision base. It builds a path to power.

recommendations progressions help salespeople in the following ways:

- *Provides the seller with an opportunity*—to reaffirm, clarify, further explore, and prioritize objectives and problems discussed in the discovery meeting.
- *Enables the seller to continue to find, grow, and create dissatisfaction organizationally*—with the people who were involved in the discovery, and the new people who are present at the general recommendations meeting. Your offering is likely to impact multiple departments and multiple levels of the organizational chart, so there should be plenty of opportunity to uncover additional concerns, opportunities, and goals.
- *Builds a Path to Power.* A key strategic outcome of general recommendations is that it helps you gain access to other key individuals in the organization who have power and influence on decisions regarding your type of offering.
- *Fosters alignment between the seller and buyer, and between members of the buying team.* General recommendations is also used as a consensus mechanism internally in the buying organization. It sparks discussion among members of the buying team about the existence and severity of problems, and the threat they pose to the accomplishment of objectives. Equally important, general recommendations put the seller on the same side of the table as the buyer—working together to remove productivity constraints and move toward the achievement of the buyer's objectives.
- *Progresses the selling cycle.* The general recommendations document enables the seller and buyer to *mutually* establish specific next steps (progressions) that advance the cycle forward. This is

the end result of the general recommendations progression—
agreed action toward final commitment.

- ◆ *Adds Value.* The general recommendations step helps the seller
  answer the buyer's primary satisfaction stage questions: "How
  serious are my problems? Are the problems severe enough to warrant action? Do I have potential other constraints of which I'm
  unaware?" Helping the buyer acknowledge, discuss, and answer
  these questions is consultative, and represents significant value to
  the buyer.

Fast-forward a few weeks. You're sitting in the lobby waiting to
meet with this same buyer. Remember, you executed a great discovery,
and your buyer is looking forward to meeting with you again. *You have
momentum!* Per your suggestion, the buyer has invited another department head to this meeting.

How do you introduce the general recommendations document?
After doing your *approach* for the benefit of the individuals who were
not present at the discovery meeting, you'll describe the *purpose* of your
visit as follows:

Thanks for taking the time to meet with me today. As promised,
I've spent some time thinking about your situation. Based on that,
I've documented some of the important information you shared
with me at our last meeting. I've also included some ideas and
options that might help you resolve some of your challenges.

If it's okay with you, I'd like to hand out this document one
page at a time. This may seem a bit unusual, but it will keep us all
focused on the same page and ensure the most efficient use of your
time. Is that okay?

Your buyer will agree that is acceptable. By asking approval to hand
out your document one step at a time, you'll avoid resistance. This step-
by-step sequence is essential. It ensures that each page of the general recommendation is given the proper attention necessary to build sufficient
psychological momentum toward solution buy-in. It's also important to
hand out the document page by page because you don't want the buyer
to lose focus and flip ahead—often to the options section. The seller
needs to control the discussion and make certain that the key elements
of each page are discussed collaboratively.

The seller should also ask the following at the beginning of the meeting to ensure that the members of the buying organization get the value they desire from the discussion:

Any questions before I begin?

Is there anything specific you want to discuss, learn, or accomplish today that I should be aware of?

The buyers' response to these questions may also give the seller additional insight regarding where the buyers are psychologically in their decision-making process.

You're now ready to share your general recommendations document with your buyer(s). We will sequentially discuss each section of the document in detail.

Section I: Situation Summary

This section contains factual information learned via your fact questions during the discovery. No more than one page in length, it quickly summarizes data such as:

- How the buyer originally learned about you, or how you learned about the buyer.
- When the discovery call occurred (date), and who was originally present at this meeting. This is historical information that will help new buyer entrants to the sales process catch up and understand what has occurred.
- It's important to show in this section that you understand the buyer's business. Therefore, briefly include some general information you learned that you feel is important to mention such as:
  - Core or existing product and/or service offerings.
  - New innovations, products, services.
  - Uniqueness and history of the company.
  - Target market focus or niche.
  - Trends or emerging patterns.
  - General comments and observations about finance, operation sales marketing, distribution, competitive climate, and so on.

List broad facts about the business, and more specific facts that relate to your product or service.

The situation summary should set the tone for the general recommendations themselves. For example, you might finish the situation summary section as follows:

> **The purpose of this document is twofold:**
>
> 1. To clarify XYZ Co. objectives.
> 2. To gain clarity on constraints and issues preventing XYZ Co. from accomplishing these goals or operating in a best-practice manner in critical areas of the business.

Hand out the single sheet. Let the buyer read it quickly, get agreement that you've got your facts correct, and ask the members of the buying organization if any key facts have been left out of the situation summary. Then, move on. There is no reason to dwell on this area since there is little buyer or seller value to be gained from such information. What this section accomplishes, though, is demonstrating that you listened, learned, and are ready to add value.

Section II: Goals and Objectives

The goals and objectives section documents critical objectives at two levels: organizational and departmental. Don't confuse objectives of the buying organization with objectives related to your specific product/service. Rather, this section highlights what's important from a future accomplishment perspective of the enterprise. Examples you might document:

Organizational
- By end of year, establish an ISO certified program in three core areas of the business.
- Grow sales by 15 percent.
- Improve gross profit margin by 2 percent.
- Achieve a better mix of sales whereby new products account for 20 percent of total sales volume.

Departmental
- Hire six new programmers in the IT area.
- Reduce cost structure in operations by 3 percent.
- Begin using outsourcing as a mechanism to reduce cost.

The most important objectives should be listed first, followed by objectives of lesser importance. Typically, broad organizational goals should come before departmental goals. Key organizational goals drive most key departmental goals.

How did you originally find out about these critical objective areas? Of course, by asking objective questions, a key element of the FOCAS structure. This information was gathered during the discovery process. Now it's time to simply transfer this data to a document that can be shared with your buyer.

Remember, a common mistake made by less experienced sellers is to assume and document objectives around *their specific product or service with buyers who have no active needs.* For an organization that sells accounting software, an example of such an invented or assumed buyer objective might be: "To change to a more functional and cost-effective accounting system that better meets XYZ Company's needs." This is a mistake since the audience for a general recommendations document is satisfaction stage buyers who have *dormant* needs. If a buyer verbalized the objective "to change to a more functional, more cost-effective accounting system that better meets XYZ Company's needs," the buyer would have active needs and no longer reside in the satisfaction stage. To document a specific product or service offering goal at this juncture in the selling cycle would undoubtedly create *severe psychological resistance* from the buyer.

As mentioned in previous chapters, when selling divergent offerings that satisfy new applications demand, *problem solving will not be enough to trigger change.* To be successful, you must appeal to the other side of the influence equation: *achievement* and *accomplishment.* One potential basis of a relationship is problem removal or prevention. The other is opportunity attainment. In effect, focus on dissatisfaction, but simultaneously demonstrate that you can make "a good situation even better." How? By accelerating or streamlining the goal achievement process, or enabling even more aggressive goals to be set and reached.

In summary, when you document goals that are critical to the buyer, you communicate to the buyer that you not only understand their objectives, but can accelerate the achievement of those objectives as well.

Always assume that you may never meet some of the key decision makers or decision influencers, up or down the organizational ladder. Based on this reality, you'll need a way to show this invisible decision base that your offering strategically aligns with the future direction of the

company. Also, when selling an offering
that represents a new application, there
will be no existing budget if the buyer
resides in the satisfaction stage. The
buyer is not already using the application,
and the buyer doesn't yet believe they
actually need it. So, the buyer won't have
budgeted dollars available for the new
application. As a result, there must be a
very strong case built that will ultimately
motivate the organization to change.

At the end of the day, unseen decision makers must review how your offering helps further their strategic agenda.
Simply removing tactical or departmental problems will not be enough to gain
the type of momentum throughout the
decision base necessary to counter the
extreme high cost of change for a new
application.

To be successful selling divergent
offerings, you must appeal to
achievement and accomplishment
in addition to problem removal.

Now, let's turn our attention to how to deliver the objectives and
goals section to the buyer. A good way to begin is by verifying and clari-
fying documented objectives with the individuals you met during the
original discovery meeting. Since organizations are dynamic entities that
experience constant change, you'll want to inquire whether there have
been any changes in their key goals since your last meeting.

Again, you will often have one or two new individuals present at
this discussion. Those individuals typically represent different departments, agendas, rungs of the food chain, and politics. Because of this,
you'll often learn about other key goals previously unexplained or discussed. Return to your objective questions and ask these new individuals if they have any goals or objectives they would like to add. This is
critical, as you still need to remain consistent with your *strategic intent,*
which is to find objectives, uncover dissatisfaction, grow dissatisfaction,
and, if necessary, create dissatisfaction.

Remember, your buyer is still in the satisfaction stage. As such, tactics may change, but strategic intent should not.

As a rule of thumb, it generally takes only a short time to present the goals and objectives section. On different occasions, though, it can stimulate some interesting and often lengthy dialogue. Regardless, the key here is that this section positions you as that rare individual who has a broad strategic perspective. As a result of this businessperson who sells positioning, you will gradually gain additional buyer time, trust, and candor. In effect, through FOCAS and general recommendations, you are quickly and assuredly gaining credibility. From the eyes of the buyer, you are not a salesperson anymore, but a *customer productivity expert.*

Credibility will be gained in even greater amounts as you move into the next section of the general recommendations process: constraints, issues, and challenges.

Section III: Constraints, Issues, and Challenges

This pivotal section of general recommendations reveals the problems, and the implications of those problems, that the seller originally uncovered in the discovery visit . . . and then some. These issues should be documented on one or two separate pages. A bullet-based layout often seems to work best.

Problems documented in this section come from two sources:

1. *The buyer.* Via shared problems learned in your discovery. The buyer shares these problems when asked good concern questions. Follow-up anchor questions get the buyer to think about and share the implications of those problems as well.
2. *The seller.* (a) *Your observation* of problems you suspect they may be having now, or will be having in the future, and (b) your perspective on some of the potential *consequences* of problems the buyer expressed during the original discovery.

The first source of problems and their implications offers moderate value to the buyer in a general recommendations document since it simply yields a historical summary of a previous discussion. The latter source of problems and their implications provides tremendous value because it incorporates the seller's insight, perspective, and experience. As a result, buyer thinking is challenged, which is a critical step if pervasive dissatisfaction is to be created throughout the decision base.

Good questions, acute observation, and experience are the keys to identifying issues and constraints of which the buyer was previously unaware. This recognition of previously unrecognized needs is the province of the *customer productivity expert*. CPEs are those rare and highly productive professionals who understand that they can be catalysts in generating buyer desire for change. Demand creators do not rely on external events to stimulate buyer demand—they *are* the external event. As a result, these best-practice sellers have the luxury of operating in a wider opportunity sphere that goes well beyond the limits of shopping stage buyers.

Perhaps this explains why top salespeople see opportunity everywhere, while marginal salespeople never seem to have enough selling opportunities.

Below are some examples of problems one might document in the constraints, issues, and challenges section:

- Overall, a 5 percent across-the-board price increase has been implemented in this fiscal year to offset the significant rise in raw material costs. Customers have complained, and many have likely explored other competitive sources.
- The business is losing market share to overseas competition at a rate of 2 percent per year. Low-cost foreign manufacturers have also led to price pressure and commoditization.
- Selling new products and innovations, which represent higher margin potential, has been a real struggle for the sales and marketing team.
- The accounting department is using manual processes to meet reporting requirements for Sarbanes-Oxley, which is highly inefficient and costly. The accounting department is also now stretched very thin.

You can get as elaborate as you want here. For example, you might estimate the specific financial cost of a problem. As a rule of thumb, though, keep it simple. This is meant to be a casual first look at the buyer's constraints. Your intent is to progress to the next step, not necessarily close a deal (depending on the buyer's psychology, of course). Again, the key to this section is to examine buyer problems, grow them even further, and find potential new issues.

When discussing buyer concerns, it is completely acceptable to make comments like, "That is a perfectly normal issue. We see that problem a lot." By doing so, the buyer feels the problems are solvable, and that you have the experience to do just that. Moreover, buyers are less likely to become defensive if they feel they are not alone in having the constraints you are pointing out.

When discussing each concern or issue that you have documented within general recommendations, suppress the impulse to offer solutions. Instead, as you discuss problems, use preplanned anchor questions about issues in which there is potential to grow dissatisfaction. Your questions might sound like this:

- ◆ "How have the rising material costs affected your margins? Has your increased pricing led to any customer attrition? Is that preventing you from investing in the new technology you need?"
- ◆ "Has losing market share led to any layoffs? Have any of your key customers left you? If not, do you anticipate this happening?"

The key here is to come prepared with a good inventory of concern and anchor questions that can help you find and grow additional dissatisfaction. Ask these strategically significant questions to those new to the discussion as well as the people who were at the preceding discovery meeting.

During the dialogue, make sure to take good notes. Where appropriate, add to the list of concerns. Attempt to get the buying team to prioritize the problems and highlight those that are most dangerous. Remember, these problems are theirs—not yours. You are simply facilitating a discussion. As such, try to get agreement from the participants about how they see their constraints from both an individual and group perspective.

Please note, once again, that organizations are dynamic, not static. Therefore, new problems may have arisen since the discovery meeting, while others may have been resolved. Never assume that a situation you discussed three weeks ago has not been altered by some unforeseen random event.

How much additional dissatisfaction do you need? When is enough . . . enough? The correct response is that you should grow dissatisfaction to the point where the buyers consider their problems as serious enough to warrant action. What type of "action"? Specific action in response to one of the options you're about to present.

Before leaving the constraints, issues, and challenges section, ask some solutions questions. These questions are a good way to get a sense of the buyers' state of mind around their current level of dissatisfaction. For instance:

- "How serious is that problem?"
- "If that constraint could be eliminated, how would that help?"
- "Do you agree that this needs to become a front-burner issue?"

The answers that buyers offer to these solution questions will provide some indication about their position in the buyer decision model. Perhaps the buyers are still in the satisfaction stage. Another possibility is that the discussion has convinced the buyers of the need to take action, which would likely place them in the hedging stage.

In summary, the constraints, issues, and challenges section enables buyers to more clearly see, discuss, and prioritize their constraints. If written and delivered appropriately, this section also allows buyers to see how their problems are interrelated. As a result, salespeople have a value-adding format for helping buyers determine if the combined cost of their multiple problems warrants the consideration of actions that can be taken to remove them. Often, what were formerly back-burner issues move to the front burner, which is a necessary step if buyers are to seriously consider your next section: options and solutions.

Section IV: Options

Up to this point, the dialogue between the buyer and seller is predominantly focused on the buyer's issues and objectives. The buyer, though, soon needs to have some idea about where the seller is leading him.

The options section of the general recommendations document is the seller's first opportunity to show the buyer some practical alternatives to:

- Eliminate some of their costly constraints and,
- Achieve their objectives more quickly or assuredly.

In effect, the options set forth the seller's general recommendations (hence the name of the progression step). A solution path(s) is presented, which may or may not touch on actual product and service offerings.

The seller's job, as a customer productivity expert, is to construct and present some well-crafted options that help buyers take positive action on their issues and frustrations. As you will learn in a moment, various types of options have differing purposes and deliver unique buyer value.

When writing the options section of a general recommendations document, no more than four options should be presented. As a rule of thumb, three is an ideal number. Too many options confuse the buyer.

Only one option should be written on a page. This is important for several reasons. First, if you give the members of the buying team multiple options at once, the buyer will read ahead. It is much better to focus on and discuss one option at a time so that each option is clarified and adequately considered in the seller's presence. Second, placing one option per page enables the seller to improvise by removing an option. This is done by simply not showing it to the buyer. Why would a seller do this? Perhaps information uncovered during the general recommendations meeting reveals that one of the seller's options is inappropriate or impractical. If this occurs, it is better to not present the option.

After each option is read and discussed, the seller should gauge the reaction of key members of the buying team. This can be done with nonthreatening solution questions such as, "Do you think this option may be helpful or add value?" or "How do you think this option might be helpful?" Buyers are typically fairly candid at this point. If they aren't, encourage them to be honest, direct, and open.

The Three Primary Option Types

Essentially, there are three major types of options that you are likely to include in your general recommendations document. They include demand creation options, service demand options, and risk-mitigation options. Although we'll focus on these key options in Chapter 7, let's briefly discuss each type now and provide some examples.

DEMAND CREATION OPTIONS

Demand creation options are meant to appeal to buyers that are still in the satisfaction stage with no commitment to act. These options, if selected, grow the dissatisfaction of the buying team. They also find, clarify, and measure additional buyer problems.

Demand creation options are powerful psychological mechanisms that position the seller as an ally—one more interested in *sincerely impacting* the buyer versus jamming a premature solution down the buyer's throat.

An example of a demand creation option is to conduct an analysis or study in a certain area. These in-depth looks might be called a functional analysis or productivity study. Analyses can range from informal to highly intensive. A seller might actually have the capability to do two or three different types of these. Such an arsenal enables the seller to select one or more of them as appropriate for the buyer's situation. Each might differ in terms of what is being analyzed or the degree of the analysis.

There are three types of options you can present in a general recommendations document: demand creation options, service demand options, and risk mitigation options.

An analysis helps the buyer answer, "How serious are my problems?" and "Do I need to act?" These assessments represent real value to buying organizations. In fact, whether you charge buyer organizations for such studies, the organizations should receive sufficient value that they are willing to pay for the analyses to be conducted. Ideally, the buyer should be asked to pay for the analysis to gauge their interest, to increase their level of commitment, and to increase the buyer's walk-away cost.

"Why would a buyer agree to do a study of this nature?" your skeptical side may be asking. Simply, buyers appreciate an *outside expert opinion* of how efficient or inefficient they are in a specific area of their business. *Most* businesses understand the importance of being best practice. Yet, most have no way to measure how they stack up. A study—and the subsequent findings report—gives them a yardstick in this pursuit.

General recommendations are precisely that . . . general. By engaging a seller to conduct some form of analysis, buyers give the seller a forum for gathering information and returning with more specific recommendations and options. The options portion of a general recommendations step is simply a catalyst for getting the buyer involved in the problem-solving and decision-making process.

Conducting demand creation options, such as an analysis, are often necessary as a preliminary step for the salesperson to best serve a buyer organization. As a customer productivity expert, you may also be unsure at this juncture about the *total impact potential* of your offering on the buying organization (financial and otherwise). In effect, you require a closer look for a better handle on the scope and scale of the buyer situation. Without this perspective, it may be impossible to prescribe specific solutions that best fit the buyer's situation.

SERVICE DEMAND OPTIONS

Service demand options are a second type of option. They are ideally suited for buyers with active needs. In other words, a seller would present a service demand option to a buyer who is committed to taking action on an offering category. Obviously, the buyer motivation behind the active need is either the removal of specified problems, the achievement of objectives, or a combination of the two.

An example of a service demand option is to list a specific end solution that the buyer can acquire. The end solution would be the product, service, or combination that would enable the buyer to achieve its desired outcome (problem removal, goal achievement, etc.).

Why list a product or service as one of your options? The buyer may have arrived psychologically at the shopping stage by the end of this process. If you anticipate this possibility, listing a service demand option (a.k.a., your product) as one option makes sense.

Even though you may have listed a product option, don't go into great detail (verbally or written) about its specifics during the general recommendations meeting. You also would not list the investment required to implement the solution, preferring to cover this verbally. You would, however, simply and generally describe the solution, its implementation, and the final deliverable. Of course, depending on the level of customization of your solutions, you (the seller) may not yet have enough information to determine the exact form or scale of the solution, anyway.

Although the buyer is probably not ready for a full rollout of the end solution at the time of a general recommendations meeting, it is situationally appropriate to list the specific solution as an option. Doing so helps define a solution path for the buyer. Listing a final solution tells the buyer how the seller envisions delivering the desired outcome. Also, by mentioning the solution in general terms and without a specific investment, it begins preparing the buyer for the end solution, which absorbs most of the shock the buyer would otherwise experience if suddenly confronted with this information.

Last, logic dictates that buyers cannot make a decision about a problem removal until they first understand the cost of the solution. Therefore,

Remember Wayne Gretzky? Some consider him the greatest player in the history of hockey. When asked what differentiated him from other players, he would answer, "I never skated to where the puck was—I skated to where the puck was going to be." Your options strategy within general recommendations is analogous to Wayne Gretzky. Don't think where the buyer is at the beginning of the general recommendation meeting. Rather, anticipate where the buyer will psychologically be by the time you begin introducing options.

once you enter into a discussion of final solutions, buyers will ask the seller about the relative investment, and the seller will have to answer.

RISK-MITIGATION OPTIONS

Risk-mitigation options are the third type of option that may be included in a general recommendations document. Risk-mitigation options are meant to appeal to buyers who now have active needs, but are not yet ready to accept the risk or burden of a full rollout solution. In other words, this type of option is designed for buyers in the hedging stage of buyer psychology.

Risk-mitigation options are designed to do two things:

1. To get the buyer to commit to going down a path toward a specific solution.
2. To reduce the amount of risk the buyer perceives with regards to committing to a full rollout of a specific solution.

Risk-mitigation options essentially say the following to a buyer: "We think that you should buy Solution A in order to achieve your desired outcome and satisfy your active need. But, we recognize that committing to a full rollout of Solution A might be too risky right now. Therefore, we've designed another option to help you determine if Solution A really can deliver what we say it can."

One obvious example of a risk-mitigation option is a trial. Such an option would allow the buying organization access to the product or service for a defined period of time in order to get a sense of how it works, how difficult it is to learn and implement, and how effective it can be for them.

Listing risk-mitigation options and demand creation options jointly prevents buyer shock. Whereas service demand options represent buying the whole cow to the buyer, risk-mitigation options tell the buyer they can buy some milk without committing to the entire cow. Demand creation options enable the buyer to push forward without even having to buy a glass of milk! Remember, demand creation options allow the buyer to have an outside entity (the seller) take a closer look and make more specific recommendations about the buyer's problems and goals.

The Significance and Sequence of Options

Options are also the first *true gauge* of the buyer's dissatisfaction level. When creating the options section, it can be helpful to vary them in terms of the level of financial commitment you are asking for. Obviously, buyers willing to choose options that require higher commitment and investment see their problems as severe and disruptive.

It may also be worthwhile to vary the types of options you present in the general recommendations document. Why is it often valuable to include varied options?

After conducting a discovery, you have a sense for the buyer's psychological stage (satisfaction stage, etc.). Therefore, when crafting your options, you know the buyer is most likely going to be in a similar psychological stage at the start of the upcoming general recommendations meeting. However, you won't know where the buyer's psychological stage will be after discussing the situation summary section, goals and objectives section, and constraints, issues, and challenges section. The buyer may remain in the satisfaction stage with dormant needs or develop active needs and creep into the hedging stage. Therefore, per your Wayne Gretzky strategy, it is worthwhile to include demand creation options that appeal to satisfaction stage buyers, risk-mitigation options that appeal to hedging stage buyers, and service demand options that are necessary for hedging stage buyers to understand the destination for the solution path.

Listing multiple options not only brings the buyer into the decision process, but also puts the buyer on the same side of the table with you. In other words, multiple options put the buyer and seller together as collaborators in solving the buyer's problems.

Options allow freedom of choice. Without options, a buyer is suspect that he is being forced down a path that benefits the sales organization, or perhaps getting a solution that only partially meets his needs.

The order of options can be important. For example, the buying organization may have multiple problems that need to be addressed separately. The option you list first should be one that addresses the biggest need of the buyer during your discovery discussion. Other times, it is helpful to begin with the option that would be the least risky and require the smallest level of commitment from the buyer. This allows for a positive discussion around the initial option, and lays a foundation for options that require more significant investment to implement.

To finish our discussion on options, please note that presenting options to a buyer at this stage is a highly effective way to accomplish some or all of the following:

- Expand *higher* and *deeper* into the decision base, those currently unmet individuals who have influence or power in a decision about your offering.
- Lay a *strategic path* for the buyer that can either prove or disprove the need for change concerning the change initiatives.
- Offer a way for the buyer to understand a *solution path* for your offering on a smaller-scale, less risky, basis.
- *Advance* your selling cycle forward with your buyer.
- By offering choices, you'll more quickly gain *credibility* and *trust,* the two essential ingredients necessary to any productive, meaningful, and lasting relationship.

Presenting options that are creative, empathetic, and strategically rooted makes buying easy. Furthermore, presenting buyer options is a strategic mechanism that truly qualifies a salesperson as a consultative customer productivity expert.

Section V: Value

Value is actually not a separate section of the general recommendations document. Rather, the value section is integrated with the options section. Each documented option is followed by a brief discussion of the value of selecting that option. In essence, the value component is a brief description of the buyer takeaway as a result of potentially implementing a specific option.

Well-devised options need to address the buyer's problems and objectives that are listed in related sections of the general recommendations document. Therefore, the value component of each option needs to explicitly link to solving specific buyer problems (or removing specific buyer constraints) listed in the constraints, issues, and challenges section. The value component should also link to the more expedient or assured achievement of specific buyer objectives listed in the goals and objectives section. In this age of innovation, the most meaningful value is the ability of the selling organization to help the buying organization realize significant productivity gains—to do more with less.

The value of demand creation options and risk-mitigation options is not always straightforward for the buyer. Keep in mind that demand creation options and risk-mitigation options do not solve systemic buyer problems or directly enable buyers to achieve their objectives. However, they are valuable to the buying organization. As an example, let's briefly look at the value of a demand creation option such as some form of functional analysis. Such an analysis is valuable to a buyer in its ability to better define and measure problems and determine whether these problems are significant enough (with regards to goal achievement) to warrant change to remove them. Risk-mitigation options are also valuable because they allow the buyer to determine if specific solutions have the ability to remove some of their specific constraints and better enable the attainment of specific goals.

The value description gives you a way to raise buyer enthusiasm for the option(s) as a means to gain the additional buy-in required to move forward. The value component helps the buyer visualize the value of agreeing to take the next step.

Every option you propose to the buyer offers a different type of value to that particular buyer. The value element gives you an opportunity to document this specific payoff. Why is that necessary? Here are a few thoughts.

- ◆ Don't assume the buyer understands the benefit of a particular option. Some buyers have limited perspective, depth, or scope with your area of specialty. Most buyers are simply not experts in your domain. The value description helps buyers become cognizant about how a particular option would most help their unique situation at a specific moment in time.

Here's a sample of what the value description might look like in a general recommendations document.

Option 1: Functional Analysis. We propose doing an in-depth study of your current situation. This study would evaluate the strength and weakness of your finishing department. The deliverable would be a report on how your department compares to best practice in the areas of cost, turnaround, productivity, and service.

Value. There are indications that problems currently experienced in this area have led to bottlenecks and inefficient raw material usage. Even at a 2 percent inefficiency rate of raw material, the current cost being absorbed by XYZ Company is over $750,000 annually. This analysis would help XYZ assess the severity of this problem and examine potential solutions. Improving efficiency and eliminating bottlenecks could also lead to less labor dependence, a factor that would help XYZ become more competitively advantaged in its market due to a lower cost structure.

♦ The value description also gives you an opportunity to put in some general, broad *financial estimates* of how this option might economically impact the department or organization.

♦ Not to be overlooked, the value element ultimately helps *your* key contact eventually *sell* to higher-ups in the organization. Everyone has a boss; even the CEO reports to a board of directors! Make it easy for your key contact to sell to their decision base by documenting value, financial and otherwise, into each progression option you recommend.

Value is the final icing on the general recommendations cake. It ends each proposed option in a positive tone. The key here is to keep it simple. Don't get overly elaborate in your description; a paragraph or two, or a few bullet points, should clearly communicate your thoughts in this final segment of general recommendations.

Wrapping Up Your General Recommendations Progression

After you have presented and discussed all of your options, get a sense for which option(s) the buyer may want to pursue. Again, accomplish this with solution questions such as: "Do you think any of these options would address your needs? Where do you think you need to focus your attention first? Which option do you see as the most appropriate, and why? How else might this option be helpful? Does one of the options stand out as something you would like to consider?"

By asking these solution questions, you allow the buyer to express both the psychological and financial payoff of a specific option. As always, the key in this summary portion is good questioning and great listening. This is your first foray into any serious solution talk, so solution questions (the S in FOCAS) will be most effective at helping raise buyer enthusiasm for the particular option(s) the buyer seems to find most appealing.

A successful general recommendations meeting would include achieving one of the following progressions:

- Getting a commitment from the buyer to return with a more specific and detailed proposal for implementing one or more of the options.
- Returning with new or revised options, based on the general recommendations meeting discussion.
- If the buyer is interested in pursuing an option and terms can be set in the general recommendations meeting, an acceptable progression would simply be to set up a follow-up call to find out if the buyer will move forward.

Should you try some fancy closing techniques at this point regarding one of the options? Absolutely not! Stay appropriate and consultative. Although some decisive buyers will often tell you they want to move ahead immediately on one of the options, most need additional time to discuss the options internally (a meeting to which you will not be invited). Encourage buyers to discuss and debate your suggestions and ideas. If you have done your job, you'll get your minor commitment soon. Perhaps, though, try to set a specific date and time to either talk on the phone or meet in person to get their final decision about your options. This way, both parties have a targeted date for commitment.

How to Deliver a General Recommendations Document

There are three primary methods to deliver a general recommendations document: in person, over the phone, and via the web.

In-person delivery is the ideal method, but not always the most practical due to geographic constraints. As we've discussed ad nauseum, hand out the document page by page in order to control the discussion and keep the buyer(s) focused when you are delivering the general recommendations personally.

The second option, the phone, is sometimes the only practical channel for having a general recommendations meeting. Simply e-mail the document prior to the scheduled meeting. We suggest sending it the day before, allowing time for e-mail problems to be worked out and for members of the buying team to print the document. Once the phone meeting begins, go through the steps of discussing the document page by page. Obviously, this is far from ideal since it does not allow you to help shape the buyer's perspective as you might in person. Buyers who have pre-read the document have a tendency to be more rigid in their thinking. Also, the members of the buying team may misinterpret some points or formulate positions on the options before the seller can clarify and build the case for the options.

Web delivery, the third option, is much better than the phone. The web enables you to deliver your general recommendations document one section at a time without having to travel to the buyer's location.

If you deliver through the web, turn your general recommendations document into a PowerPoint presentation. This presentation can be delivered one section at a time through any one of many versions of web-based meeting and presentation software available. This technology allows you to deliver slides to multiple buyers at your desired pace and sequence. Microsoft Live Meeting (a registered mark of Microsoft Corporation) is a popular software tool in this category of meeting software.

In effect, as long as the buyer has access to a personal computer, you have a way to deliver a general recommendations document without the high cost and inefficiencies associated with travel. What's ideal about this delivery method is that you can deliver your general recommendations document to multiple buyers who:

- Are at the same location in the same room.
- In the same building, but in different offices.
- In remote, geographically dispersed locations.

This is a wonderful example of how technology can improve sales productivity by saving valuable time otherwise spent traveling. With this technology, everything is conducted in real time (live). Essentially, the same sequence of events occurs as in a live presentation, and you preserve the crucial element of surprise and opinion shaping.

Final Thoughts on the General Recommendations Progression

Congratulations! You have just learned a critical step in the influence chain—the general recommendations progression. Most important, you have added a business tool that buyers will find extremely helpful in furthering their decision process. Furthermore, you have learned to build the type of bridges that help buyers cross the steep psychological divide between curiosity and commitment to change. As a result you'll create more and better accounts for your enterprise.

General recommendations documents get more people involved in the buying process. This document, which captures your business case for change, is often distributed to other members or influencers of the buying team. Such a tool is especially helpful for your internal sellers and advocates because it communicates a strong value proposition for them.

Possibly our most important comment on the general recommendations progression is that, if it is to be successful, you first must execute an effective FOCAS discovery. The contents of your general recommendations document are only as good as the FOCAS questions you asked in the discovery. Master both competencies and you'll have achieved a role that adds significantly more value to you, your organization, and your buyer. That role? Customer productivity expert, of course!

The Three Steps to Bridge the Divide

How does one bridge the psychological divide from buyer curiosity to commitment to change? We've discussed the general recommendations progression as a possible means for accomplishing this feat. However, we need to take a step back and consider the mechanics involved with bridging the divide.

Fundamentally, we see best-practice divergent offering sellers undertake three steps to accomplish this passage:

1. Validation
2. Verification
3. Valuation

Step 1: Validation

Good sellers excel at quickly validating problem severity and under-achieved goals. They do this with the multiple constituents who comprise the decision base. In other words, early on in a selling cycle, the better sellers spend the vast majority of their time helping buyers *validate* that their organizational and departmental realities dictate the need for further action.

Interestingly enough, although valuation (Step 3) is typically built on economics, validation (Step 1) is often based on *emotional issues.* What type of emotional issues? Customer complaints, poor morale, inconvenience, image, and so on, are all examples of emotional impediments that may not make for a sale, but will progress a sale to the next phase of the buying cycle.

Remember, economic value is the true driving force in almost all divergent, new application decisions. Yet it is extremely difficult to determine economic ROI early in a cycle due to lack of information. As a result, best-practice sellers capitalize on the emotional frustration of buyers as a means to gain buyer commitment to the next phase—verification.

Both the discovery and general recommendations steps play a role in accomplishing validation. During a discovery, sellers use FOCAS to uncover and understand a buyer's goals and issues. Both the objectives and goals section and the constraints, issues, and challenges section further enable the seller to validate a buyer's problems and objectives. These sections provide the seller with a forum for documenting and discussing the severity of issues and problems, as well as the gap between current realities and unrealized goals.

Step 2: Verification

In this phase, sellers must conceptually verify to buyers that they have a *feasible solution(s)*—a solution that, at first glance, appears practical and affordable to the buyer. Buyers will not want to go down an investigative path too far without first getting a sense of the trade-offs and economics associated with the potential future solution.

Verification may appear simple and straightforward, but it is a very delicate step. Here's why. As previously mentioned, demonstrating solutions to buyers at this early phase is dangerous because buyers typically think cost when they see new capabilities. When this occurs, buyers naturally resist. Their reluctance manifests in objections—a buyer reaction that research indicates will cause a failed sales outcome.

Therefore, a detailed presentation of capabilities at this sensitive juncture has a tendency to scare away buyers *no matter how impressive the demonstration.* Although buyers' initial knee jerk will often be enthusiasm for all of the wonderful possibilities of your offering, a delayed reaction of reality is soon to come. In other words, it's only a question of time before apprehension sets in. Two weeks later, the buyer gets collective cold feet when they begin to seriously consider all the costs associated with change. As enthusiasm wanes, so does the motivation to move forward.

This is a typical scenario when an opportunity is lost not to the competition, but to the depths of the divide.

The verification step should generally show that you have some effective, practical solutions, but in a way that is fairly low key, unobtrusive, and nonthreatening. The key is not to arouse cost anxiety. Remember, buyers simply need to *verify* that the general costs associated with a solution are not prohibitive should they decide to eventually invest. Verification, which we will discuss later in more detail, fills this psychological need for the buyer.

The general recommendations progression also accomplishes the verification step. More specifically, the options section of the general recommendations document allows the seller to show a general solution path or general capability for helping the buyer remove constraints and speed up goal attainment. This section does not scare the buyer away with details about the solution. It does allow the seller a chance to generally discuss investment, which the buyer will certainly be interested in.

Step 3: Valuation
This final step allows both buyer and seller to examine the ROI associated with the new application. This is the final step to bridge the divide

before final buyer commitment can be achieved and the hedging stage realized.

Valuation enables both parties to examine the full-scale returns—economic and otherwise—that can potentially be achieved by the new, divergent methodology. Remember, economics are the major motivator in all high-risk purchasing decisions, and this step enables you to present financial evidence to support the proposed change.

The valuation step should give you logical access to other key players in the decision base (those individuals who have both power and influence in the decision regarding your offering). These influential people will be interested in the economics of change. In effect, this step entails an analysis (ranging from casual to formal and comprehensive) that will either economically prove or disprove the validity of your concept.

Buyers will go through the valuation step with or without the seller. Therefore, it is better that the seller employs strategies and methods to be actively involved in this process.

By building bridges to others in the decision base, the valuation step also allows sellers to uncover additional unrealized objectives and harmful constraints at three levels: organizational, departmental, and personal. Often, this information fills in the final missing pieces of the puzzle for both buyer and seller. The end result of valuation is organizational consensus to move toward the next probable phase of buying behavior, the hedging stage.

A final important note to consider regarding valuation: Rarely do the costs associated with one problem area justify change. Rather, it's the summation of the total costs of multiple problem areas that win the day in valuation.

The general recommendations progression also contributes to the accomplishment of the valuation step. In the options section, the seller should present options that serve to analyze the economics around buyer change; in other words, that look at the cost of the problems and unattained opportunities. The value discussion in the general recommendations document also provides the seller with an opportunity to highlight the expected economic impact of an option, which is based on the problems the option can remove or the objectives that the option can facilitate.

Summary of the Three-Step Process

The most effective sellers already execute this three-step process. However, most do it on an unconscious level. Therefore, we saw value in making this process formal.

The essence of the validation, verification, and valuation processes is to satisfy the psychological needs of a satisfaction stage buyer. These strategies should do the following for the buyer:

1. Answer the question, "Are my problems serious enough to consider change, and does this help us better accomplish unrealized goals?" (*validation*)
2. Generally demonstrate that there resides a reasonable and feasible solution down the road should the buyer decide to purchase. (*verification*)
3. Clearly prove that the buyer can get a healthy ROI based on the uniqueness of the solution. (*valuation*)

Summary

In Chapter 6, the key points are:

- General recommendations is a critical post-discovery progression step that enables sellers to manage opportunities with buyers in the satisfaction stage. There is also a set of skills necessary to execute this step properly, as well as a best-practice process for delivering the document to buyers.

- A well-constructed general recommendations document consists of five parts:
  1. Situation summary
  2. Goals and objectives
  3. Constraints, issues, and challenges
  4. Options (from which the buyer can choose)
  5. Value of each option, which should be integrated with the options section

- ◆ There are three classifications of options, including:
  1. Demand creation options, intended to appeal to buyers with dormant needs and to find, grow, and create buyer dissatisfaction.
  2. Service demand options, intended to appeal to buyers with active needs and to lay out a solution path when dealing with divergent offerings.
  3. Risk-mitigation options, intended to appeal to buyers with active needs who want to reduce the risk of a final rollout before fully committing to the solution.

7

Navigating the Final Stages to a Consensus "Yes"

Six chapters are now in the bag. You're on the home stretch. Here's a meaty chapter that contains some practical, value-adding progression step ideas.

Chapter 7 discusses advancing the sale to final commitment. Typically, gaining buyer commitment in major account selling first requires a series of effective progressions. This chapter provides some effective progression steps appropriate for buyers in each stage of the divergent offering buyer decision model. Without having progression steps appropriate for each stage of buyer psychology, misalignment between the buyer and seller will occur and the sales process will break down.

So far, we focused on steps appropriate for managing opportunities with buyers in the satisfaction stage. Specifically, we've given you structure for doing a discovery and executing a general recommendations meeting. However, let's assume in our ongoing scenario that your buyer remains in the satisfaction stage after you have conducted these two steps. You managed to find, grow, and create dissatisfaction, and you

Without the right steps, friction and resistance will cause the sales process to falter.

identified some critical objectives the buyer is trying to attain and may need help with, but your buyer is not yet committed to change. You've made progress, but the buyer's psychology still revolves around, "Are my problems serious and costly enough to warrant change?"

Visually, your efforts with the buyer have yielded the results shown in Figure 7.1.

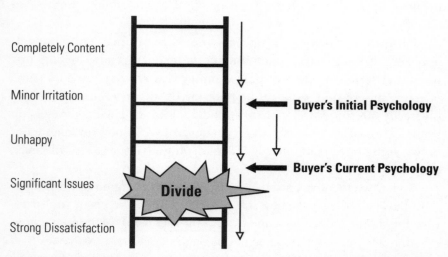

Divergent Model's Satisfaction Stage "Divide"

Figure 7.1 The FOCAS discovery and general recommendations steps have driven the buyer down the satisfaction stage ladder, but not across the divide.

Before you achieve a full buyer commitment, you now need to execute some progression steps that will:

♦ Get the buyer to cross the psychological divide between curiosity and commitment to change.

♦ Reduce the buyer's risk of making the large commitment to rolling out your offering.

♦ Build consensus within the buying organization's decision base to implement your offering.

Remember, though, that the sales process in your major account sales environment is not linear. You should not—and will not—manage each opportunity in the same sequential way. Instead, with the large sale, you will have a portfolio of progression steps to deploy situationally based on each specific buyer's decision process. Each buying organization moves through its decision process at its own unique speed. Some organizations are more open to change and less averse to risk than others, for a wide variety of reasons. Therefore, linear, step-by-step processes will misalign with most buyers.

Your portfolio of progression steps should contain the types of progressions listed in Table 7.1.

The three main types of progressions, which we have listed in previous chapters, are demand creation, risk-mitigation, and service demand progressions. In this chapter, we discuss the demand creation and risk-mitigation progression categories in greater detail. This chapter also covers consensus-building progressions. We reserve further discussion of service demand progressions until Chapter 8.

As for implementation progressions, we do not discuss this category in detail because we are required to keep this book to a manageable length. Implementation progressions are also least important concerning

Table 7.1

Buyer's Divergent Decision Stage	Appropriate Progression Category
Satisfaction Stage	Demand Creation Progressions
Hedging Stage	Risk-Mitigation Progressions
Consensus Stage	Consensus-Building Progressions
Rollout Stage	Implementation Progressions
Shopping Stage	Service Demand Progressions

new client acquisition, which is the main focus of this book. The roll-out stage, where implementation progressions are appropriate, occurs post-commitment. Therefore, implementation progressions are more about client management than client acquisition.

You may be curious about why we did not mention consensus-building or implementation progressions in the previous chapter, which was on the general recommendations progression. The reason is it would be unlikely you would include either of these two progression categories as options in a general recommendations document.

Here's another key point about progressions steps: *Within each category, there are an infinite number of possible progression steps that can be developed.* We've seen our clients create many unique progressions after they have a logical understanding of the buyer decision model. Therefore, when you adopt these buyer models, be creative with the types and variety of progression steps you develop.

We'll provide you with some examples of effective progressions used by various organizations. As you create your own, always ask yourself whether each progression is value-adding to the buyer and aligned with the psychology of the buyer. If not, go back to the drawing board.

Demand Creation Progressions

We've already spent a great deal of time discussing demand creation progressions in Chapters 5 and 6, so we'll spend little time here. Conducting FOCAS discoveries, general recommendations, and analyses are examples of demand creation progressions.

The key with this progression category is that these steps are meant to help answer the questions satisfaction stage buyers contemplate, which include, "How serious are my problems?" and "Do I need to take action to remove these problems?" and "Does this fit with our strategic direction and objectives?" In other words, this category is meant to grow dissatisfaction, enable goal achievement, and to create active buyer demand.

Following are some interesting examples of demand creation progressions utilized by some organizations.

Demand Creation Progression Case Study: Tribute, Inc.

An excellent example of a demand creation progression comes from Tribute, Inc., and its vice president of sales and marketing, Bill Horrigan.

Tribute is a provider of industry-leading enterprise-wide distribution management software for the industrial distribution industry. The vertical markets served by Tribute and its software products include distributors of hose, hydraulics, pneumatics, pumps, instrumentation, gaskets, conveyor belting, and rubber products—along with their related industries.

Tribute's distribution management software can solve problems experienced in multiple functional areas of distribution businesses. It encompasses financial management, inventory management, sales, services, and other areas. Tribute's solutions can have a significant ROI for its clients.

When confronted with satisfaction stage opportunities, Bill Horrigan often employs a survey-style demand creation progression, which helps him build a compelling business case for his prospect to change.

To clearly articulate this survey-style demand creation progression, we'll describe an actual example of how Horrigan used this step to advance a prospect out of the satisfaction stage of buyer psychology. Tribute calls this type of progression a diagnostic study.

Bill had conducted a discovery with the owner of a hose and hydraulics distributor. The owner responded to a Tribute direct-mail piece, but was still in the satisfaction stage. The discovery revealed that the owner was relatively content with his company's existing inventory management software. However, he was generally discontented with his organization's overall productivity. As with most C level executives, he was opportunity-focused and saw great potential in capitalizing on some market opportunities. The owner felt significant growth was possible, but the organization was constrained by inefficiencies. Under the circumstances, growth could only be achieved by the addition of more personnel, making his business difficult to scale up.

At the end of the discovery, Bill had identified several deficiencies with the existing inventory management software that the owner was aware of. However, the cumulative cost of these recognized deficiencies was not significant enough to warrant changing the organization's inventory management software.

Bill needed to identify additional problems with the existing inventory management software being experienced by the organization. He suggested that the owner allow him to meet independently with several key managers and executives to gauge whether the existing solution may be contributing to some unrecognized inefficiencies and unnecessary costs. Because Bill tied this diagnostic study to the owner's desire to increase productivity and make the business more scalable, the owner gave Bill permission to perform a diagnostic study (Bill's demand creation progression).

As part of this study, Bill executed a FOCAS dialogue with each of the following individuals: the accounting manager, inventory control and warehouse manager, VP of operations, and customer service manager. Through these discussions, Bill found several significant problems related to the organization's existing inventory management software that the owner had not known about, which included:

- The inventory control and warehouse manager had a pair of problems with the existing software. First, the software didn't allow him to load updated vendor prices automatically. Instead, he and his staff had to manually change vendor prices, which consumed considerable time considering the company's catalog listed 5,000 parts. This work added up to a cost of 1 percent of margins, or tens of thousands of dollars. The second major problem experienced by the inventory control and warehouse manager was that the existing software did not enable him to determine what was dead stock, excess stock, or overstock. He estimated that between 25 and 30 percent of the organization's $3 million of inventory fell into one of these categories. That represented between $750,000 and $900,000 of undesirable inventory that could be managed out with better tools and practices.
- The accounting manager was mailing invoices. The existing software did not allow for the convenient e-mailing or faxing of invoices. It cost the company $1.05 per mailed invoice (not including labor), with approximately 300 invoices mailed per week. Factoring in holidays, this represented over $15,000 per year. Worse, whereas faxed or e-mailed invoices would be received instantly by customers, mailed invoices took 4 or 5 days to be received. This meant that the mailed invoices were delaying payment. The estimated cost of delayed cash flow was $40,000 per year.
- The FOCAS dialogue with the VP of operations yielded another

cost not realized by the owner. The existing software required the company to buy preprinted forms for reporting, invoicing, documentation, and so on. Tribute's distribution management software, by contrast, would allow the organization to use much less expensive plain paper. The preprinted paper added between $10,000 and $13,000 in unnecessary costs annually.

◆ The FOCAS dialogue with the customer service manager yielded another serious problem. The existing inventory management system enabled inconsistency in quoting by the customer service team. Each customer service person quoted differently on the same items. Customers quickly realized this and often called two or three customer service representatives within the company to get the best price. Productivity was diminished, the organization paid for more calls on its toll-free line, and margins were compromised. Another estimated 1.5 percent of margins were shaved off.

Many of these problems were actually discovered by Bill during the FOCAS discussions. The various managers accepted these inefficiencies as necessary because they did not know that better practices were available. In other words, they did not previously view some of these costs and inefficiencies as problems because they were accepted as the regular costs of doing business in their industry.

Bill returned to the owner with all of these issues documented in a formal findings report. This report became a working document that tied together all of the associated costs and inefficiencies of the existing inventory management software. Although none of these problems independently warranted a change from the existing system, the total sum builds an overwhelming case for change. In effect, it created demand for change by the owner.

This study process not only built the necessary case for change with the owner, it also produced other benefits. First, the documentation of these problems forced each manager and executive to take ownership of his respective problems. This ownership of problems helped establish consensus agreement among the company's leadership to change. The study process also helped Bill later calculate the projected ROI on Tribute's distribution management software solution, which Bill calls the economic cost-benefit analysis.

Bill Horrigan's progression of a diagnostic study is a classic example of how one creates demand with satisfaction stage buyers.

Final Thoughts on Demand Creation Progressions

Before moving on to risk-mitigation progressions, let us first spend a little more time discussing studies and analyses on a conceptual basis.

We have already established that it will be necessary to build a case for change among the decision base before an organization will commit to your offering. This is especially true in selling new applications where:

- No budget has been created yet.
- The application is discontinuous (no existing infrastructure is in place).
- The buyer's risk associated with change is high.

You may also be faced with a situation where your offering solves *multiple problems* for *different departments*. Furthermore, in many instances, no single problem by itself is great enough to justify the high cost of change. It's the *cumulative cost* of multiple problems that buyers must see before becoming dissatisfied enough to go down the risky path of change.

Based on this, a functional analysis enables sellers to continue their strategic intent of:

- Finding additional objectives that can be motivators of change.
- Uncovering further dissatisfaction, and growing it.
- Creating dissatisfaction (in areas where buyers are unaware they are having problems).
- Tying constraints together in a uniform fashion as a means to show potential ROI.

In our experience, many salespeople are reluctant to offer a study or analysis to buyers. Yet this closer look analysis is one that separates average from excellent salespeople. Ordinary salespeople have difficulty creating demand because most do not understand the strategic importance of taking a more in-depth look at a buyer's situation. As a result, these salespeople end up dealing in tactical problems only—problems that buyers do not see as serious or strong enough to justify the investment for change.

Customer productivity experts are anxious to get a better look at buyer processes, systems, and methodology. By doing so, they also gain:

Good salespeople used analytics and studies to create demand deep and wide in the buyer organization.

- *The path to power.* Access to other influencers and people who comprise the decision base, which is typically wide and high. *Wide* means different departments; *high* means senior management levels.
- *Impact assessment.* By gaining valuable insight through further investigation, salespeople and buyers begin to understand the scope and scale of how solutions can impact organizational performance and the bottom line.

The form a study takes will vary both by industry and subject. Typically, though, a study consists of three elements:

- The study process.
- The documented report.
- Delivery of the report to the buyer.

The study process typically entails one or a combination of surveys or interviews with key individuals (inside or outside the buyer organization), direct observation, benchmarking, and other forms of analyses. Regardless, the real process is simply a continuation of the FOCAS discovery process. In other words, the seller works to learn about additional goals and objectives in that specific domain as well as uncover additional constraints or problems that are preventing the buyer from optimizing in a particular area.

During the analysis process, the seller should focus on both recognized and unrecognized constraints. The latter includes issues and challenges that the buyer may be experiencing but is unaware of at the time of the study. Remember, many times buyers accept a certain way of doing things because they don't know what they don't know. In these

Table 7.2

Findings Report Sections	Description of Section
Overview	This section updates the reader on the purpose of the study, relevant company objectives, who was included, how it was conducted, and relevant dates. You might also include how you originally learned of the buyer (or they of you). Simply put, this section is meant to ramp up the reader on the pertinent facts of the situation. Always assume that there will be people reading this report who you have *not* met but have influence in the decision. This part helps them get up to speed quickly on the situation.
Strengths/Assets	This section lists the positive elements you found in your analysis. Jumping in with problems too soon in your report will alienate some buyers. Also, some of the upcoming problems you'll soon be discussing may be personally or emotionally difficult for your buyer. You don't want to start your findings report by putting people on the defensive. The strengths section gives you permission to subsequently discuss dissatisfaction areas by first discussing what the buyer is doing well. Companies want to know not only where they are falling down, but also where, what, why, and how they excel. Documenting the strengths you've uncovered positions you as a credible person who can objectively see both sides of the buyer equation.
Constraints/Vulnerabilities	This section highlights all areas where the buyer has current or potential problems. Some of these you may have uncovered via your initial discovery. Your analysis simply confirms or substantiates these constraints. On a higher value-adding level, this is your opportunity to document those problem areas of which the buyer was previously unaware. This is the domain of creating dissatisfaction, a strategic hallmark for best-practice demand creators.
Specific Recommendations	This is the feel-good part of the report in the sense that solutions can now be discussed. In this section, you'll attempt to arrive at conceptual agreement relative to which direction the buyer wants to take to remove some or all of the dissatisfaction areas and achieve key objectives. Often you'll be introducing product/service solutions at this point. Remember, buyers like options, so if you can show a few different alternatives that help the buyer, all the better. You should also list the value of each option, which includes the specific problems the option can remove and goals that are facilitated by the option.

instances, the buyer may think they are doing something well. In reality, though, the buyer is often inefficient or ineffective. Sales productivity experts are capable of finding and quantifying unrecognized constraints through analysis.

The findings of an analysis or study need to be documented and presented to the buyer team. The delivery of this report should be done just as a general recommendations document is presented. An effective structure for the findings report is shown in Table 7.2.

Risk-Mitigation Progressions

As alluded to in Chapter 6, risk-mitigation progressions are appropriate for buyers in the hedging stage of decision making. Once a buyer's needs become active and they commit to change, the buyer will be motivated to reduce risk of a divergent offering. Remember, risk is high in a divergent offering, so it is natural for a buyer to proceed with caution. Unless buyers are afforded opportunities to reduce their risk, they will either return to the satisfaction stage or shift into a shopping stage mentality and search for alternative solutions. Either buyer reaction is obviously undesirable for you, the seller.

Risk-mitigation progressions are meant to provide buyers with methods of building confidence that your solution is appropriate for their situations and capable of delivering on your promises. Effective risk-mitigation options enable buyers to attain at least a threshold level of comfort with your solutions and the corresponding investment. Once this comfort level is achieved, buyers will make a formal and final commitment.

Risk-mitigation progressions range from very casual to highly sophisticated. Ideally, buyers should be asked to make a financial commitment regarding risk-mitigation options, which raises both their walk-away costs and their attention. Some very general forms of risk-mitigation progressions include:

- ◆ *Trial.* The buyer may prefer a trial of your product or service in a limited or full-scale capacity. This may be an actual usage or some simulated endeavor aimed at allowing the buyer to experience your offering with little risk.

- *Demonstration.* The buyer may want to see your offering produce results for the buyer's specific application.
- *Implementation of solution analysis.* Dollars may be budgeted to study the best way to integrate your solution in the organization. The psychology here is not "Should we do it?" but "What is the best way to integrate the solution we've selected, and what would the implementation process entail?"
- *Visitations.* Site visits to your location or visits with your existing clients with similar applications are good examples of risk-reduction strategies for the hedging phase.
- *Modeling.* Creating accurate and elaborate models that can simulate the effects of the new application on the buying organization, using data or scenarios that precisely represent the actual buying organization.
- *Reference checks.* The most common of all risk-mitigation progressions are providing buyers with lists of references and getting them to speak with several who have had similar situations, challenges, and so on.

You should have an adequate sense for what constitutes a risk-mitigation progression and the purpose of these valuable sales process steps. Now, let's look at some examples of risk-mitigation progressions utilized by effective sellers.

Risk-Mitigation Progression Case Study: Physicians Imaging Solutions

Physicians Imaging Solutions (PhIS) is in the business of creating additional revenue streams for physicians. More specifically, they help physicians capture more patient revenue through diagnostic imaging projects. Physicians Imaging Solutions does this by *partnering* with physician groups to launch and operate diagnostic imaging centers within the physicians' facilities. These imaging centers enable physicians to generate income from MRI scans as opposed to referring patients to hospitals or other outside imaging centers, where the physicians earn no income from the scans. The partnership provides the physician groups with new capabilities, and the decision for such a partnership is a divergent one.

Developing these imaging centers represents tremendous risk to physicians groups. Risk comes from multiple directions, including large financial investments for construction and the acquisition of MRI equipment, the additional cost of MRI technicians, regulatory risks (primarily from Stark Laws), and operational risks.

Once physician groups reach a commitment to change, the high risks of moving forward can be a substantial barrier that can prevent finalizing deals for PhIS. Therefore, David Kelly and Joe Palmisano, the principals of PhIS, have developed an effective strategy for mitigating this substantial risk.

When PhIS senses that a physicians group prospect has moved into the hedging stage, they begin taking measures to reduce the total risk perceived by the group. They begin by ensuring that the physicians group understands all of the risk. Often, the physicians aren't aware of all of these risks, and they appreciate that PhIS informs them accordingly.

PhIS then separates the risks into separate *buckets,* attacking each independently in the form of progressions. The three primary risk buckets include financial risk, operating risk, and regulatory risk.

Financial risk of such imaging projects can be broken down into two related components:

1. Whether the physicians groups will produce enough patient scan volume to cover the additional costs and turn the desired profits.
2. How much the physicians groups will be able to collect from these scans in the form of reimbursements.

PhIS has developed a straightforward method of answering these questions and measuring the actual financial risk the physicians face.

PhIS tracks the number of patients the physician group refers for MRI scans over a 30- or 60-day period to project a likely scan volume. PhIS also has a formula for determining the revenue the physician group should expect to receive from the projected scan volume. In order to have numbers to plug into this formula, PhIS studies the breakdown of the purpose for types of scans. The purpose of scans is significant because reimbursements vary according to the circumstances for the scans. PhIS also has to factor in the disparate reimbursement practices of insurance companies. For example, BlueCross/BlueShield and Medical Mutual may provide different reimbursements to the physician group for an identical scan.

The sophisticated model used by PhIS produces the expected monthly incoming and outgoing cash flow from the imaging center. The results of this risk-mitigation progression clearly demonstrate the true financial risk to which the physicians are exposed. Financial risks subsequently cease to be a roadblock. This process also enables PhIS to prove its ROI case for the project.

Regulatory risk is also mitigated by PhIS. Physicians are provided substantial legal documentation and case study analyses that prove the installation of in-house imaging centers would not violate Stark Laws or other regulations. Therefore, regulatory risk ceases to be a roadblock.

The third major risk for physicians lies in operating risks. The primary component of operating risk lies in how the imaging center will be used and in selecting the optimal imaging equipment for the physician group. As you might guess, imaging equipment requires a large investment and comes with many expensive options. The proper equipment and options vary from group to group. Therefore, PhIS performs extensive surveys with each and every physician in the group to determine equipment and center needs. PhIS also integrates its knowledge of imaging trends into the center design decisions and equipment selection processes.

This analytical process, conducted before a formal commitment is made by the physicians, eliminates the operating risks associated with imaging center design and use, as well as machine selection.

The principals at PhIS believe these risk-mitigation progressions are critical. They have told us that they would not get final commitment from physicians without these important sales process steps. Obviously, these steps represent tremendous value to their prospects—enough so that the physicians frequently pay for these steps. The PhIS principals also feel these risk-mitigation efforts endear themselves to the physicians, and create the level of trust required for such partnerships to be successful.

One last note on risk mitigation progressions used by PhIS: When PhIS charges for these steps, the fee is contingent on whether the physician commits to moving forward with a partnership. In other words, the fee is waived if the group enters into a partnership with PhIS, and charged if the physician group walks away from the deal.

Risk–Mitigation Progression Case Study: JMS Elite

JMS Elite is a business development firm that works with organizations to generate sales leads. Essentially, JMS is a teleservices firm that represents organizations that sell complex and expensive (frequently $100,000-plus) business solutions. The business development personnel at JMS are uniquely trained and experienced in engaging senior level executives in strategic business dialogues as a means to create selling opportunities for JMS clients. Most of JMS's clients are technology companies, although JMS has worked outside the technology sector as well.

A full rollout of JMS Elite's business development services entails a structured 3 to 6 month commitment from clients. For clients, these engagements with JMS represent a significant investment and high initial risk. Not only would an unsuccessful project mean a poor return on a fairly large sales and marketing investment, but also the potential for lost market opportunities.

Because of the large risk associated with a full and contractual rollout of JMS services, JMS has developed an effective risk-mitigation progression that it calls a pilot program. In a pilot program, a prospect only commits to a 6-week project rather than the full 3 to 6 months.

A pilot program represents an opportunity for prospects to experience JMS services at both reduced risk and investment levels. Pilot programs enable prospects to get a sense of the volume and quality of leads that JMS is likely to produce during an ongoing relationship.

The duration of each pilot is carefully chosen by JMS Elite's principals. The pilots are set to be only long enough for JMS to ramp up and begin delivering the high level of results that JMS business development personnel are capable of producing. The investment required by JMS is also determined carefully by JMS principals. The amount is low enough to prevent prospects from perceiving substantial risk, but high enough to get enough buyer skin on the table. JMS understands that charging for such progression steps elevates a prospect's walk-away costs and increases their commitment to the success of the pilot.

Because of JMS's focus on managing buyer risk, JMS occasionally offers an out clause in its initial full rollout contract. Again, such an option reduces a prospect's risk toward an acceptable level, and increases the likelihood that the prospect will advance into the next stage of buyer decision-making psychology: the consensus stage.

Consensus-Building Progressions

When the buyer decision base reaches the consensus stage, the members of the buying team are primarily motivated to confirm, secure, or regain organizational consensus to commit to your specific offering. They have already selected your offering and limited the *functional risk* ("Will the offering perform sufficiently?") to an acceptable level while in the hedging stage. However, members of the decision base are now trying to mitigate their *personal risk* in the event implementation of the offering goes poorly.

Achieving a consensus agreement to go forward is key for proponents in the decision base. Again, a consensus agreement to commit to your offering reduces their political vulnerability if implementation is difficult or if results are less than expected. Consensus, though, is also critical for establishing support from all of the people who are involved in making implementation successful. If buy-in isn't wide and deep, there is a greater likelihood that implementation will go poorly.

The consensus stage typically includes three phases: a reevaluation of the concept behind the divergent offering, an internal lobbying process by proponents, and a final vote. These phases can range from fast and informal to long and intense. Logically, the higher the organizational risk and the greater the political charge in the organization, the longer the consensus stage.

Process steps in the consensus stage should not include gimmicky closing techniques. It would be foolish to waste all of your

Good sellers not only get to "yes," but build a coalition of support that leads to successful rollout.

previous hard work and value-adding steps by trying to pressure the buying team into a commitment.

Instead, you will need to be an influencer. We'll explain later.

Consensus among the buyer decision base is something that you, the seller, must constantly be aware of during the sales process. Remember, you need the critical mass of the decision base to make psychological shifts and advance through each stage of buyer behavior. It's a bit like herding cats—a tricky endeavor when dealing with individuals up and down the organization chart.

Before we can explain effective consensus stage strategies, we need to explain two of the most critical elements in this stage: *buyer roles* and *political structure*.

Buyer Roles

Effective sellers not only know who is in the buyer decision base by name and title, they also learn each person's specific role in the buying decision process. In other words, each person in the decision base has a certain function in the decision-making process.

In their successful book, *Strategic Selling,* Robert B. Miller and Stephen E. Heiman identify the various roles that members of a buying organization predictably play in complex buying decisions.[1] *Strategic Selling* also describes how these roles should affect selling strategy.

We have our own classification system of buyer roles. We created it because the *Strategic Selling* system did not adequately cover all of the roles a seller will face, especially in a large, divergent sale where the risk of mistakes have dire consequences. Members of the buyer decision base tend to fall into the following seven general categories:

1. *Early evaluators* are the experts who evaluate your offerings on a technical level. They are screeners who can shoot down your offering, but cannot make the ultimate "yes" decision.
2. *End users* use, or supervise the use of, the types of offerings you sell. They are not only concerned with performance and functionality, but with how your offering will affect them personally.
3. *Ultimate deciders* are the economic decision makers. They can actually say "yes." This buyer role looks at the bottom-line performance of your offering relative to their organization.

4. *Strategic coaches* help you navigate their organizations. They are your champions. They trust you and want you to succeed because they feel your offering is good for the organization.

5. *Devil's advocates,* whether sought out or naturally part of the decision base, are contrarians. Whereas technical evaluators poke holes in your product or service, devil's advocates are quick to point out the deficiencies, risks, and downside of your concept. Their role is to shoot holes in high-risk concepts, especially divergent ones. They exist because leaders see value in building productive contrary opinion into their major decision processes so that all angles and perspectives are considered.

6. *Change managers* are relied upon to make sure that adoption of the new application goes smoothly. Change managers play multiple roles in this endeavor, from ensuring employee buy-in will occur to actually overseeing the foundational changes necessary for successful adoption. Since the organization is dependent on these change agents to grease the skids of change, they clearly have a voice in a decision concerning your offering.

7. *Consultants* are experienced and respected individuals asked to weigh in on decisions. Their objective perspective and insight are highly respected. They may be internal or external to the organization.

Not every role is filled in every selling scenario. Sometimes, an individual can play multiple roles. Moreover, we have not listed all of the possible buyer roles because members of an organization can influence a decision in many ways. For instance, one could make a case that any person who perceives the offering negatively might potentially sabotage your offering.

Obviously, these roles are not equal in weight. The critical mass tends to move as the ultimate decider moves. Unfortunately, sellers often don't get any, or sufficient, direct interaction with ultimate deciders. Therefore, sellers must have strategies for influencing these important people through other channels, such as general recommendations, value-based proposals, and strategic coaches or champions.

Our purpose is not to go into great depth about the implications of each buyer role within a divergent sales process. What we will do is explain these roles in relation to our consensus-building progressions. However, before discussing this in detail, let's investigate the other key factor in large organizational decisions: *political power and influence*.

Political Power and Influence

Jim Holden, in his excellent book *Power Base Selling*, discusses the *who* aspect of how major decisions are made.[2] His contention is that decisions are made less by organizational chart hierarchy and more by political influence.

We agree with Holden. Political power and influence strongly impact buyer decisions, especially in the complexity of making decisions for large divergent offerings.

Political roles and influence are difficult to understand and assess by sellers. These roles are not always consistent with an organization's formal structure. Titles can be deceiving when attempting to determine who has influence within an organization.

The four most common political roles, as we have adapted for our own purposes, are categorized by the combined levels of title and influence a person possesses. These political roles include:

- *Power core.* These people have power due to their organizational chart status and are influential in strategic decision making. They are frequently presidents, owners, other C level executives, and influential senior VPs.
- *Figureheads.* These people have a big title and the authority that accompanies such a title, but lack influence.
- *Rank and file.* These are people who lack both power and influence. They are the workers and implementers.
- *Fast-Trackers.* These are people who lack a powerful title and formal authority, but who possess a great deal of influence. They are often trusted confidants of those with authority.

Visually, the various political roles can be represented as in Figure 7.2. Obviously, the individuals you will focus on are the power core and the fast-trackers.

To get a sense of the political roles of each member of the buyer team, you should ask who is in involved with key initiatives and who is

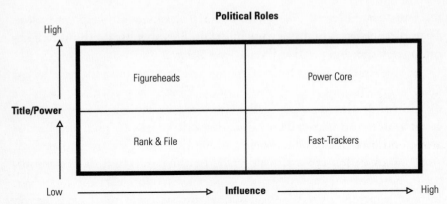

Figure 7.2 Salespeople must account for the political realities of buyer organizations and the political roles of each member of the decision base.

responsible for the accomplishment of key objectives. Yesterday, organizations put their key people on their biggest problems. But times have changed. Innovation is a much more important element in the sustainable success of a company. Therefore, today's organizations put their best and brightest on their biggest opportunities. This is where you'll find the fast-trackers who have an important say in whether your divergent offering ever gets to second base.

To understand the political structure of the organization, you also need to continuously seek answers to the following questions:

- Where is the action (i.e., key projects, etc.) within this organization, and who is involved?
- How credible is the person you're dealing with to higher-ups in the organization?
- How much influence does this person ultimately have, and how is she perceived by other key people?

Consensus–Building Strategies

When you are trying to advance a buyer decision base through the decision process (from satisfaction stage to hedging stage to consensus stage), the critical shift from one stage to the next will not truly occur until ultimate deciders (buyer role) and the power core (political role) move forward simultaneously. You cannot have a consensus "yes" until both psychologically commit to your offering. Fortunately, these individuals often represent both roles in a decision base.

However, the power core often will not commit until their respected fast-trackers (political role) also concur. Leaders respect these people's opinion and often depend on their buy-in. Similarly, ultimate deciders often won't commit until they get a majority sign-off from early evaluators, end users, change managers, and consultants (all buyer roles).

Paradoxically, when the decision base has reached the consensus stage, none of these buyer roles will be who you rely on the most. Instead, your efforts will be focused on the strategic coach, the person who is your confidant and advocate on the buyer team.

Consensus-building progressions will mostly be focused on and through the strategic coach. Remember, these are people who have psychologically committed to your solution and who want to see you succeed. You will need a steady stream of feedback from the strategic coach about who is still involved in the decision, the political *and* buyer roles of each person in the decision (everyone serves both a political and a buyer role), the influence of each person, where key people are with each decision (decision stage), and what impediments stand in the way between each person and psychological commitment to your offering.

Therefore, consensus-building progressions mostly include:

- Progressions you take with the strategic coach.
- Progressions you get the strategic coach to suggest and implement with other members of the decision base.

The former type of consensus-building progressions include periodic debrief and update sessions with your strategic coach. These meetings allow you to craft strategies to be employed by your strategic coach for the purpose of building team consensus.

The latter type of consensus-building progressions include the specific steps you ask your strategic coach to take with key members of the decision base who have not yet psychologically committed to your offering. These steps may include:

- Getting a power core or fast-tracker of the decision team to call a relevant reference or two.

- Getting a power core or fast-tracker to review your value-based proposal. Although you, the seller, may not have direct interaction with key people, your proposal (and even the general recommendations document) are likely to be reviewed by higher-ups (especially if strategic coaches are charged with facilitating this review).
- Reviewing the key points of the value of your solution and the results of hedging stage progressions with power core or fast-tracker members.
- Setting time for the entire decision base to allow you to make a presentation that covers all of the final details, what to expect upon implementation, the ROI/economics they should receive, the implementation plan, and so on.

Another key with a consensus stage selling strategy is to get the decision base to commit to a specific timeframe for making a decision. Ask them how much time they realistically need to make a decision, double it, and agree upon a specific date for the formal decision to be made. Include some negative ramifications of not having a decision by that time, such as a price shift or change in delivery dates. This can be a delicate scenario. But if suggested well ahead of the decision and agreed to by both parties, it can create buyer urgency and momentum toward a final "yes."

As you can see, a consensus stage selling strategy can be difficult to create because organizations have diverse risk tolerance, politics, culture, and so on. Our goal in Chapter 7 is to provide you with models to help simplify the complexity of gaining a final buyer for your divergent offering.

Summary

In Chapter 7, the key points are:

- Best-practice sellers have a portfolio of progressions that solve the purposes shown in Table 7.3.
- Once a buyer commits to a divergent offering, a lot of work still has to be done by the seller before a formal commitment to rollout can be achieved.

Table 7.3

Buyer's Divergent Decision Stage	Appropriate Progression Category
Satisfaction Stage	Demand Creation Progressions
Hedging Stage	Risk-Mitigation Progressions
Consensus Stage	Consensus-Building Progressions
Rollout Stage	Implementation Progressions
Shopping Stage	Service Demand Progressions

◆ In order to get critical-mass shifts and consensus from a decision base, salespeople need to understand the buyer roles and political roles played by each person in the decision base and plan strategies and tactics accordingly.

◆ The political roles include power core, fast-trackers, figureheads, and rank and file.

◆ The buyer roles in a divergent buying decision include ultimate deciders, strategic coaches, early evaluators, end users, devil's advocates, change managers, and consultants.

Notes

1. Gardner, H. (1983). *Frames of mind: The theory of multiple intelligences.* New York, NY: BasicBooks.
2. Holden, J. (1990). *Power base selling.* New York, NY: John Wiley & Sons.

8

The REAP Strategy for Harvesting Active Needs

Up to this point, we've mostly focused on the essentials required to create buyer demand. As mentioned, demand creation is the competence that most often distinguishes top sellers from average sellers. For this reason, and because 90 to 99 percent of your market is likely to have inactive needs for your offerings, we encourage you to invest the necessary time to master this most valuable of all selling dimensions.

In this chapter, we turn your attention to the province of servicing buyer demand. When we talk about servicing demand, we refer to those buyers (likely between 1 and 10 percent of your market at any given time) who already have active needs for your offering. In other words, these buyers are already convinced of the need to change and are actively evaluating alternatives.

When a buyer has active needs and is evaluating alternatives, the buyer is in the shopping stage of buyer psychology. Sellers must utilize a separate set of strategies, steps, and skills when selling to buyers in the shopping stage and servicing their demand. We often see less-effective

When buyers have active needs, they are in the shopping stage. Effective sellers apply a unique set of strategies when managing opportunities with buyers in this stage.

salespeople employ satisfaction stage strategies with shopping stage buyers—a sure recipe for failure.

Although a relatively small percentage of your market will be in the shopping stage at any given time, you may spend the largest percentage of your time with these types of opportunities. Therefore, increasing your effectiveness at managing shopping stage opportunities will have a high payoff for you.

Since buyers in this decision-making stage have defined and active needs, buyer budgets are more likely to be in place or in the process of being created. Sales cycle times also tend to be shorter. However, these types of opportunities frequently are competitive because buyers with active needs logically shop for alternative solutions in order to best meet their needs. Therefore, if you commonly find yourself in competitive selling situations, pay attention. This chapter will be especially meaningful for you.

Before discussing shopping stage strategy, let's first answer the following question: *How does a buyer get to the shopping stage?* Let's review.

The buyer can enter the shopping stage in several ways. When buying concurrent offerings (which satisfy aggregate, continuous improvement, or economy demand), buyers go through the decision-making process shown in Figure 8.1.

When buying concurrent offerings, buyers realize active needs, either independently or with help from a seller, and then predictably progress into the shopping stage from the satisfaction stage. Once buyers have chosen the offering they feel best meets their needs, they progress out of the shopping stage and into the apprehension stage. If the seller mismanages the opportunity once the buyer has reached the apprehension stage, or if some other disruption occurs that makes the buyer uncomfortable with the chosen offering, the buyer

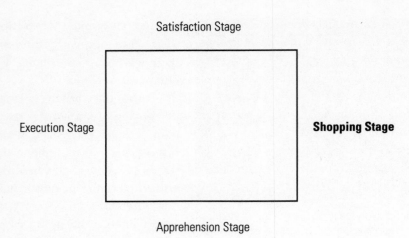

Figure 8.1 The decision process used by buyers of concurrent offerings includes a shopping stage, which often represents a competitive
challenge to sellers.

may revert back to the shopping stage or even back to the satisfaction
stage.

When buying divergent offerings (which satisfies new application
demand), buyers go through the decision-making process illustrated in
Figure 8.2.

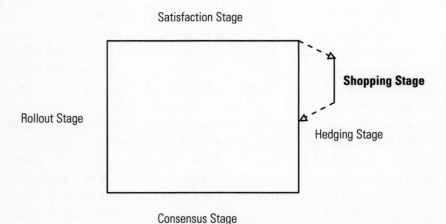

Figure 8.2 A buyer of divergent offerings may or may not enter the shopping
stage depending on when engaged by the seller and the effectiveness of the
seller.

When making decisions about divergent offerings, buyers who re-alize active needs with the help of a proactive seller (a.k.a., customer productivity expert) typically enter the hedging stage and then advance to the consensus stage. However, buyers who realize active needs for a divergent offering on their own typically enter the shopping stage before moving into the risk-mitigating hedging stage. Also, with diver-gent offerings, a buyer in the hedging stage or consensus stage can revert back to the shopping stage if the buyer decision base cannot reduce risk sufficiently or build consensus around the offering. Again, this may occur if the seller fails to offer the buyer risk-mitigation options or fails to achieve consensus support within the decision base.

So, these models show that a buyer can enter the shopping stage from a variety of angles, regardless of whether the offering is concurrent or divergent.

Now, let's review a little more about the shopping stage.

A buyer in the shopping stage no longer attempts to determine whether problems are serious enough to warrant change. Instead, the buyer has determined the total cost of the problems justifies the cost of action, and therefore acknowledges a need for change. The buyer seeks a solution and is driven to understand how to make the best choice among alternatives.

So, how does selling to shopping stage buyers differ from satisfaction stage selling? Although there is some strategic overlap, they are generally as different as night and day. That's because buyers' *needs* are so vastly dif-ferent from one stage to another. A satisfaction stage buyer's psycholog-ical needs revolve around answering the questions, "Are my problems serious enough to warrant change?" and "Will this help us achieve our critical objectives?"

The driving psychology of a shopping stage buyer is, "How do I choose the best alternative for my needs?" This buyer is attempting to determine how to select the option that best removes a specific problem, helps achieve a specific objective, or better enables the buyer to capital-ize on a specific opportunity. All shopping stage buyer behavior and activities revolve around this critical psychological dynamic. Proper sell-ing strategy, therefore, should focus on helping the buyer understand how to make the best possible decision, and then helping the buyer actually select the most appropriate offering given the buyer's needs.

Table 8.1

	Satisfaction Stage	Shopping Stage
Seller Strategy	Create demand	Service demand
Buyer Needs	Dormant (need development)	Active
Initial Contact Most Often by:	Seller	Buyer
Is a Buying Process in Place?	No	Yes (even if early generation or informal/casual)
Has a Decision Been Made to Change?	No	Yes
Dollars/Budget Committed?	No	Yes
Receptivity to Meeting with You?	Low to moderate	Highly receptive
Urgency around a Decision?	No urgency	High urgency—generally wants to move fast

Table 8.1 illustrates some ways in which the shopping stage differs from the satisfaction stage.

Determining if a Buyer Is in the Shopping Stage

It is imperative that a seller quickly identifies in which stage of the decision-making process model the buyer resides. Many perfectly good sales opportunities have been lost by salespeople who employed the wrong strategy with the right buyer because they misread the buyer's psychology.

On the surface, it would appear to be a fairly easy and straightforward endeavor to determine where the buyer is in the decision-making process. Quite often this is true. Other times, though, it can be fairly challenging to pinpoint a buyer's psychological status.

The primary tip-off that a buyer is in the shopping stage is when the buyer makes the original contact and requests information or a dialogue. This is a strong indication that the buyer has active needs, or at least a sufficiently high level of dissatisfaction that the tipping point for needs to go active is very near.

Be careful though, because buyers who initiate a dialogue do not always have active needs. Similarly, when the dialogue is initiated by a salesperson, the buyer's needs are not necessarily dormant. Moreover, the needs of one individual do not always reflect the needs of the organization. For instance, consider the following two examples:

- You were contacted by a senior manager who is in the shopping stage actively looking for solutions. The critical mass of the buying organization's decision base (including the critical economic decision maker), though, remains in the satisfaction stage and is perfectly content with the status quo. In other words, the senior manager who contacted you wants to change, but the rest of the decision base does not.
- You were referred to a company who you feel has major account potential. You called this company, and they agreed to an appointment. Since you initiated the original contact, you assumed the buyer is in the satisfaction stage. Approximately halfway through your sales call, though, you discover that the buyer actually agreed to meet with you because they are actively shopping your category.

Satisfaction stage buyers who are in the beginning phases of *contemplating* change, but not yet *committed* to change, are often mistaken as shopping stage buyers by salespeople. Rather, these buyers are still in the satisfaction stage, although psychologically planted at the bottom of their needs ladder (some growing problems). Consequently, these buyers often contact sellers to begin preinvestigating the feasibility and cost of potential solutions. They project common characteristics of shopping stage buyers, but are not fully committed to change and making a purchase. In such a situation, the proper selling strategy to deploy is satisfaction stage strategy.

Again, understanding where the buyer is in the decision-making process is essential. Misinterpreting where the buyer is in the process will almost always lead to a failed sales outcome. Following are a couple of stories to illustrate this point.

Story 1

Barry, a business development vice president for a regional accounting firm, received a phone call from Trexcel, a sizable technology organization.

Trexcel requested information about their firm. Barry persuaded the buyer, Trexcel's CFO, to agree to a face-to-face appointment.

One week later, Barry met with the CFO. Barry asked a great deal of questions. His questions seemed to hit their strategic mark as, not only did he uncover some critical organizational goals, he also found specific areas of dissatisfaction. After about 90 minutes, Barry summarized the key buyer goals and problems he had heard. The buyer agreed that Barry had a good understanding of their concerns.

Unfortunately, Barry found out weeks later that the buyer had awarded their accounting business to one of Barry's key competitors.

Story 2

Lisa was clearly excited about her upcoming meeting with GeneSor Companies. GeneSor had contacted Lisa a few weeks ago requesting a visit. One of the better salespeople in her company, Lisa knew this was a major opportunity.

During her initial visit, Lisa quickly learned more details about GeneSor. She also uncovered who the decision makers were, and their decision-making process. She spent time understanding what specific criteria GeneSor valued most in a solution. Before leaving, she did an improvised presentation that clearly showed how her offering was the best fit for GeneSor's needs.

Unfortunately, Lisa did not get the business. Unlike the previous case study, though, Lisa did not lose to formal competitors. Instead, GeneSor decided not to make a change at the present time. Instead, they chose to stay with the status quo versus incurring the significant expense associated with an investment in Lisa's offering.

Can you guess:

- What went wrong in each scenario to cause the failed sales outcome?
- What is the *common factor* in each story that led to negative results?

The Answer

Story 1: Barry was dealing with a shopping stage buyer—not a satisfaction stage one. Therefore, spending the majority of his time asking questions to find and grow dissatisfaction *did not* meet the buyer's needs. In effect, the buyer already knew that change was necessary. They didn't need Barry wasting their time reconvincing them to change.

Story 2: Conversely, Lisa was actually dealing with a satisfaction stage buyer—not a shopping stage one. GeneSor was curious about her offerings—which is why they originally contacted her company. Some problems they had experienced recently motivated them to pre-investigate solutions. Lisa, though, misinterpreted the situation, assuming GeneSor was in the shopping stage. In fact, GeneSor was not committed to change and was still planted in the satisfaction stage.

Lisa chose to spend the vast majority of her time learning what offering would best suit GeneSor and then presenting capability in a customized manner. Although GeneSor found the demonstration somewhat helpful, this process didn't meet the real psychological needs of GeneSor's decision base. What were those psychological needs?

The primary psychological need of the decision base was for Lisa, the seller, to help them answer the question, "Should we make a commitment to change?" It would have been fairly easy for Lisa to tip this buyer's dormant needs into active ones by building a case for change. But, because she employed the wrong strategy (in this case, shopping stage strategy) with the right buyer, she lost the GeneSor opportunity to the divide—the real nemesis of almost all major account sellers. GeneSor's interest in change never culminated into a commitment to change.

Ultimately the sellers' faux pas in both scenarios is identical—the *wrong strategy* employed because the seller failed to accurately recognize which decision stage the buyer was in. Barry assumed the buyer was in the satisfaction stage. Lisa assumed GeneSor was in the shopping stage. Both assumptions were incorrect. As a result, their strategies did not sate the true psychological needs of their prospects.

Now that we've discussed the importance and occasional complexity of determining the buyer's psychological decision stage, let's learn some methods of properly determining where the buyer is in the decision process.

The best way to make accurate determinations is to avoid making assumptions and directly ask the buyer where the organization is in the buying process. The following question should help you quickly understand the buyer's current decision-making status.

Janet, I want to meet your needs in our meeting today and make the best use of our time together. Just so I am clear about the situation, can I ask where you are in regard to this category? In other words, are you actively shopping this category and committed to implementing a solution?

Don't be afraid to be direct. The buyer will be honest and happy to answer. Consider your own buying experiences. Isn't it better to deal with a seller who is directly addressing your psychological needs? All buyers want to gain value from a sales interaction. For instance, buyers always have questions for you that they need answered. The questions simply vary depending on their buying stage. Therefore, directly asking where the buyer organization is in the decision process allows them to steer you in a way that best meets their psychological needs for discussion.

If the buyer responds that active shopping within the category has begun, it is important to make sure the entire organization is committed to change and not just the individual person (unless the decision maker is the economic decision maker). Therefore, ask these follow-up questions:

- Are you actively shopping the category and have decided as an organization to definitely implement a solution in this area?
- Or, are you perhaps personally committed to a solution, but the rest of your organization is not yet convinced of the need for change?

These are actually solution questions. Essentially, properly worded solution questions can also be used to *gauge* buyer needs.

Without spending a lot of time here, we've listed some other obvious and subtle methods of determining if buyers have moved out of the satisfaction stage and into the shopping stage:

- An RFP or RFQ has been issued.
- An internal buying team has been formally created.

Good sellers delineate whether an individual or the entire decision base is in the shopping stage.

- A budget has been created.
- The buyer uses language that signals active needs (a commitment to act) such as "I need to . . ." or "I have to do something about. . . ."
- Interest is coming from higher-level executives, which indicates a level of seriousness and commitment.
- The buyer's level of sophistication is often a key indicator, especially when the offering represents a new application to the buyer's organization. If the buyer seems to have done some homework and has a sense of competitive offerings, the buyer is likely in the shopping stage.
- If all else fails, do your own research. Identify someone in the buying organization who might help you or is potentially willing to do some digging. Tactfully ask them for input into where the decision base is in the decision process.

A Note of Caution: Here Today, Gone Tomorrow

Another common pitfall encountered by less experienced sellers is to *assume* that a buyer's decision-making state is static. Quite often, as we mentioned earlier, buyers bounce back and forth between stages. For example, a shopping stage buyer can quickly revert back to satisfaction stage status literally overnight. *How can this happen?* A myriad of events can alter decision-making circumstances or put a buying decision on hold. For instance,

- Your key contact is fired or leaves the business.
- The buyer loses a critical customer.
- Acquisition/merger talks begin.
- A new CEO or president with a different set of objectives joins the organization.

All experienced sellers can recollect stories of major account shopping stage opportunities that were lost *not* to their competition, but to unforeseen circumstances that reverted the buyer back to the satisfaction stage. In such occasions, the seller either loses out to "no decision" or must attempt to resurrect the opportunity by redeploying a satisfaction stage strategy.

Shopping Stage Decision Factors

Let's discuss effective shopping stage sales strategy. *What is the most criti-cal element of effective strategy when dealing with shopping stage buyers?* In two words: decision factors.

Decision factors (DFs) are the stuff of which decisions are made. DFs are criteria that can be used by a buyer to select a solution and make a buying decision. Remember, during the shopping stage, buyers are motivated to make the best choice and to learn how to make that deter-mination. In order to do so, they need to *differentiate* between alternative solutions in the market. DFs are the *components* that help buyers frame out which solution offers the best value relative to their needs.

In *Major Account Sales Strategy,* Neil Rackham drives home this point effectively.[1] Although best known for his *SPIN* work, Rackham has written some excellent material on competitive selling. Many of our ideas in the remainder of this chapter are deviations or extensions of Rackham's original thinking. His work has provided a solid foundation on which to build.

As a buyer, you instinctively recognize that decision factors are the essential DNA of a good decision. For instance, you've probably been in a shopping stage situation for a new house at one time in your life. How did you decide which house best fits your needs? *Decision factors!*

Let's take a closer look. What would be the most critical decision factors for you if you were to buy a house today? In other words, what criteria are most critical in deciding which home best fits your unique needs? You would probably list a whole array of decision factors such as size, location, neighborhood, cost, yard, number of bedrooms, school system, taxes, architectural style, garage capacity, commute, and so on.

Now, what happens to these decision factors as you look at different houses? If your answer is, *they change,* you'd be correct. For instance, you might go to an open house where you see a home theater in the lower level. Being a movie buff, you begin thinking that having the capability to add a home theater at a later date would be nice (to the horror of your spouse, of course). This lower-level space flexibility now becomes part of your criteria. Or, consider the fact that you might have 13- and 15-year-old children who will be driving soon (a terrifying thought of a different kind). After talking to a few other parents of teenagers, you decide that a three-car garage is essential. Another new criteria added to the list.

Essentially, there are two types of decision factors:

1. *Hard decision factors.* Those factors that are clearly measurable and quantifiable to both buyer and seller. For instance, three-car garage, 3,500 square feet, central air conditioner, 2.5 baths, or $250,000 maximum price are all hard criteria.
2. *Soft decision factors.* Those factors that are more subjective and less easily quantified. For instance, with regard to our home example, safe neighborhood, good school system, convenient location, and coziness all represent soft, difficult to measure criteria. Other examples of soft DFs include quality, reliability, and service. Why? Because each can be interpreted differently depending on the unique perspective of the buyer and seller.

Regarding soft DFs, there are two important points to keep in mind. First, *more effective sellers do not accept soft DFs at face value.* In other words, best-practice salespeople turn soft decision factors into hard decision factors. Simple questions like, "What do you mean by reliability?" or "What would good service entail for you?" help sellers define soft DFs and transform them into less ambiguous criteria. The primary reason experienced sellers do this is to gain a clearer picture and understanding of buyer needs. Think of soft decision factors as criteria buried within a murky fog. Until the fog lifts, it is difficult to get a clear vision of the actual situation. Sellers need the clearest picture possible of the buyer's DFs in order to get on the same page with the buyer and add optimal buyer value.

The next point is significant for all major account sellers. In large sales, soft DFs are typically *dominant* buying criteria. Conversely, in smaller sales, hard DFs are the criteria that win the day. Rackham's research in major sales environments validated this key point.

This is critical because we often see less effective salespeople apply their own definitions to a buyer's soft criteria. In other words, they assume they know exactly what the buyer wants when the buyer mentions a soft criterion, such as good service. Unfortunately, this is a common error that leads to misalignment and, eventually, a lost sale.

DFs such as quality, reliability, service, support, flexibility, durability—

all soft DFs—become the critical, differentiating elements in *high-risk* decisions. Why is this so? Common sense dictates that when buyers invest higher amounts of capital in categories they deem critical to their lives or businesses, they want to mitigate or reduce as much present and future risk as possible. Therefore, they create more decision factors. Unfortunately, many of the decision factors they create are difficult to measure and are therefore soft.

We will discuss decision factors in more detail in a moment.

Shopping Stage Strategy

Let's now examine shopping stage strategy. Essentially, there are four broad phases of best-practice shopping stage selling strategy for the *large sale.* Each phase has distinct steps—a total of 12 across the four phases.

Remember, good strategy must not only help the seller, but the buyer as well. Good sellers never lose sight of the fact that effective influence is best accomplished when the buyer's psychological needs are continually addressed. *Alignment* reduces buyer resistance, objections, and friction, paving the way for collaboration—not a win-lose scenario.

For sales strategy to be applied across a sales organization, it should be in the form of a model. Good models make strategy memorable, understandable, and systematized.

FOCAS was an effective questioning model. It is the mechanism best employed with satisfaction stage buyers. It is not, however, the acronym of choice in a shopping stage opportunity.

When you engage a buyer with active needs, *it's time to REAP.*

REAP is a strategic tool that will help you harvest existing buyer demand. Remember, a shopping stage buyer has already decided to change and is actively evaluating alternatives. The driving psychology is to find the best value for the situation and make the best choice. The activities of the seller, therefore, should be helping the buyer understand how to make the best choice based on the situation and objectives. These activities are seen as value-adding to buyers.

Harvesting buyer demand can be a fairly simple, straightforward process with little or no competition. Alternatively, it can be a long, complex, and highly competitive one. Whether a selling scenario falls at one of these extreme scenarios or somewhere in between, certain com-monalities always apply to the shopping stage situation. First, buyer demand is in place. Second, a buyer decision about the offering category will be made. And, last, capital will be spent (hopefully with you).

REAP: The Strategic Overview

REAP is the strategy for harvesting shopping stage opportunities.

When you, the seller, first meet a satisfaction stage buyer via phone or in person, you should conduct the type of discovery that was described in Chapter 5. We call the satisfaction stage brand of discovery a FOCAS discovery because the primary element is the FOCAS questioning model. The strategic intent behind FOCAS is to find, grow, gauge, and create dissatisfaction and to learn key buyer objectives.

When you initially engage a shopping stage buyer, you will also need to conduct a discovery. However, it won't be a FOCAS discovery and FOCAS won't be the primary element. Rather, when dealing with buyers who possess active needs, you will conduct a REAP discovery.

The REAP acronym is a guideline that effective sellers use when facing a shopping stage opportunity. It serves as a broad road map to ensure that buyer and seller needs are being addressed. Although the REAP process extends beyond the discovery phase, the four-phase REAP model provides a best-practice structure for discoveries with buyers in the shopping stage.

The letters in REAP represent the following phases:

Ramp-up
Establish decision factors
Assess dormant need areas
Present capability

Ramp-Up

The initial objective of the seller with *any* shopping stage opportunity is to get ramped up on the situation as quickly as possible. Many times, the buyer with active needs has contacted you. This may be a current

customer, future cus-
tomer, or noncustomer.
Regardless, you'll begin
the ramp-up phase of the
shopping stage strategy
by immediately gather-
ing some important base-
line information.

Below are the five
essential elements that
need to be covered in an
efficient Ramp-up pro-
cess:

1. Why shopping?
2. Approach
3. Expectations of initiative
4. Facts and familiarization of buyer
5. Big four

Why Shopping?   This is your starting point. You need to not only
confirm that the buyer is in the shopping stage (see earlier part of the
chapter), but learn what circumstances drove the buyer into this shopping mode. The following questions can help you quickly determine
the why of the situation:

- "What problems were you experiencing that have caused you to
  look at solutions? What were the costs and implications of those
  problems?"
- "Why are you actively looking at making a purchase?"
- "What situation, problem, or goal has put you in the shopping
  mode?"

Once you've confirmed that the buyer is in the shopping stage—*and
why*—you're ready for your approach.

Approach   If appropriate (noncustomer situation), take time to give
the buyer your background (who you are, what you do, what value

you deliver, type of customers you work with, the purpose of your visit, etc.). You've already learned a good approach earlier in this book.

Note that you have just asked the buyer to tell you why he is shopping and what problems drove him into the shopping mode. Therefore, you can and should tailor your approach to reflect what he has just said. For example, you can mention in your approach that you solve the types of problems he is experiencing, who you've solved similar problems for recently, and the type of value your clients have received from your offerings.

What might be the purpose of your visit? It's to understand the buyer's situation, exactly what is being looked for, what solution might best fit the situation, and whether you've got the best value alternative.

Expectations of Initiative   Inquire about the buyer's *expectations* of the purchase. An effective way to phrase this might be, "I'd like to understand what you're hoping to gain here. What are your objectives for this purchase, and what do you want to be the end result of implementing the solution you eventually select?" You might also say, "Let's imagine that you've purchased the offering and it's one year later. What's different, and what benefits and advantages have you ideally realized?" This is important because you're beginning to learn the specific goals associated with the purchasing initiative. This information will be essential when you later craft an effective value-based proposal.

Facts   This is a good time to step back and ask some fact questions. You're going to need some basic information about the company, the situation, how it is currently doing things in the area of the active need, what alternative solutions it is considering or planning to consider, and so on, before you can begin formulating the best solution. Perhaps begin by saying, "Although I've done some research on your company (visited the company website, etc.), would it be okay if I ask you a few questions to better understand your company's situation and how you currently go about doing things in this specific area?"

Big Four   At some point during the call, you'll want to learn the following four essential pieces of information:

- Timeframe of the decision and implementation
- Decision maker(s) and role(s) of each person
- Decision–making process
- Budget for the initiative

You don't need to find this information at once *or* at this specific point. The Big Four, though, need to be uncovered at some point during the visit.

Ramp–Up: Is It Value–Adding?

The ramp–up phase of shopping stage strategy is necessary for the seller to be effective. Buyers will want the seller to fully understand their situation. Buyers will also appreciate a seller who asks good questions and who ascertains the situation and what the buyer is trying to accomplish.

With that said, *Is the ramp-up phase of the REAP model value-adding for the buyer?* It's a good question, especially since research—and the premise of this book—suggests that sellers who add value beyond their offerings have a greater chance of sales success.

Contrary to popular sales folklore, the elements of ramp–up add *little value* to buyers. As a result, this tactic does little to differentiate a seller favorably. Salespeople and sales managers who put a great deal of emphasis on always finding the decision maker, budget, and timeframe are often dismayed. Yet, think of it from the buyer perspective. During ramp–up, he is simply educating the seller on his situation. Due to this, there is very little, if any, value received from the buyer's end.

The good news, though, is that the next phase of REAP—Establish decision factors—clearly adds value to buyers in their quest to determine the best choice for their unique situation. It is also an area of strong differentiation between top and average sellers. The primary reason is that less effective sellers seem to put a great deal of emphasis on the R portion, spending most of their time learning facts that do not help buyers make an educated choice.

Effective sellers, though, spend more time in the E segment of REAP—a strategy that helps them gain credibility, trust, and appreciation from the buyer.

Establish Decision Factors

As mentioned, deci-
sion factors are the
ingredients that com-
prise how a buyer
determines the best
choice. As a result,
the E phase of REAP
is a critical strategic
area for both buyer
and seller.

There are four main steps that make up this phase of shopping stage
sales strategy:

1. Learn current decision factors.
2. Turn soft decision factors into hard decision factors.
3. Introduce new decision factors.
4. Challenge the ranking of decision factors.

Learn Current Decision Factors

Now it's time to learn what decision factors, if any, your buyer has currently established. These decision factors should be grouped in three
primary areas:

- ◆ Critical must-haves
- ◆ Nice-to-haves
- ◆ Unimportant

Remember, some buyers can situationally be clueless about how to
make a good decision, especially if the offering category represents a
new application for them. Other buyers can be very sophisticated,
armed with specifics and certainties about what they want, when they
want it, and how much they have budgeted. Most buyers, though, usually fall between these two extremes.

Regardless, your initial strategy is to inquire what DFs are currently
on the buyer's table. Your question might sound like this, "Mr. Buyer,

can you share with me any factors or criteria you currently feel are important in your decision? This would include any features, functionality, specifications, services, etc., you think will comprise an ideal solution for your situation." Start with broad questions about the buyer's decision factors to see what is foremost on his mind. Subsequently, ask more specific questions about certain criteria to help narrow the buyer's focus.

Now, with pen in hand, it's simply a matter of getting a thorough understanding of your buyer's perspective into the makeup of a good solution.

Often, you'll want to pepper the buyer's responses with questions like the following:

- "Have you looked at other competitive alternatives in the market?"
- "Can I ask which ones?"
- "What did you like?"
- "What didn't you like, or perhaps feel was unnecessary?"
- "Why is that so important?"
- "What are some nice-to-haves you might like to see, ones that would be helpful, but not necessarily essential?"
- "What about unimportant criteria—things you see little value in and aren't important for your situation?"

Overall, this should give you a quick understanding of not only the buyer's perspective, but level of sophistication as well. You may or may not agree with some of the buyer's opinions at this point. The key, though, is not to debate or offer wisdom, but to listen and learn.

When we watch effective sellers do this in the field, we often hear the question, "Why is that important?" after the buyer mentions each decision factor. Understanding why the buyer values each decision factor will later help the seller collaborate with the buyer on ranking DFs, challenge the importance of DFs held by the buyer, and introduce new and relevant DFs not previously considered by the buyer.

After gaining a moderate to thorough understanding of the buyer's decision criteria, it's time to move on to the next step—turning soft DFs into hard DFs.

Turn Soft Decision Factors into Hard Decision Factors

Many of the decision factors you'll hear from buyers will be soft. They are *subjective*—very much open to interpretation.

Earlier in this chapter we discussed the fact that soft DFs are the *dominant criteria* in decisions that involve moderate-to-high buyer risk. As a result, they are often the key determinants regarding who ultimately wins the business. Therefore, you'll want to take some time to have the buyer explain exactly what is meant by some of the stated soft decision factors. Soft criteria like good service, excellent support, durability, flexibility, and uptime can have wildly different interpretations from buyer to buyer and organization to organization.

Best-practice sellers realize the importance of quickly gaining a deep and thorough understanding of a buyer's decision factors. These more effective sellers understand that accepting soft decision factors at face value is a monumental mistake. Therefore, it is necessary to get buyers to define their soft decision factors by asking questions such as:

- ◆ What do you mean by good service?
- ◆ I want to make certain my definition of support is the same as yours. How do you define excellent support?
- ◆ What are your expectations in terms of durability?

Remember, more experienced sellers never impose their own definition for a buyer's soft criteria. Doing so would lead to misalignment, miscommunication, and lost credibility.

Conversely, we often see less experienced sellers *tell* the buyer the "right" definition of soft criteria. Educating buyers is often valuable, but this isn't education. It's usually ignorance or arrogance. Most important, it can put a perfectly healthy opportunity into critical condition. Buyers, no matter how unsophisticated, get frustrated very quickly by sellers who unilaterally presume to know what's best for them at the expense of their own opinions.

One final point on soft decision factors is that subjective criteria are bad for both buyers and sellers alike. Each party has a definite interest in differentiating the alternative solutions under consideration. Let's look at it from both perspectives.

If multiple buyer decision factors are soft and unclear, the seller will certainly be unable to build a case that the seller's offerings directly and uniquely match or exceed the buyer's criteria. The seller will also have difficulty tailoring solutions to specifically meet the buyer's unique needs if those needs are not sufficiently defined.

To understand the buyer's motivation to turn soft criteria into hard criteria, return to the shopping stage buyer's driving psychology: *How do I make the best decision for my unique needs?* To reduce the likelihood of making a poor decision, it is beneficial for the buyer to have hard, measurable decision factors—not soft, subjective decision factors. The buyer cannot accurately compare and contrast alternative solutions without hard metrics.

Introduce New Decision Factors

Your next tactic within the Establish decision factors phase of the REAP model is to introduce meaningful new decision factors to the buyer.

Since most buyers are rarely experts in your category, they are often open to advice about decision factors they may not have considered. Shopping stage buyers often don't know what they don't know, especially when the category represents a new application for them. Many buyers readily admit their naiveté. As a consequence, they are open to education about how to make a more informed decision.

From your perspective, you genuinely want to help the buyer make the best decision. You also know that you have certain advantages that the competition does not possess. Based on your understanding of the buyer's situation, you feel that some of these unique advantages would help the buyer. Subsequently, it follows that if you can get some or all of these unique advantages on the buyer's critical decision factor list, your chances of winning will improve dramatically.

Consequently, you'll want to suggest some of these criteria to the buyer. This can be done in a few different ways. For instance, your company might have a tremendous amount of experience in the specific industry of the buyer. You know that your competition does not. Thus, you can take any of the following approaches to potentially get this criterion on the buyer's list:

- ◆ *Suggest.* "Mr. Buyer, we feel it's really helpful to us and our clients when we have a lot of experience in their industries. How important is the industry experience of the vendor you choose as a means to reduce your risk in start-up and implementation?"

♦ *Concern question.* "Mr. Buyer, have you had any past problems dealing with vendors who are experts with their product, but lack practical experience in your industry?"

♦ *Third party.* "Mr. Buyer, we just did an installation of a similar product in a company whose situation mirrors yours. One of the critical decision factors for this buyer was industry experience. They didn't want to spend time educating new vendors about the uniqueness of their business. They were also concerned that initial implementation might not go smoothly with a vendor who wasn't familiar with their industry. Is industry experience an important factor for you in your decision?"

Buyers welcome sellers who educate and introduce meaningful decision factors. Again, as already mentioned, that's because shopping stage buyers not only want to make the best choice, they need to *differentiate* vendors as well. This last point is counterintuitive for many sellers. In other words, buyers who are shopping do not want to commoditize offerings. In fact, they need to do the opposite—differentiate. Why? Without understanding how vendors and offerings are unique, it is difficult for buyers to make a clear decision on which solution is best.

Effective sellers spend appropriate time ensuring that the *uniqueness* of their offering gets full consideration. This uniqueness can manifest in many ways, including:

♦ Product functionality and versatility
♦ Company personnel and experience
♦ Education and training
♦ Financing and terms

Preparation is key here. Be as fully prepared as possible about which decision factors you feel need to appear high in the buyer ranking.

Challenge the Importance of Decision Factors

The last step of the Establish decision factors phase of REAP is to challenge the importance—or unimportance—of the buyer's decision factors. Two things must be accomplished here.

First, now that all of the decision factors are listed and defined, the seller should review the list and ask the buyer to rank and prioritize any criteria about which the seller may be unsure. Remember, a practical prioritization scale is: critical, nice-to-have, and unimportant.

Second, after the buyer has ranked the decision factors, the seller should work with the buyer to reprioritize them in a way that:

- Better suits the buyer's needs.
- Positions the seller's offering(s) advantageously against possible alternatives.

For instance, let's consider the following hypothetical scenario. You are attempting to sell a piece of production equipment to a buyer. *Speed* is a critical factor for the buyer. The buyer wants to purchase the fastest possible equipment, and defines speed in terms of the output of units per minute. Unfortunately, you are not especially strong in this area. Your key competitor has the fastest piece of equipment in the market in terms of units per minute, and the buyer is also in discussion with this competitor.

Your equipment, however, is extremely reliable and has shorter set-up times for new production runs, and you have data to prove it. Consequently, you can attempt to reframe the meaning of speed to favorably suit your offering. How? Perhaps by suggesting that the buyer rethink the definition of speed from units per minute to total units per month. Your equipment may not be the fastest, but it requires less downtime for set-ups and is the most reliable. It never breaks. Your competitor's unit is fast, but fairly unreliable and experiences extensive downtime before each new production run. By having the buyer rethink speed as *predictable output,* you improve your chances of being compared favorably in this critical area.

Customer productivity experts, through a combination of experience, quick thinking, and planning, are able to challenge the importance of decision factors and persuade buyers to rethink and reprioritize their decision criteria.

Buyers generally understand that there is no perfect solution. They are aware they'll need to make trade-offs to make a decision. Due to this, your goal should not be to design the perfect solution. Rather, your objective should be to position your offering as the alternative that best meets the decision factors.

That's why the E portion of REAP is absolutely critical. Done properly, it adds tremendous value to the buyer because it educates the buyer how to make a better decision.

Remember, buyer decision factors can be a moving target. As buyers look at different alternatives, their criteria often shift and change. As a result, good sellers consistently retake the pulse of shopping stage buyers when revisiting.

In summary, Establishing decision factors is a lot of hard work. It can also be a bit frustrating since buyers can appear fickle—changing their criteria every time they talk to someone new or see something different. The key is to stay patient, flexible, empathetic, and above all else, helpful. Buyers appreciate sellers who understand their plight of choosing the best alternative. As a result, your attitude of helpful consultation can serve as a positive and differentiating criteria all by itself.

Be Smart—Use a Strategic Cheat Sheet

Good sellers are thorough. They are careful not to make any strategic oversights. This can be difficult, though, when engaged in a complex sales discussion with multiple buyers.

A remedy is to consider the use of a shopping stage strategy reference guide (Table 8.2), essentially a strategic cheat sheet.

Table 8.2 Shopping Stage Strategy Reference Guide

Strategy (REAP)	Common Decision Factors: Standard Categories Used by CRM Buyers	SalesEye Online Differentiating Decision Factors
Ramp-Up	◆ **Company**	◆ **Nonlinear sales**
1. Why shopping?	- Industry experience	**process manager**
2. Approach	- Stability	◆ **Sales mapping**
3. Expectations of	- Technical knowledge	◆ **Designed for**
initiative	◆ **Platform**	**complex, multistep**
4. Facts	- Web-based vs. client	**sales processes**
5. Big Four	server	◆ **Sales manager red**
	- Offline version	**alerts**
Establish Decision Factors	- PDA/cell phone/	- Process logic alerts
6. Learn current	laptop versions and	- Customer touch
decision factors	compatibility	alerts
7. Turn soft DFs into	- Integration with	- Pipeline versus goal
hard DFs	enterprise systems	alerts

Table 8.2 *(Continued)*

Strategy (REAP)	Common Decision Factors: Standard Categories Used by CRM Buyers	SalesEye Online Differentiating Decision Factors
8. Introduce new DFs 9. Challenge DF priority **Assess Dormant Needs** 10. Use FOCAS to uncover additional need areas—any problems in other areas? **Present Capability** 11. Customized presentation or demonstration 12. Value-based proposal	◆ **Functionality** - Contact database (contact level vs. company level) - Customizable reporting at sales rep, territory, region, and company levels - Customizable dashboard - E-mail - Marketing manager - Schedule - Document manager - Sales process builders - Outlook integration - Data export/import ◆ **Support** - Training (initial and ongoing) - Tech support (toll-free, site visits, account manager) - Representative's knowledge ◆ **Total Lower Cost Value** - Price vs. functionality - Maintenance costs - Quality	- Progression alerts - Rep activity alerts ◆ **Multilanguage (up to 40 languages)** ◆ **Sales rep usage monitor** ◆ **Industry benchmarks** ◆ **ROI guarantee** ◆ **Adoption guarantee** ◆ **SalesEye consulting services**

By simply putting this on a sheet of paper, it can be easily glanced at during a sales call to keep both you and the buyer on track. Consider the following example, based on a scenario where you are selling a hypothetical web-based CRM solution called SalesEye Online.

Assess Dormant Needs

Now it's time to park your conversation regarding the buyer's active needs. Why? To explore whether problems may exist in other areas in which you can be of help. In other words, once you take the discussion of the buyer's active need(s) as far as you can, begin looking for dormant needs that can be developed.

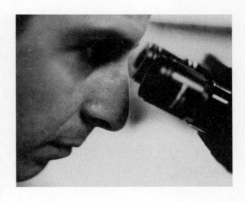

As a rule of thumb, the more integrated and broad your offerings, the more critical it is that you execute this strategy. Why? Consider the following rationale:

- *Flexibility.* The broader your solution to the buyer, the more flexibility you have in solution design and pricing.
- *Value.* By developing and meeting additional buyer needs, you can add more value to the buyer and make a larger, more positive impact on the buyer's business results.
- *Differentiation.* An integrated value solution makes you more difficult to compete with—especially for competitors who have a narrow product line. Situationally, you become nearly unbeatable if you convince a buyer to expand beyond the initial active need area.
- *Larger sale.* You can increase the size of your sale by developing and servicing additional buyer needs.
- *Change costs.* Buyers who commit to expanded solutions, products, and services are typically making a stronger commitment to you. As a result, you are more difficult to fire in any one area if a buyer is purchasing a multitude of offerings from your company. Put another way, the buyer's cost of changing from you to another vendor are increased in an integrated scenario.

So, how do you assess whether other dormant needs exist? Assuming you've spent sufficient time Ramping up and Establishing decision factors, you might segue as follows:

John, thank you for sharing this information with me today. I believe I have a good understanding of what you're looking for. I know you need to make a decision fairly soon, so I'll move quickly to show you our alternatives. But, before I do so, would it be okay if we parked your current active need for a moment so I could explore a few other areas of your business where we might potentially be of help?

That's it. Just communicate that you understand their current situation, promise to move quickly, and ask permission to field a few questions outside the active need area.

Case Study: How Conferon Global Services Learned to REAP the Rewards of Its New Total Solutions Business Model

Consider an example from Conferon Global Services (CGS), the meeting and event management company discussed in earlier chapters. CGS was formed when Conferon acquired two companies (ExpoExchange and ITS) that offer services consistent with CGS's market and existing service offerings. The two acquired companies both offer services that fall outside Conferon's core offerings as well as variants of Conferon's existing offerings. Although different, these meeting and travel-related services are used by the corporate and association buyers that Conferon typically does business with.

Essentially, the combination of these three market powerhouses produced a robust collection of synergistic services. No other organization in the world could match the total and integrated solutions that CGS was now capable of delivering. Bruce Harris, the president of CGS, and David Peckinpaugh, the EVP of sales and marketing, made a strategic decision that the entire CGS sales network would sell *all* of the new conglomerate's services (versus all three companies only selling their specific offerings). The salespeople from each of the three original organizations were now armed with tremendous potential for cross-selling and up-selling, and an unprecedented value proposition.

Unfortunately, the first 9 months yielded very few sales of integrated solutions. Overall revenue and profit also failed to climb as much as expected. The average sales size also didn't grow. Ownership and management were obviously very disappointed that the sales team was struggling to leverage the new value proposition into larger sales and greater dominance in the market. We were engaged by David Peckinpaugh to look into the matter.

We found that there were two primary reasons for the CGS sales network's inability to capitalize on the new model and sell larger, broader, and more integrated solutions, and accelerate the growth of CGS:

1. The sales network, which still hadn't fully embraced strategies for engaging satisfaction stage buyers and creating demand, was highly dependent on buyers with active needs. Most of the opportunities the sales network had were with buyers in the shopping stage.

2. With buyers in the shopping stage, the CGS salespeople would (ironically) REP, not REAP. In other words, they would engage buyers with an active need, ramp-up on their situation as it related to the active need, establish decision factors around the active need, and present CGS's impressive capabilities around the active need. The presentations and proposals were narrow in scope and focused on one or two CGS services at a time that were appropriate for the pre-defined active need. At such a narrow scope, where only one or two services were at play simultaneously, CGS had many, many competent competitors. The CGS companies won their fair share of the business, but no more than before the acquisition and not enough to represent an acceleration of growth.

What are we saying? When presented with a narrow, active need opportunity, the salespeople from the three CGS entities would get excited and try to service it without looking at the buying organization from a broader perspective. They didn't try to Assess for dormant needs in other areas. Consequently, they never tried to or were able to sell broader, integrated solutions that only CGS was capable of delivering. Therefore, on an opportunity-by-opportunity basis, the salespeople failed to differentiate their capabilities and found themselves in unnecessarily competitive situations. Lots of waste resulted.

We subsequently worked with the CGS sales network on strategies to park active needs and assess for dormant needs before presenting capabilities. We trained them to become more comfortable managing broader opportunities and simultaneous dormant and active needs. The result: CGS is now capitalizing on its unmatched capabilities and seeing its revenue, sales size, and profits increase significantly.

Assessing dormant needs can be accomplished through the FOCAS question model. Use these questions to find, grow, gauge, and create dissatisfaction as well as business–critical objectives that can be used to build a case for buyers to change.

Once a dormant need is identified, apply the proper buyer model (divergent or concurrent) and the corresponding set of selling strategies necessary to move the buyer through the decision-making process. Therefore, situationally, you may have to manage the dormant need and active need separately. For instance, after the REAP discovery, you may move to a general recommendations progression for the dormant need and a formal, specific value-based proposal for the active need.

Remember, when a buyer has an active need, speed is important because the buyer is shopping and, if not quickly addressed, the active need could become inactive, or you could lose the business to a fast-moving competitor. Speed is less important to dormant needs. Therefore, if you identify both dormant and active needs with the same buyer through the REAP process, do not allow the management of the dormant need to significantly delay the process of servicing the active need.

Presenting Capability

You've now Ramped up on the buyer's situation. You've helped the buyer Establish and prioritize decision factors. You've also parked the active need and used FOCAS questions to Assess the buyer's dormant needs.

Presenting capability is the final piece of the REAP strategy when engaged with a shopping stage opportunity. This is the area that salespeople typically enjoy most—the show-and-tell portion.

Since so much has been written on the subject of delivering a good presentation, we do not feel it is necessary to go into any great detail. Suffice it to say, demonstrating the functionality of one's offerings can vary drastically from industry to industry. Yet there are some rules of thumb that are important to consider as one moves into this phase. We'll discuss these momentarily.

Generally, there are two categories of Presenting capability: (1) presentation/demonstration and (2) value-based proposal.

Presentation/Demonstration

As observers of sales behavior, we've seen some pretty effective presenters over the years. The personality types can vary significantly—some charismatic and relational, others more logical and reserved.

Our interest is in the common components—the rules of thumb—that make for a good presentation. Based on that, we see three basics that seem to lead to an effective demonstration of capability:

1. Later rather than sooner
2. Resonate
3. Educate

LATER RATHER THAN SOONER

We wish all sellers would follow this advice. Many salespeople, excited at the prospect of a sale, have the fatal habit of presenting and demonstrating far too quickly; in effect, before the seller understands the buyer's situation, establishes decision factors, and assesses for dormant needs.

The problem with this scenario is that, done too early, the features and benefits one communicates are often misaligned with the needs of the buyer. Features are presented by the seller that have little relevance to buyers. Benefits in which buyers have zero interest are also introduced.

The negative outcomes of a premature presentation are multifold:

- Sellers lose credibility with buyers who wonder why they are discussing irrelevant capabilities.
- Buyers resent their time being consumed by salespeople who do not have a thorough understanding of their situation.
- The natural reaction of a buyer who learns of unnecessary features is, "How much are these irrelevant features adding to the expense?" All buyers want the best value, so excessive and unneeded capability screams out, "More cost!"

Sellers are much better off spending time early on learning a buyer's unique situation and needs (or decision factors). Remember, buyers appreciate sellers who spend time thoroughly understanding their condition before launching into a presentation. Stay patient. Learn, listen, and understand before presenting. If you make a mistake, error on the side of presenting later rather than sooner.

RESONATE

Another rule of thumb for effective presentations lies in buyer relevance. When a capability is shown in a manner that is meaningful to the buyer, receptivity to the message increases. In other words, when a presentation *resonates* with a buyer, the probability of influence increases. Salespeople who have spent sufficient time learning, introducing, and challenging buyer decision factors have a huge advantage in making their presentations resonate.

What should factor into a presentation to make it resonate? Your tailored presentation should tie in the buyer's problems that caused the buyer's needs to turn active, the buyer's objectives for implementing a solution, and a comparison of your offering to the ranked and prioritized decision factors of the buyer. If you include these elements in your presentation, it will likely resonate with the buyer.

EDUCATE

Often, the presentation portion of REAP is a way to educate the buyer on how to make a sound decision. In other words, by showing capabilities that the buyer may not have considered yet, you help the buyer better prioritize between critical, nice-to-have, and unimportant decision factors.

The key to educating buyers properly is to refrain from *telling* them what's important in a decision. You can *suggest* what they might consider. You can also *ask* whether they feel a certain feature or benefit might be advantageous. Remember, people only take their own advice. Make it their idea, and you're far better off in the short and long run.

Presenters who position themselves as educators come across as collaborative. Today's buyer wants to be brought on the same side of the table as the salesperson as soon as possible. They will only do so, though, if they trust the seller. By educating versus preaching, the buyer's trust of the seller increases. The result is more openness, honesty, and candor—essential components in any healthy relationship.

Value-Based Proposals

Good proposal construction can be a huge area of advantage in the competitive selling situation. This section examines some of the better practices associated with composing an effective proposal.

Proposal writing can take many shapes, sizes, and forms. Sometimes a buyer has issued an RFP and expects a proposal that conforms to a specific, rigid protocol. Other buyers are more open to entertaining different types of proposals. Regardless of whether your proposal must conform to a strict buyer–imposed structure or not, our intent is to supply you with the components of an effective proposal.

Many salespeople face the challenge of selling higher-priced offerings than their competitors. For these sellers, crafting and delivering an effective value-based proposal is especially critical. The challenge in these situations is to clearly demonstrate that your offering is worth the higher price. In other words, you'll need to supply a proposal that persuades a buyer that the added value of your total offering justifies a larger buyer investment.

Table 8.3 lists an effective value-based proposal structure. It isn't meant as a rigid structure, and situations will dictate which proposal elements are appropriate. With that caveat, it's a solid value-based proposal structure.

Table 8.3

I.	Overview
II.	Objectives of Initiative
III.	Critical Needs
IV.	Proposed Deliverables
V.	Value, Compatibility, and Needs Alignment
VI.	Investment and Terms
VII.	Expectations a. You of Us b. Us of You c. Anticipated Trade-offs
VIII.	Implementation Timeline
IX.	Guarantee
X.	References
XI.	Addendum

Each section is ideally one page—two pages maximum. If you use more space than this, you risk turning off your buyer by not respecting her time. For those descriptions that legitimately require more space, simply delegate this information to the Addendum portion of the proposal.

I. OVERVIEW
This is a brief introduction for the reader of your proposal. Remember, some individuals who are reading this document may not be entirely familiar with your company or the situation. This section quickly ramps up the reader on some pertinent facts, such as:

- How you originally became engaged in the opportunity.
- What has taken place thus far in the buyer–seller interaction.
- Some data and facts about the company and buying situation.

Nothing fancy here—just a quick recap. This is an opportunity to communicate to your buyer that you understand the buyer's business and the context of the situation from a factual standpoint.

II. OBJECTIVES OF THE INITIATIVE
This section enables you to list the goals of the buying initiative. These goals can be at multiple levels: organizational, divisional, departmental, and even personal. The key here is to communicate that you clearly understand *why* the buyer is investing in the offering category and what the buyer hopes to achieve as an outcome of the investment. By documenting these buyer expectations, you lay a foundation of credibility with your forthcoming solution. You are also *differentiating* from your competition who, at this point, is probably quoting.

Many sellers overlook this very important section, but buyers appreciate this section because it reaffirms their reasoning for the large investment. Often, as the discussion progresses and the buyer gathers information, the buyer's objectives migrate and change, so the seller must be flexible. By documenting and discussing the strategic motivation behind an initiative, buyers begin seeing you as something beyond a salesperson—*a businessperson who sells.* This is a strongly differentiated role and position in a competitive selling scenario: a partner helping buyers achieve their strategic objectives.

Show the buyer that you fully understand the economic and strategic logic behind an initiative. The buyer will reward you with the capital of respect and trust.

III. CRITICAL NEEDS

This section gives you additional opportunity to differentiate and further distance yourself from the competition. It also helps the buyer answer the overriding question, "How do I make the best decision for my specific needs?"

The critical needs section lists the buyer's decision factors that you learned and helped formulate in previous meetings. This was accomplished during the Establishing decision factors portion of your REAP strategy.

Remember, decision factors are the elements that buyers use to choose from among all category alternatives. This is your opportunity to demonstrate that you understand *exactly* what the buyer deems important in this decision.

During earlier discussions with the buyer, you likely unearthed two types of decision factors—hard (quantifiable) and soft (subjective). You'll now want to define these in a manner that removes the ambiguity associated with soft decision factors. Examples of how to define otherwise soft DFs follow:

- *Flexibility.* Unit must be upgradeable as new technology enters the market.
- *Service.* Should a problem occur, 24-hour-minimum service turnaround is critical.
- *Speed.* Range—50 units per minute to 60 units per minute.
- *Price.* On a lease/purchase basis, budget is $10,000/month maximum.
- *Training.* One week minimum onsite training of your personnel with a 1-day follow-up 30 days after installation.
- *Support.* 16-hour phone support during the first two shifts of operation (hrs. 7–4 and 4–midnight EST).
- *Terms.* 60-month lease purchase with $1 buyout at term.
- *Delivery.* Must receive unit by December 31 to take advantage of investment tax credit and first-year depreciation schedule.

Many of these decision factors were originally soft (flexibility, service, etc.). Note how a definition now makes these ambiguous terms hard and quantifiable.

Here are a few additional considerations:

- Using matrices, colorful pie charts, scatter diagrams, etc. can be a visually appealing way to display decision factors. Research proves that displaying relevant information in varied formats is a *strong* influence mechanism.
- Consider listing the buyer's decision factors in a hierarchy of importance. In other words, you might have critical DFs listed first, nice-to-have DFs listed second, and unimportant DFs documented last.
- You may also list *why* each DF is important from the buyer's perspective. Doing this not only reminds the buyer of the importance of each DF, but also demonstrates you fully understand the buyer's situation, objectives, and the value she is trying to extract from the investment.
- Efficiency and brevity are important. Ignore the impulse to turn the section into something that might overwhelm your buyer.
- Again, consider this section a working document. Because buyers have often experienced your competitor's capabilities and functionalities since your last communication, decision factors may have changed somewhat. Don't resist this—embrace it. Your role is to help the buyer make the best decision. By working in a spirit of helpful collaboration, you'll stay well ahead of your competitors who are eager to pressure buyers to close deals.

IV. PROPOSED DELIVERABLES

This is where you specifically and briefly list and describe the offering you are proposing. List the key specifications only—no need for minutiae. Include only the amount of detail necessary for the buyer to have a broad understanding of your offering and the specific deliverables.

You can explain the details associated with your offering in an addendum section. The addendum is simply a catch-all at the end of your proposal where you can put detailed specifications, spreadsheets, and so on.

Again, you're attempting to stay on a 1,000-foot level with the buyer for now. If your key buyer is a CEO, a 5,000-foot level might be more appropriate. Conversely, if you're dealing with technical and user buyers, you'll need to spend the appropriate time explaining technical and nuance details important to these parties.

V. VALUE, COMPATIBILITY, AND NEEDS ALIGNMENT

Okay, here's the pivotal question at this point of the proposal process: *How does your offering stack up against the specific needs of the buyer?*

This is the value discussion within the proposal, which makes this section very meaningful. After all, the buyer is investing in value and results, not a product or service.

This section really must tie your total offering to the buyer's situation, the problems the buyer is experiencing, the objectives and motivation for the investment, and the key decision factors the buyer is using to make the decision. If you effectively use this section to show that your total offering will help the buyer remove problems and achieve desired objectives within the parameters of the decision criteria, you will have a tremendous value argument for the buyer to commit to your offering.

Remember also that, at the end of the evaluation process in competitive situations, the seller who best meets buyer criteria *wins!* This is your opportunity to match your offering's features, benefits, and advantages to the specific buyer criteria you highlighted in Section III.

One effective format for this section is a three-column spreadsheet. The first column lists buyer criteria. The second column lists the compatibility of your offering to the buyer's criteria. The third column gives you the opportunity to note or highlight the value the buyer will extract and unique competitive advantages of your total offering.

Let's provide an example. Because production equipment examples tend to be easily understood, a good illustrative scenario comes from a subsidiary of 3M called Combi Packaging Systems.

Combi designs and markets sophisticated packaging equipment and is an industry leader. In a hypothetical scenario, Combi is trying to sell a piece of packaging equipment to ABC Nutrition Company, a maker of bottled nutritional supplements. The category of equipment that ABC Nutrition is shopping for is called a pick-and-place machine. This type of machine will automatically pick up ABC Nutrition's bottles of supplements and place them in cases for shipment. Combi offers a piece

Table 8.4 Needs Alignment and Compatibility

ABC Nutrition Company's Needs	SPP's Compatibility with ABC Nutrition's Criteria	Value and Notes
Flexibility: ABC utilizes a wide array of bottle sizes and packaging case sizes for its supplements.	◆ SPP can be used for bottle sizes ranging from ⅜ inch to 10 inches, which is a range that all ABC bottle sizes easily fall within. ◆ SPP can be used for case sizes ranging from 20″ × 13″ on the high end and 8.5″ × 4.75″ on the low end, a range that encompasses all current ABC case sizes.	SPP's flexibility will allow ABC to expand to both smaller and larger bottle sizes and case sizes than currently used. SPP will provide ABC with the maximum flexibility in experimenting with and selecting future packaging alternatives.
Footprint: Minimum space required by the machine is preferred. Approximately 90 sq. ft. is available in a facility that is near capacity.	SPP is 6 feet by 7 feet (42 sq. ft.). Combined with ABC's case builder, it will easily fit in available space.	SPP leaves the smallest footprint in the industry, allowing ABC to make optimum usage of its limited plant space and contributing to a delayment of plant expansion.
Speed: Minimum of eight cases per minute of output.	SPP offers 10 cases per minute of output.	SPP is the *fastest* unit in its category on a speed/price basis. SPP achieves speed without driving up operating costs, enabling ABC to reduce packaging costs.

Changeover Time: ABC requires the changeover time between runs to be no more than 30 minutes.	The changeover time for SPP is 10–15 minutes.	SPP's changeover speed is unmatched in the industry. ABC will experience less downtime between product runs, representing significant cost savings.
Compatibility: The machine must integrate with existing Case Erector (machine that erects the cases that hold the bottles).	SPP will integrate seamlessly with existing Case Erector.	SPP will delay any need to invest in a Case Erector. However, Combi offers multiple options for highly flexible and efficient Case Erectors should the need eventually arise.
Service and Support: Phone support line for technical issues and on-site technicians.	◆ We have a toll-free service line available 24 hours per day. ◆ Guarantee on-site techs within 48 hours, and have techs in city of the ABC Nutrition facility.	Combi's service sets the gold standard for the industry, and ensures minimum costly downtime in the unlikely event of malfunction.
Budget/Price: ABC has a budget of $80,000 for a pick-and-place unit.	The investment for SPP is $70,000 with flexible terms.	ABC will get the maximum return on its investment.
Warranty	Combi offers a lifetime warranty on the SPP frame and a 1-year overall warranty.	Combi stands behind its products and matches the industry standard for warranties.

255

of equipment called the SPP Servo Pick & Place Packer that matches up
well with ABC Nutrition's decision criteria. A highly simplified version
of the compatibility/needs alignment spreadsheet that the Combi salesperson would create might look like Table 8.4 (this Combi example has
been manipulated and fictionalized for our purposes).

You get the idea. This is a *pivotal* display of information in a competitive selling situation. Done properly, it should accomplish two things:

1. Demonstrate that you meet the *buyer criteria* in essential areas.
2. Show that you are *positively differentiated* from competitive alternatives in areas that the buyer deems important.

VI. INVESTMENT AND TERMS

Not much explanation required. Clearly list the total financial costs first.
Then follow with the terms of the investment, such as billing dates, and
so on.

Make sure you use the word *investment,* not *price* or *cost.* The word
investment is more appropriate, not just because it is more positive, but
because it also connotes that the buyer is making a financial commitment in order to generate a financial return.

To further differentiate yourself from competitors, you may also
want to list some of the nonfinancial costs of the investment, such as
change costs. Buying organizations appreciate this, and sellers earn trust.

VII. EXPECTATIONS

This section allows both buyer *and* seller to have a candid discussion
about what each expects of the other should the buyer commit.

Remember, many buyers (*especially* those of new technologies) can be
naïve about the realities of what it takes to succeed with your offering. For
instance, there may be a fairly steep learning curve. This will require that
the buying organization commit to the independent training and education necessary to facilitate a successful implementation. Or, the buyer may
have to make certain internal changes if the new endeavor is to succeed.

This is your opportunity to document expectations from the only
two perspectives that matter: the buyer's (of you), and your expectations
of the buyer.

How many times have good intentions gone awry because the

proverbial cards were not laid on the table early on? This section gives you an opportunity to have a frank business discussion about what the buyer can expect should he move forward. In other words, this is your chance to *document* that there will be some future hard work—and possible landmines to encounter—before success will be achieved. For a solution to deliver the promised return, the seller may need the buyer to do certain things and have a certain level of responsiveness. The seller's needs should be documented and discussed.

Not surprisingly, buyers appreciate this candor. Sellers are often hesitant to communicate realities at this juncture, but doing so is positive. Buyers appreciate a frank discussion on what's in store for them. Additionally, this candor gives the seller added credibility. It's also a differentiator as most competitors are reluctant to venture into these potentially disruptive areas.

Again, the rule of thumb is to keep it simple. Let the buyer know that you intend to do your job, but the buyer organization must do its job if success and optimization are to be achieved. Although this may seem counterintuitive to gaining a buyer's commitment, it works strongly to the seller's advantage.

The third element of this section is *trade-offs*. You should list the disadvantages and shortcomings of your total solution relative to your buyer's objectives for the investment and decision criteria. Sometimes, solutions can only be tailored so far, and the buyer has to make trade-offs when selecting a solution. Helping the buyer to understand these trade-offs before they make a decision is both appreciated and valued. Bad experiences occur for both parties if the trade-offs are discovered by the buyer during implementation.

Put yourself in the buyer's shoes. You're about to make a big decision. Who would you prefer dealing with—the polished presenter who describes a scenario through rose-colored glasses? Or a seller who accurately describes the reality of what it will take to achieve success?

Buyers are not naïve. They know that the steeper the change, the higher the price to be paid. Good sellers communicate, *in advance,* the anticipated bumps on the road to success.

This is your obligation as a *businessperson who sells.* It is also your *moral obligation.* These are your future potential partners. Treat them accordingly by discussing trade-offs and expectations before "yes" occurs.

VIII. IMPLEMENTATION TIMELINE

This is another opportunity to lay out what a full rollout might look like. Lay out the activities and events around implementation, starting with the signed agreement. That way, the buyer can visually see what will happen, what needs to be done, by whom, and when.

Again, keep it simple. Hopefully your competitors are not doing this.

Buyers want to do business with organizations that are thorough. They want to know what to expect. By putting in a bit of work here to lay out the steps to success, you'll gain additional advantage over your competition.

IX. GUARANTEE

If you have one, here's where to place it. If you don't have one—get one! This is an opportunity to reduce buyer fear in specific areas where anxiety can cause indecision.

X. REFERENCES

Make certain that your list of references includes people with the same title and responsibilities your decision makers have, organizations that faced similar situations and that had similar objectives, organizations in the same or similar industry, longer-term clients who have fully implemented your solution and realized results, and new clients who are still in the early stages of implementation. If you include all of these types of people and organizations, your prospect should be able to get the answers they need from your references.

Above all else, though, make sure that you list references who are accessible, and provide a phone number and e-mail address for each reference source. Prospects not only get frustrated when they struggle to reach your references, they also negatively perceive your organization's relationship with your clients. After all, if your clients were strong proponents of your organization, they should make time to respond to reference checks.

XI. ADDENDUM

The last section of a value-based proposal is the addendum. Many different types of information can go in this section such as:

- ◆ Specifications
- ◆ Literature

- ◆ Articles of interest
- ◆ Company information
- ◆ Evidence/validation

This is where you place additional data and information that you feel the buyer might find relevant. Remember, this is a big decision for the buyer. Supply the necessary information that makes it easy for the buyer to not only understand your offering, but make a decision in your favor.

Final Thoughts on Shopping Stage Strategy

That's it for this chapter on selling in the shopping stage. Our intent was not to go into overly elaborate detail since this is an area where there is already a large amount of published material.

Most salespeople feel very comfortable with the presenting capability portion of selling. Unfortunately, comfort and competence are two very different things. Comfort typically comes from the fact that sales presentations are typically rehearsed, structured recitals of information. Unfortunately, the old dog-and-pony shows of yesterday's salesperson do not translate well into effective selling today.

Competence seems best achieved by those sellers willing to ask the right questions, listen, and learn before plunging into solutions. This was the common theme of satisfaction stage strategy, but in a largely different context. Plunging in with solutions with satisfaction stage buyers will be a tremendous setback and mistake. Doing so with shopping stage buyers may have less severe implications for the seller, but will also adversely impact the likelihood of success.

We hate to sound redundant, but the critical factor to success is *preparation*. Those who have a sound market-facing strategy *and* prepare have a significant advantage over their more impulsive competitors.

Summary

In Chapter 8, the key points are:

- ◆ Selling opportunities with buyers in the shopping stage are often competitive. Regardless, success in shopping stage selling depends on proper management of the buyer's decision factors (DFs).
- ◆ A model for best-practice selling strategy is represented by the REAP acronym, which has four phases and multiple subphases:

- ◆ Ramp-up
  1. Why shopping?
  2. Approach
  3. Expectations of initiative
  4. Facts and familiarity of buyer
  5. Big four (timeframe, budget, decision makers, decision-making process)
- ◆ Establish Decision Factors
  1. Learn current DFs
  2. Turn soft DFs into hard DFs
  3. Introduce new DFs
  4. Challenge the ranking of DFs
- ◆ Assess Dormant Needs
  1. FOCAS questioning model and apply satisfaction stage strategy to any dormant needs that are uncovered.
- ◆ Present Capability
  1. Presentation/demonstration
  2. Value-based proposal

Notes

1. Rackham, N. (1989). *Major account sales strategy.* New York, NY: McGraw-Hill.

III | Sustaining Your Growth Engine

9

For Chief Growth Officers Only: Tying Your Framework Together

We hope that you are committed to rethinking your selling strategy based on what you have learned in the previous eight chapters. This chapter is for managers and executives who must implement, manage, and sustain a new selling framework. You are the chief growth officers, and the framework set forth in this book should represent your *new growth engine*.

If you are not a chief growth officer, keep reading, anyway. This chapter will be insightful because it will reflect how sales teams will be managed in the future.

This chapter presents some key management systems that hold together the strategic sales framework discussed in the book (Figure 9.1).

We have organized this chapter into two primary sections: The first is on Salesgrading and the second on measurement.

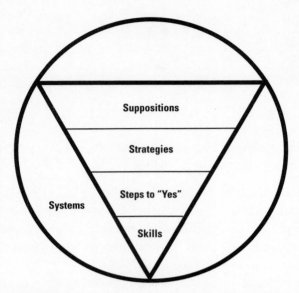

Figure 9.1 Systems are the glue holding a sales framework together.

Salesgrading: Raising the Bar on Sales Effectiveness

The Problem and Potential of Sales Effectiveness Training

We suspect that sales training is a category that has generally failed to deliver on its promise of productivity improvement. This statement is not meant to negate the importance of teaching and implementing common skills, strategies, and steps among a sales team. A shared effectiveness methodology is clearly necessary to optimize a sales team's productivity. Rather, the previous statement is a call for a careful analysis of why these important training endeavors so frequently fail. It's also a call for understanding why, on rarer occasions, these initiatives deliver meaningful advantage to an enterprise.

So why does one training initiative fail while another succeeds? It's an important question since training can be a fairly expensive and high-profile initiative. Even if the financial commitment is not seen as large, there is a significant cost of lost sales time due to training activities.

Although many factors can lead to failure in sales training initiatives, we see three that stand above the rest:

Table 9.1

Content	
Learning design and delivery	50 percent combined
Accountability	50 percent

1. Wrong content
2. Improper learning design and delivery
3. Lack of accountability to change

All three variables are not weighted equally. In fact, the primary reason sales training initiatives most often fail is due to a *lack of accountability to change*. With regard to sales training programs that fail, we believe the primary cause of the failures roughly breaks down as shown in Table 9.1.

As discussed in detail later, systems of accountability are imperative if a sales effectiveness training program is to succeed. Let's examine each contributor to a failed training initiative in more detail.

Wrong Content

It goes without saying that content is very important. Content can vary significantly, so it's important to understand your unique and specific selling challenges. Also, the wrong content for your situation can actually train your sales team to be less effective.

Unfortunately, many executives and managers feel that all sales training is created equal. This one-size-fits-all mentality is a surefire recipe for a failed sales training initiative. This is obviously not the case, as research has proven that the competencies and strategies necessary to be effective at selling large offerings varies significantly from the competencies and strategies necessary to sell small offerings. Furthermore, not all large sales are the same, and proper major account frameworks account for the different types of large sales.

Good training that eventually leads to productivity improvement has a stickiness factor. In other words, the content easily adheres to trainees because it speaks to their unique challenges, frustrations, and opportunities. Stickiness will not be achieved if the training program has generalist content.

Improper Learning Design and Delivery

Learning design and delivery is also critical. Effective learning design and delivery achieves maximum retention within the time and financial parameters set for the program. Careful thought must go into how content is taught, the types of training formats, the learning tools used, the scale and scope of programs, the level of customization, exercises, sequence of delivery, and so on. If learning design or delivery is poor, trainees will obviously have difficulty retaining the program's content. However, with the right content and a proper level of accountability, poor learning design and delivery can be overcome by trainees.

As you have probably experienced, 1 to 4 day boot camps or entertrainment workshops don't allow for retention, and surely don't lead to meaningful and sustained behavior change. Space repetition is required for teaching complex skills, strategies, and steps. In other words, proper training programs spoon-feed and reinforce learning over a reasonably extended period of time. Such spacing and repetition allows for content absorption and trial time. For behavior change to occur, trainees must learn and practice in training sessions, attempt new competencies in real-life field situations, and return to training sessions for refinement and coaching.

For a training program to be impactful, it must resonate with the trainees. For this to happen, content, materials, and simulations must be customized to reflect the uniqueness, idiosyncrasies, and vernacular of the trainees' selling environment. The program should also have tailored simulations or role-plays that enable trainees to practice skills in realistic scenarios and receive immediate and structured feedback. Unfortunately, many sales executives run their salespeople through off-the-shelf programs that aren't customized to their selling environment and that don't reflect the realities faced by their people. These programs fail to resonate with the trainees, and little learning or positive behavior change occurs.

Lack of Accountability to Change

As noted earlier, the lack of accountability to change is the primary cause of training failure with about 50 percent of the programs that do not produce the expected results.

Here's why.

Let's look at a typical training scenario. Assuming the right content is in place and proper learning design and delivery have been conducted, a typical training class will likely be segmented as in Table 9.2.

Table 9.2

25%	This section is motivated to learn and willing to pay the price to master complex skills and strategies. Positive behavior changes are made and sustained. The return for the organization will come from the improved performance of these individuals.
25%	This section has absolutely no interest in learning new material or changing their selling behavior. They are either outwardly or passively resistant to the change that is being suggested. They may go along with the new program while it is being delivered, but will continue to do things as they have been done in the past after the program is concluded.
50%	This large group is interested in new content and fairly open to learning new ideas. They believe the methodologies of the program are appropriate on the whole. Unfortunately, these individuals lack the discipline necessary for meaningful change to occur. Put another way, this large group will not give the necessary effort outside the classroom to master complex strategies, skills, and steps. Remember, for true behavior change to be realized, hard work, study, risk taking, trial and error, and adjustment will be required. Many of these elements need to take place outside the classroom. This group will predictably not pay this price despite believing there might be positive rewards of achieving mastery. As a result, productivity improvement will not be gained.

Based on this data, one can conclude that 75 percent of all participants in traditional sales training fail to learn anything of lasting impact or achieve any field behavior change. These individuals fail the training program, and the program fails these individuals. Please note that this 75 percent failure rate can occur even if the program content, learning design, and delivery are excellent. This explains why organizations often fail to meet their objectives for training initiatives.

Why is there a 75 percent failure rate with most good training programs? Most training programs do not have a built-in method of accountability that ensures participants master complex strategies, skills, and steps being taught. Most training programs allow people to hide and evade, never demonstrating their new competencies at a quantifiable level.

It could be worse. Consider a typical situation with bad content, good learning design and delivery, and no accountability. Here, 75 percent of the class would thankfully not change. Unfortunately, though, 25 percent would change—for the worse. This 25 percent would learn methodologies that actually make them less productive.

The Cycle of Training Failure

When there is a lack of accountability to a sales effectiveness program, organizations complete a cycle of training failure. When we describe this all-too-familiar cycle to executives and sales managers, we almost always get knowing nods of agreement. This cycle of training failure usually occurs as follows:

1. First, the organization is dissatisfied with sales performance (i.e., lack of sustained growth, incompetence in creating demand, inability to sell new offerings, difficulty creating new customers, ineffectiveness in penetrating new markets, inability to have strategic C level business dialogues, difficulty selling integrated value solutions, too many lost opportunities, etc.).
2. The chief growth officer decides that sales training is the best solution.
3. A program is chosen and readied for implementation.
4. The sales force, although quietly grumbling behind the scenes, acts receptive to the new initiative (with the exception of a small minority within the sales team who are more vocally resistant).
5. Salespeople are taken out of the field, and the training program is implemented.
6. During training, there are varying degrees of receptivity, although the majority agree that some good ideas are presented. Many of the salespeople are satisfied to pick up one or two new ideas that will help them in the field. Management, though, is hoping that significant behavior change will take root.

7. The salespeople return to the field. Some try a few new things, but most don't. Some would like to try

Without accountability mechanisms, trainees will sleep, hide, and evade. The outcome is little behavior change and failed sales training programs.

new things, but are afraid to fail with real buyers and choose to operate within their traditional comfort zones.

8. In a very short period of time, the team reverts back to business as usual. The critical mass of sales behavior returns to its original pretraining state. The new methodologies that were part of training, even those that were generally accepted conceptually, are forgotten. Salespeople make the same strategic and tactical missteps they made prior to training.

9. Six months later, reality sets in for the chief growth officer and other members of management. These leaders see clearly that little change has occurred, and the poor performance that plagued them originally still exists. Management begins to look elsewhere for solutions, contemplating wholesale changes in sales personnel, compensation, territory restructuring, etc.

This common cycle of failure has, unfortunately, positioned sales effectiveness training as a low-return category. This is a shame because an effective sales team can be a source of great competitive advantage, and organizations still rely on training programs to achieve this effectiveness. Fortunately, there is a proactive defense against this cycle of training failure. It's called Salesgrading.

Salesgrading: The Accountability to Change

How do you hold salespeople accountable to change around a sales effectiveness training program? Here's how:

1. At the beginning of a sales effectiveness training program, you tell the trainees that they will be rigorously and comprehensively graded at the end of the program.

2. You set and communicate positive and negative ramifications according to how each individual scores.

3. You grade every trainee at the conclusion of the training program and provide each individual with timely feedback. A scoring system should be applied (1 to 100), and overall results of the entire team should be reported to everyone.

4. You regrade each person every year or two to encourage enduring discipline, retention, and behavior change.

Salesgrading is an evaluation process that enables managers to quantify the effectiveness of their salespeople. It's a process of grading out a salesperson's ability to effectively create and manage sales opportunities. We'll give you more detail on the process momentarily.

At Sogistics, we use the Salesgrading process to evaluate salespeople in multiple areas of effectiveness: strategic acumen, skill levels, sales process (steps), suppositions, and even talent. When Salesgrading is used in conjunction with training, we also evaluate an individual's grasp of content knowledge.

We suggest that Salesgrading be used as the accountability mechanism for sales effectiveness training. Salespeople must be graded out in the key areas of the training program subsequent to the completion of the program. Each and every person should receive a score. With such a process, every member of the team is fully aware that he cannot hide in the program and evade the negative consequences of not putting in a real effort to learn the strategies, skills, steps, and content that are part of the system.

The point of using Salesgrading with training is to drive better learning and greater change with the 75 percent of the trainees who otherwise would not make the necessary effort to learn and apply the new methodologies. The real gain, however, will come from the 50 percent who see value in the training program concepts, but who lack the discipline to master and work the system. Fear of negative consequences, desire for positive rewards, and competitiveness will supply this group with the necessary motivation they otherwise lack—driving them to become training successes. The lower 25 percent who have built attitudinal barriers to learning may still be difficult to draw into the program even with the application of Salesgrading. However, this grading process is likely to lead to some positive training outcomes even with this disenchanted group. The consequences associated with Salesgrading push some of these individuals to engage in the program and attempt some new things. As a result, they'll lower some of their barriers and experience some positive results as well.

When using Salesgrading to foster some accountability to change with a training initiative, traditional pen-and-paper or computer-based tests can be used to evaluate strategic acumen and content knowledge. Grading skills, however, is an entirely different matter. Skills are best assessed through realistic simulations. For example, to assess skills in our framework, one would need to conduct FOCAS discovery simulations and REAP discovery simulations, and even role-plays around general recommendations meetings.

As mentioned previously, management must reward good grades and apply negative consequences to substandard performance. Rewards might include status, a new title or certification, monetary bonuses, opportunities to teach future training programs, favoritism in sales lead distribution, and extra educational opportunities. Ideally, a combination of disparate rewards will be provided because people respond differently to various types of compensation. Negative consequences of poor performance might include withholding sales leads, cutting marketing support in the person's territory, probation until a higher grade can be obtained, and revoking other educational opportunities. Everyone, whether they score well, poorly, or moderately, should be placed on a personal development plan by management.

Don't make the mistake of feeling guilty about withholding leads and educational opportunities from people who score poorly. Salespeople who score low have not put the time, energy, and effort into learning the new skills, strategies, and content. From a practical standpoint, you wouldn't want these less effective salespeople handling high-quality leads for fear of mismanagement. Further training and educational opportunities are also more likely to be wasted on these individuals. Moreover, if placed in additional training programs, they may actually drag down those people who are serious about learning. Time, focus, and energy will be taken away from the people who do like learning and who are willing to pay the price to apply what they learn. Therefore, the return on training will suffer if these low graders are continually included.

The matrix in Figure 9.2 should be used by management to make decisions about each member of the sales team.

A combination of Salesgrading and actual sales performance will enable managers to plot each member of the sales team in the matrix. Salesgrading results will determine where an individual lies on the horizontal axis while actual results determine where the individual lies on the vertical axis.

Obviously, the goal is to get as many people in Quadrant 4 as possible. Sales effectiveness training programs that include a combination of good content that resonates with trainees, appropriate learning design, excellent delivery, and Salesgrading as an accountability mechanism will result in the maximum percentage of a sales team in Quadrant 4.

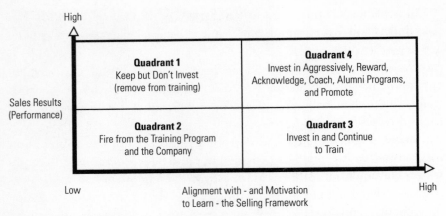

Figure 9.2 Organizations should make sales personnel decisions based on their results and alignment with the sales framework.

Final thoughts on Salesgrading: First, when used in conjunction with sales training, Salesgrading is not only a motivator and an accountability system. Its ultimate purpose is to add more certainty to sales results. In other words, Salesgrading is a mechanism that helps sales management better predict the sales team's ability to deliver on promised sales goals. Think of it as a strategic tool to determine how effectively a team can execute market-facing strategies. Armed with this knowledge, management can more accurately predict sales performance versus plans and budget, and adjust accordingly.

Second, when executed properly, Salesgrading is also a highly effective process for assessing candidates for sales and sales management positions. Since it is very rigorous, Salesgrading will inform management about the candidate's incoming alignment with the organization's market-facing strategies, process, and values.

The Power of Measurement

If an organization is to succeed in raising the productivity of its sales team, it must become serious about *measurement*. Similarly, if an organization hopes to hold its sales framework together and ensure that people are executing it properly, management must have a process of measurement. By measurement, we are not referring to the measurement of results. What we are talking about is measurement of *effectiveness processes* that most positively influence desired results.

Successful sales executives understand that more activity *does not* equal more sales in the large sale environment. This is especially true when selling large divergent offerings. Although high activity may correlate to better sales achievement in small sales, it is the polite blend of quantity and quality that rules the day in large sales. Neil Rackham, the author of *SPIN Selling* and other leading books on sales, proved this point

Better managers control revenue growth by measuring individual and team effectiveness within sales process.

well in his extensive research with major account sellers such as IBM, Motorola, and Kodak.[1] We've cited this research earlier and encourage you to read Rackham's works.

Effectiveness (skill, steps, and strategy) is the primary variable that determines large sales success. Conversely, efficiency (activity) is the more dominant key to small sales achievement. Unfortunately for the sales manager or executive in the major account or large sales environment, it is significantly more difficult to measure effectiveness than efficiency.

Without effectiveness metrics, sales managers have tremendous difficulty gaining certainty, predictability, and control over sales results. In the absence of these metrics, growth becomes less a function of planning, design, and strategy than luck, fortuitousness, and timing. Therefore, best-practice selling organizations must always strive to quantify the effectiveness of both individual salespeople and the team as a whole.

When you measure results, you only measure the effect of the results-inducing process. If results are poor, you have no metrics that can indicate where breakdowns in the sales process occur. As a result, applying the proper corrections can be extremely difficult.

Therefore, it is absolutely critical to measure process. More specifically, the sales process should be broken into the critical success activities that contribute to sales effectiveness. When you measure these critical success activities on an opportunity-by-opportunity basis and on a sum-of-opportunities basis per salesperson, data will clearly indicate the specific areas where a salesperson is effective and ineffective. When using process metrics, you can also benchmark salespeople against each other in all critical success activities to see who is best practice at each activity and who is struggling. Thus, learning can be extended and shared across an entire sales team.

This is likely to be very ambiguous to you. So, let's look at an example. Let's say that you have three salespeople on your team and you want to measure the effectiveness of each person in managing satisfaction stage opportunities. The critical success activities in this process might be FOCAS discoveries, general recommendations, a casual functional analysis, a formal optimization study, a risk-mitigating trial, a value-based proposal, and a commitment. Remember, major account selling is nonlinear. The only steps that are certain in a successful sales process with a buyer initially in the satisfaction stage are the FOCAS discovery, the proposal, and the commitment. General recommendations, the analysis, the study, and the trial are only deployed as appropriate and necessary. (Note: Critical success activities will vary from organization to organization.)

Let's say that the sum of each person's critical success activities for sales opportunities over a 3-month period (10 opportunities each) is as listed in Table 9.3.

Now that you have metrics, you can begin to assess the effectiveness of each person for each critical success activity. Although many more effectiveness ratios can be drawn from this example, Table 9.4 shows some interesting ratios that would enable the manager to see and react to costly effectiveness issues.

When armed with these comparative effectiveness metrics, a sales manager can see where people are struggling and succeeding. Managers are then able to quickly intervene and help salespeople in the specific areas where they are underoptimized. In our example, the manager would need

Table 9.3

Person	FOCAS Discovery	Gen. Rec.	Functional Analysis	Study	Trial	Proposal	Commitment
Bob	10	7	4	1	4	4	4
Sue	10	8	4	3	6	5	4
Jane	10	5	2	0	0	3	1

Table 9.4

Person	Commitments as a % of Discoveries	Proposals as a % of Discoveries	Commitments as a % of Proposals	Commitments as a % of Gen. Rec.	% of Gen. Rec. that lead to any next step
Bob	40%	40%	100%	57%	86%
Sue	40%	50%	80%	50%	100%
Jane	10%	30%	33%	20%	60%

to spend a lot of time with Jane to help her be more effective at executing FOCAS discoveries. Although Sue and Bob are both producing satisfactory results, they also could be better optimized in certain areas. The manager may want to help Bob work on the general recommendations step. As for Sue, the manager may coach her on value-based proposals, demand creation progressions, or risk-mitigation progressions. As you can see, managers can be more effective with regard to both skill coaching and strategic coaching when they have metrics at their disposal.

Proactive sales managers and executives constantly monitor effectiveness metrics so they can react before goals are missed and valuable opportunities are squandered. Metrics also enable managers to benchmark their team's effectiveness, and perhaps determine how their team stacks up against other best-practice teams.

These measures also allow sales managers and executives to more accurately predict sales results and performance versus budgeted results and plans. In other words, these managers can determine in advance whether predetermined growth strategies were built on a solid foundation or quicksand.

Measurement has been the true missing link preventing sales from becoming a manageable business discipline. This is an essential precept to grasp for any organization wishing to better control the elusiveness and randomness associated with sales outcomes.

One cannot manage what one cannot measure. And, if one agrees with the premise that there is a reason for every failed or successful outcome, then measuring sales effectiveness is not only possible, but absolutely necessary.

Yet, measurement is meaningless if the sales organization doesn't have a best-practice selling system in place. If the activities prescribed by the selling system are not validated, researched, and proven effective for the organization's sales environment, there is a good chance management will be measuring and reinforcing the wrong things.

For instance, it is quite common to see linear, step-by-step selling processes based on dated selling systems. Managers are often the biggest proponents of such a selling system because they feel linear systems give them control over outcomes. From reading this book, though, you know this is folly. Since selling and measuring in a linear fashion cannot possibly take into account the psychology of a buying organization, the wrong data is collected and salespeople waste time submitting their process data. Simply put, if you start with the wrong selling system, you cannot properly measure.

Another thought on measurement: It can be a significant driver of growth. With some of our clients, we have implemented what we call measurement-feedback-reward (MFR) systems that have pushed sales teams to new levels of growth. Such systems combine the measurement of critical success activities, feedback to each person about how she stacked up against other individuals and the overall group, and recognition and rewards for those individuals achieving excellence in various areas of effectiveness. To provide an example, consider the following case study.

Final Thoughts on Salesgrading and Measurement

We encourage all sales teams to not only commit to a *framework* of effectiveness, but also *accountability* to change. Without accountability, there can be no real productivity gains and the framework will fail at or soon after implementation. Yet, without a proper framework, it is impossible to hold salespeople responsible to a higher level of effectiveness. Clearly, frameworks and accountability are inexorably linked for those desiring significant sales productivity gains.

There also cannot be initial or ongoing accountability without *measurement*. It's an extra function, but it's the difference between sales managers who achieve advantage and differentiate, and sales managers who are willing to settle for the chains of mediocrity.

Last, the consistent advances in CRM technologies have made measurement and reporting much easier and more efficient. There are no longer any excuses for not applying metrics to your selling effort.

Case Study: Using a Measurement-Feedback-Recognition System to Drive Growth

In January 2002, we began working with a small manufacturer of capital equipment whose market included the steel, aluminum, and forging industries. The previous year had been the worst in the company's long history, during which it acquired only eight new customers and lost many more due to the terrible market conditions experienced by the industries this company served.

When this company engaged our firm to help them return to growth in early 2002, we found a capable team that had a fairly good sales process in place. However, the team had become stagnant and disenchanted due to the terrible market conditions they were facing.

Because the sales team had a good sales framework in place, we did little more than help them install a measurement-feedback-reward system. In creating this system with the organization's sales manager, we created sales results goals for the team. We then identified the type and volume of critical success activities necessary to achieve these goals. These goals and expectations were then communicated to the four-man sales team.

Next, we established a game, complete with a scoring system in which certain points were awarded for each critical success activity. We also created bonus points for selling in new markets and taking other risks. Each person had to compete not only against personal goals, but the rest of the team. The previously stagnant team turned into a highly energized machine.

For each of the 12 months in 2002, we diligently measured the critical success activities of each salesperson on an opportunity-by-opportunity basis and on a cumulative basis. At the end of each month, we published the results of each individual so that everyone could see how they stacked up against everyone else. Monthly and then annual awards were handed out, not based on volume of activity, but based on effectiveness of activity. The metrics also showed areas of weakness for each individual, which allowed the sales manager to offer coaching to reduce the number of sales process breakdowns.

Despite the very poor market conditions in 2002 (which were actually worse than those in 2001), the organization's sales team created 48 new clients, growing new business revenue exponentially. They also did a much better job of growing existing customer revenue. Morale began soaring early in the year, and intense but friendly competition ensued. All salespeople exceeded their goals, and the organization was in a strong position for the eventual return of better market conditions.

The Branded Salesperson: A Broader View of Sales

We conclude with a brief discussion on the broader view of selling in a large sale environment.

We mentioned in Chapter 1 that *Selling Is Dead* will have meaning and implications for various nonsales domains such as product development, customer service, marketing, and so on. The point is that optimization can never be achieved unless a framework is embraced by the entire organization. Here, we discuss the implications of salespeople and the sales framework on what is traditionally the domain of marketers.

The integration and alignment of sales and marketing is a critical topic for organizations that have a large, complex sale. Yet despite the close relationship between sales and marketing, many organizations remain misaligned in these two key areas. Many organizations invest tremendous resources to implement best-practice sales frameworks, but then fail to create marketing strategies that synergistically enhance their sales efforts and properly feed their sales engines.

How are sales and marketing strategies frequently misaligned with sales organizations?

Best-practice salespeople understand that 90 to 95 percent of the buyers in their market have no active needs for their offerings at any given time. Buyers with inactive needs represent the largest source of opportunities for salespeople who have effective demand creation strategies and competencies. However, most marketing is consciously or unconsciously aimed at buyers with active needs—only 5 to 10 percent of the market. As a result, marketers fail to engage the bulk of their markets, and sales productivity is constrained and suffers.

Similarly, branding has become a hot topic in the business community. Unfortunately, most thought leadership on branding fail to consider the impact of the salesperson (and the salesperson's process) on the total brand.

Differentiation and branding are not separate topics from sales. With regard to the large sale, you can no longer talk about selling or create selling strategies without understanding their impact on brand and positioning in the market.

Business-to-business organizations that have large, complex selling environments typically ignore the salesperson's impact on the company, product, and service brands. In many longer-cycle sales environments, salespeople are the face of their organizations and determine the buyer's

experience. In other cases, *they literally are the buyer's experience.* At minimum, large account, B2B salespeople are always a significant part of the
total brand equation. From a formula perspective, consider Table 9.5.

Organizations that are highly effective in how they face their markets
understand that the salesperson, and the salesperson's process, should
strengthen the *total brand.* Most organizations, and most marketing, mistakenly fail to acknowledge or emphasize the salesperson's brand.

New realities of selling (such as the Internet, speed of information,
global competition, rapid knockoffs/copycatting, innovation, and market
disruptors) are all weakening company and product/service brand components and making meaningful differentiation short-lived and tenuous.

Smaller companies, especially those without a highly defined and
narrow niche, lack the firepower to establish strong corporate and prod-
uct/service brands. Fortunately, for those smaller organizations who face
a complex sales environment, the salesperson's brand is always the most
important component of the total brand. It's also often the fastest and
cheapest component of the total brand to strengthen.

Larger companies used to be able to rely on the strength of their
company and product/service components of their total brand to secure
their stability and growth. The company and product/service brand
components were often so strong that they could compensate for poor
salespeople. No longer. The increases in competition, copycatting speed,
marketing chatter, and so on, have weakened these brand components and
made them less differentiated. In addition, buying organizations increasingly value, if not demand, salespeople to be customer productivity
experts. Now, for these larger companies, the strength of the total brand
is more contingent on the strength of the sales team's brand component.

Here's another interesting and related point. Innovation that leads to
new products and services (especially divergent offerings) has no brand
momentum—making branding of these innovations a difficult and
expensive undertaking. And, with ever faster birth-to-death cycles of new
products, the company and salesperson brand components offer the
biggest opportunity for brand stickiness. In other words, this age of innovation is making it wise to invest more in the corporate brand component
and salesperson's brand component, because products and services (and

Table 9.5

Total Brand = Company Brand + Product/Service Brands + Salesperson's Brand

thus their brand components) will be increasingly short lived. Innovation is shortening the useful and relevant lifespan of product and service offerings. All of these changing market conditions and disruptors are making the product/service brand component more and more irrelevant.

Therefore, we hope you accept and understand the importance of the Branded Salesperson to your organization's total brand. In the large sales environment, salespeople must be differentiators.

How does one accomplish a strong brand for salespeople? Salespeople must deliver relevance, value, and sticky messages. Salespeople must also constantly refresh their experience with customers by constantly adding new value and proving themselves to be customer productivity experts.

Starbucks has one of the most powerful brands in America. It's one that we admire. With that in mind, we challenge you to hire the right people and drill into them the right selling framework . . . and turn them into powerful *walking, talking, brands* for your prospects and clients (think walking, talking Starbucks).

Notes

1. Rackham, N. (1988). *SPIN selling.* New York, NY: McGraw-Hill.

Salespeople are often the face of your organization. They are the walking, talking experience for your buyers. We hope this book will help your salespeople create and deliver more meaningful buyer experiences, and strengthens your organization's total brand. But *you* are the Growth Manager, and *you* are in control. Will *you* use the concepts in this book to revitalize the growth of *your* enterprise?

Epilogue: Selecting Talent to Execute Your Large Sale Framework

Lisa Banach, Director of Assessment Services, Sogistics

The two authors have spent the last nine chapters and some 70,000 words introducing you to *demand types,* buyer decision-making *models,* and disciplined selling *frameworks.* They've taught you critical strategies, sales process steps, and skills that salespeople must employ in order to become best-practice *businesspeople who sell.* It's been a lot to digest. Perhaps even difficult to get through at times. But you've made it this far and we just need you to hang in a little longer. It's worth it, we promise!

With all this talk about models, frameworks, and strategies, it looks as though selling organizations are now equipped with all of the knowledge and tools needed to improve sales productivity and increase revenues. Right? Not quite.

One critical element still needs to be examined and understood. What is this element? It is the *makeup* of the people hired and charged with the daunting task of going out and effectively *applying* the elements of a sophisticated framework on a daily basis. Without the *right* people, companies can have best-practice strategies and management systems in place, but still fall short when it comes to execution and, ultimately, meeting their growth goals and other critical selling objectives.

At this point in the book, sales executives and senior sales managers should realize that properly executing the sales strategies presented by the authors is moderately challenging. Not every salesperson *can* do it. Not every salesperson will *want* to do it. Yet salespeople are the *bridge* between an organization and new business and thus an organization cannot *grow* without effective sellers (especially in an era of increasingly ineffective marketing).

The costs of making a poor sales hire are severe. Obvious costs include salary, commission, benefits, and training. However, the really significant costs are hidden. These hidden costs include competitive disadvantage, missed opportunities, poor morale of the sales team, lost customers, failure to sell new innovations, and the wasted time of management. In the end, companies facing a large sale environment can lose *hundreds of thousands to millions of dollars* with each hiring mistake.

Thus, significant pressure is placed on sales executives and senior sales managers to find and hire the *right salespeople* for the *right positions.* Executives who are unsuccessful at this hiring competency will quickly find themselves in possession of unproductive sales teams, poor revenue performance, and the threat of dismissal.

In Chapter 1, the authors talk about how salespeople who can navigate all four demand types effectively add tremendous value to their organizations and score high in what they refer to as demand versatility. These best-practice salespeople have a core group of talents in common that drive their behavior. We will take a closer look at these common talent criteria shortly.

At Sogistics, we interview, test, assess, and grade thousands of major account salespeople and sales managers annually. As a result, we've learned the unique disposition of those sellers who can produce best-practice results. I'd like to share some of this information with you.

Talent and Behavior

Success in large sales is contingent upon having salespeople who possess specific talents and behaviors. Therefore, it is critical for senior executives and sales managers to understand what core talents and behaviors they need to look for when evaluating sales candidates. We will use this section to discuss the makeup of a customer productivity improvement expert who has the demand versatility to sell across all four types of demand (both divergent and concurrent offerings).

When we talk about *talent,* we define this as a person's natural predisposition to quickly acquire the skills necessary to produce top performance in a given domain (i.e., sales). A person's natural predisposition includes their aptitudes (natural gifts), cognitive ability (intelligence), personality (personal identity), and character (do what they say they will do), which together drive their behavior.

The talents that we look for when assessing a candidate for a specific position vary based on the primary challenges faced by a seller in that position. Depending on the company's offering(s), market(s), and market-facing strategies, the seller's primary challenge will vary by two factors:

1. Whether the offerings will most often represent divergent or concurrent offerings to the buyers in the market.
2. Whether the seller will mostly create or service demand.

In other words, the talents and traits a sales executive or manager must look for in candidates will depend on where the majority of a salesperson's projected opportunities fall in the matrix in Figure E.1 (it has been simplified for the purposes of this book).

Again, salespeople will often find themselves spending the majority of their time selling either a divergent or concurrent offering and focus more heavily on either creating or servicing demand. Therefore, someone

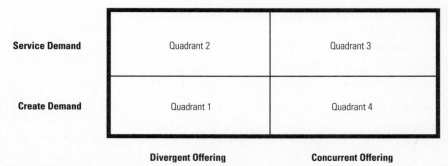

Figure E.1 Talent compatibility and talent acquisition decisions must be determined based on the types of opportunities in which a seller will be engaged.

who spends the majority of her time creating demand with a divergent offering is going to need some unique sales talents compared to the salesperson who spends a high percentage of his time servicing demand with a concurrent offering.

To make the determination about the incoming salesperson's primary selling challenges, we work with our clients to do two things. First, we have them plot their recent selling opportunities in the matrix. Next, we have them project where in that table the primary selling challenges will be in 1 to 3 years. To evaluate a candidate properly, sales executives and managers must understand how their market realities will change in the foreseeable future to determine if the individual they hire will remain relevant and effective.

The situation we would like to talk about here is when the bulk of an incoming salesperson's opportunities congregate in the middle. This is depicted in the matrix in Figure E.2 (the dots equal selling opportunities).

In the illustration, the circle shows where selling opportunities are most likely to occur. This is a common scenario. The implication is that a salesperson facing these market challenges must possess a great deal of demand versatility. She must be able to create and service demand for both divergent and concurrent offerings.

Let us show you one more graphic to help you better project future selling challenges. Figure E.3 also provides you with some indication of how the primary selling challenge typically changes over the life cycle of a product or service.

In this model, the line equals the product life cycle of an offering.

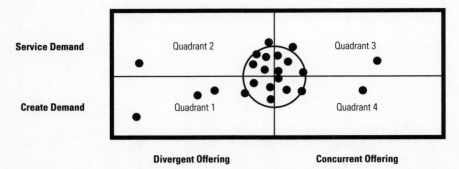

Figure E.2 Demand versatility is required of salespeople who face a multitude of selling challenges.

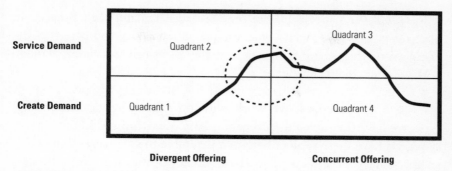

Figure E.3 Tracking product life cycles helps organizations determine future selling challenges. As offerings mature and selling challenges change, hiring managers must rethink the talents needed to most effectively sell offerings.

The circle contains the period in a life cycle during which the seller must possess the greatest demand versatility. As an offering begins to mature, the challenge begins to gradually shift from the offering representing mostly a divergent offering (new application) to representing a concurrent offering (existing application) for prospects. Further, the challenge gradually shifts from facing mostly opportunities where demand must be created to a mix of opportunities where demand frequently already exists and must be serviced.

Case Study: The Life Cycle of Trimble Offerings

Consider a company that has been discussed previously in this book—Trimble. You may recall that it sells, among other things, high-end GPS-based instrumentation for construction and survey applications. These instruments initially represented divergent offerings to their markets. The systems were discontinuous and risky to the buyers Trimble sellers called on.

Early on, Trimble salespeople had to be effective at creating demand for these divergent offerings. Little buyer demand existed in the early years, so Trimble had to rely on demand creation strategies. Success could also only come from engaging senior executives within buyer organizations.

Over time, though, as the GPS-based instruments gradually became accepted by the mainstream market, the selling challenge changed. Buying organizations began purchasing additional systems and upgraded systems. Late adopters buying their first system more readily accepted the value and

(continued)

capabilities of these instruments. Trimble salespeople no longer needed to call at the owner and president level. Mid-level sales calls became the norm because the technology had been accepted and embraced in the market. Risks had been reduced. For Trimble salespeople, building a case for change became less critical because there was more demand in the market and less resistance to change around these systems.

To summarize the shift in Trimble's sales challenges, Trimble salespeople began spending more time managing concurrent selling situations where buying organizations had already adopted the GPS-based applications. An increasing number of its opportunities was also with shopping stage buyers who already had active needs for this category of instrumentation. Much less time was spent creating demand and managing divergent opportunities.

As this shift occurred, Trimble had to simultaneously shift the skills and strategies it emphasized in both hiring and coaching.

Two notes about the previous model. The shape of the life cycle will vary by offering category. Also, the second upswing in the life cycle is caused by innovation (the production of continuously improved offerings) and market disruptors that produce popular economy versions of the offering. Continuous improvement and economy demand must be created and serviced during this period.

Now, let's return to our discussion of talent criteria.

Based on the assessments we have conducted on thousands of salespeople over the last 17 years, we have identified dozens of traits that we look for when assessing sales candidates (and a separate set for sales management candidates). However, in this epilogue, we'll only discuss the primary talent criteria that directly impact an individual's ability to successfully sell across the four demand types in large sales. In other words, we'll discuss the most significant talent criteria that combine to produce demand versatility.

The left column in Table E.1 lists many, *but not all,* of the traits we look for when assessing large account salespeople. The right column lists the most critical talent criteria that enable demand versatility in a salesperson.

This table excludes non–talent traits.

As the table shows, the six main requisites of demand versatility

Table E.1

General Large Account Traits	Demand Versatility Talent Criteria
◆ Practical intelligence	◆ Achievement drive
◆ Strong communicator	◆ Strategic orientation
◆ Financial astuteness	◆ Situational flexibility
◆ Persistence	◆ Embraces learning
◆ Demonstrates initiative	◆ Business acumen
◆ Competitive	◆ Problem recognition
◆ Analytical	
◆ Conceptual	
◆ Resourceful	
◆ Patient urgency	
◆ Mature	
◆ Good esteem	
◆ Appropriate blend of independence/dependence	
◆ Accountability	
◆ Aggressiveness	
◆ Energy	
◆ Work ethic	
◆ Thick-skinned	
◆ Integrity	
◆ Creative	
◆ Influence competency	
◆ Problem solving	

include achievement drive, strategic orientation, situational flexibility, embraces learning, business acumen, and problem recognition.

Let's look at each of these in greater detail.

More than likely, just about any book you read that talks about hiring salespeople is going to mention achievement drive. We are not identifying something new here. However, this talent criterion makes a tremendous impact on a salesperson's demand versatility, and success in general.

You know that selling is very difficult, particularly in large account settings where the buyer's change costs are high. Creating and managing the four types of demand yield a wide variety of selling situations and challenges. Consequently, without a strong internal drive pushing them to overcome obstacles, salespeople will fail.

The key element of *achievement drive* is a bias to action. Individuals who have strong achievement drive are very proactive and make things happen relative to getting the job done. Achievement drive is directed at task accomplishment. People with strong achievement drive demonstrate results-focused behavior and set challenging personal goals. By challenging, we mean that there is a 50/50 chance of hitting the goal—it is a definite stretch, but not unrealistic or impossible. Hiring organizations should find examples of situations where the person has not quit easily in the face of adversity, but instead took repeated or different steps to overcome an obstacle (high persistence). People with strong achievement drive are opportunistic and have an efficiency orientation, using tools to help them work smarter.

The second talent criterion is *strategic orientation*. Strategic sellers understand how to adjust their process to the various types of demand they encounter. They take the long, broad view. Each of their activities has an underlying intent—strategic intent. In other words, most everything they do is meant to produce a specific, desirable, and predetermined outcome. The days when a salesperson could go into an organization and simply wing it and still get the sale are long gone. Today's sellers are faced with much more sophisticated buyers.

Often, these individuals win before they ever engage a prospect because of solid pre-call planning—as opposed to simply winging it. Strategic sellers take a broad look at each situation before selecting the steps or tactics they employ. Best-practice sellers also strategically adjust their process and recommendations to better suit the uniqueness of the company and opportunity.

Our third talent criterion is *situational flexibility,* and it relates to the previous criterion. This criterion refers to an individual's ability to change her behavior, sales strategy, and approach based on the demand type, where the buyer is in the decision-making model, and other unique situations that arise during the sales cycle. This criterion has become extremely important because, as was mentioned early in the book, demand cycles. Therefore, today's salesperson is typically managing a mix of opportunities for each demand type simultaneously. If an organization hires a salesperson who takes the same approach and applies the same strategies with each of these opportunities, the organization has created a recipe for failure.

Senior executives and senior sales managers need to remember that sales is nonlinear and, therefore, they cannot afford to hire people who take a cookie-cutter approach with opportunities. Salespeople need to be able to respond quickly and appropriately to the curveballs thrown at them during the sales process. Best-practice sales professionals demonstrate an ability to remain fluid and flexible in the sales process.

As the path to new growth becomes increasingly fragmented and conventional growth strategies are rendered ineffective, a person's sales productivity and performance will be tied to his ability to remain flexible and adaptable. However, to be able to consistently and quickly adapt requires a person to also be an active learner. This leads us to our fourth talent criterion: one who *embraces learning*.

Best-practice sellers seek out additional learning and coaching, and apply what they learn and are taught. They search for new concepts, methodologies, and strategies that can significantly impact their performance. They must be willing to delay gratification and pay the price of applying what they learn.

Active learners obviously must be bright people who are capable of learning quickly. However, they must also have good esteem, which enables them to admit that they need to adjust. They also must have some tolerance for taking risks. Change is risky, and applying new methodologies is change. We also typically see natural curiosity in good, active learners. These people are curious about their industry, the markets they serve, and the buyer organizations they engage.

The fifth talent criterion is *business acumen*. Large account salespeople are faced with the challenge of constantly engaging high-level executives in intelligent business dialogue, especially when selling divergent offerings. This conversation is often conceptual and strategic. It is conducted at the 10,000 feet level. It is not a discussion of tactical problems, products, or services. Such a conversation challenges the executives to think more deeply about the business—and that is the value. Salespeople also need a general sense for how businesses operate and function.

The sixth and final criterion in demand versatility is *problem recognition*. This differs significantly from problem solving, which is a more common trait. Problem recognition means starting with nothing—a blank sheet of paper—and creating something of value. That value is the opportunity.

In other words, better-practice sellers ask questions in a certain sequence that helps them see whether recognized or unrecognized problems exist in the buyer environment.

Problem solving is an overappreciated trait. Problem recognition (transforming nothing into something) is the trait that will produce a great volume of selling opportunities, and subsequent sales.

Beliefs / Suppositions

When assessing a candidate for a sales position, hiring managers must understand the individual's sales *beliefs* (or suppositions). As you may recall, beliefs are a person's conviction or acceptance that certain things are true. As mentioned earlier, sellers will think, act, and behave in a manner that is consistent with their beliefs and suppositions. Consequently, the individuals who hold beliefs about selling that are flawed or untrue will not be productive in the long term.

Why is it important to learn about a candidate's beliefs in the assessment process? Although you can typically train people to learn new strategies and skills (if you have some accountability to change), a person's improper and unproductive beliefs about sales and buyers can be almost impossible to change. For instance, if an individual holds inaccurate beliefs about large sales (e.g., "I need to close early and often"), she will likely not be open to change or new ideas. Because beliefs can be strong motivators and drivers of action, an organization typically does not want to hire a candidate whose beliefs are fundamentally misaligned with the organization's beliefs.

Sales Strategies, Process, and Skills

Salespeople can be taught better sales strategies, skills, and steps with appropriate learning design, delivery, and accountability to change. Therefore, a sales candidate's strategies, steps, and skills are often less important than talent—which cannot be taught. However, it is important to get a snapshot of the individual's large sale effectiveness.

In sales hiring decisions, the relative importance of a candidate's effectiveness in terms of strategies, skills, and process steps depends on three things:

1. The acceptable ramp-up time. In other words, how soon does the person need to become a consistent producer?
2. Whether the hiring organization has effective sales training and coaching programs readily available.
3. Whether the person is an active learner.

If the organization needs the hire to begin producing immediately, the individual's existing effectiveness is more important. If the organization does not have good training and coaching in place, the individual's existing effectiveness is more important. Similarly, if the candidate is not an active learner, he must already have effective strategies, skills, and process steps because of the anticipated difficulty in learning a new selling framework.

Tools for Your Hiring Obstacle Course

Best-practice senior sales managers and sales executives understand the importance of creating a thorough obstacle course through which candidates can be processed before making a hiring decision. The course should involve a number of steps and incorporate a variety of valid and reliable tools that help the organization identify each individual's strengths, weaknesses, and overall fit. Effective managers know that if executed properly, a well-constructed obstacle course can be an efficient way to significantly reduce the chance of making a poor hiring decision. Ultimately, this saves the company from absorbing the tremendous cost of making poor hires.

An effective obstacle course should consist of the following elements.

Behavioral Interviews

One of the most powerful tools that can be used to assess an individual's talent and behavior is the behavioral interview. The behavioral interview is based on the premise that past behavior is the best predictor of future behavior and ultimately future performance. No hypothetical questions are asked. Instead, candidates are asked to tell a behavioral story describing examples of times in the past when they have demonstrated specific behaviors.

Compared to traditional and situational interviews, it is difficult for a candidate to give a socially desirable answer that is untrue to his character in a behavioral interview. Most interviewers ask far too many hypothetical questions that are only effective at determining how well the candidate interviews—not sells!

Listed below are a few examples of behavioral questions that can be asked when interviewing a sales candidate to uncover the talent criterion

achievement drive discussed earlier. As you can see, behavioral interviewers must probe deeper and deeper to get the candidate to tell an
entire behavioral story.

- ◆ Give me an example of an account from this past year that was
  difficult to penetrate. Describe the situation, action you took, and
  the results. *Is the candidate challenge-oriented and persistent?*
- ◆ Tell me about two or three personal goals you set for yourself this
  year. Why did you set these goals? Have you accomplished any of
  those goals? What specific actions have you taken in an effort to
  achieve these goals? *Does the candidate set stretch goals?*
- ◆ In the past 2 years, what has been your most important individual
  accomplishment at ABC Inc.? Which of these accomplishments
  came most easily to you? Why is that? Which of these accomplishments are you most proud of? Please elaborate. *Is the candidate challenge-oriented, ambitious, results-focused?*

Testing

Another mechanism that can be useful in the assessment of sales talent
(if used appropriately) is a battery of tests measuring personality and
temperament, as well as intellect and cognitive sales ability.

A word of caution, though, on personality testing. While personality tests (validated ones) can be very helpful in determining the likelihood of fit and success of candidates in a specific selling role, clearly
there are limits. With personality tests in particular, there is room for
candidates to be evasive or attempt to manipulate the outcome of the
test. Therefore, a certain slop factor should be taken into consideration
when interpreting the results. This is why personality tests are often
intended to supplement and enhance the quality of good behavioral
interviews rather than be the primary criterion in hiring decisions.

We suggest that you should not use generalist personality and apti-
tude tests. It's much more meaningful to utilize tests that measure specific personality traits and cognitive abilities that correlate to success in
the large sale environment. Based on the theory of multiple intelligences, hiring organizations should not necessarily look to measure how
bright an individual is, but rather the many ways an individual is bright
related to superior sales performance.[1]

Role-Plays in Assessment

It is important to employ role-plays or simulations that allow you to take a closer look at an individual's strategic acumen, sales process, and skill levels. Role-plays should force the candidate to walk you through an entire sales process, step-by-step. Utilize two scenarios: one where the buyer is initially in the satisfaction stage (dormant needs), and one where the buyer is initially in the shopping stage (active needs). Throughout the sales process, have the buyer explain the logic and strategy behind each step and then simulate around each step. The interviewer does *not* need to be an expert in the candidate's current field to conduct effective role-plays.

Higher Authority Checks

One natural predisposition of a candidate that should be evaluated is *character*. When we talk about character, most important we are interested in whether a person does what she says she is going to do. Character also has to do with a person's integrity, honesty, trustworthiness, and ethics. Unfortunately, it is difficult to accurately assess character using only the tools already mentioned, unless you catch the person giving inaccurate information during an interview. Therefore, we recommend using an additional tool called the *higher authority check*.

Higher authority checks are conducted with people a candidate has reported to directly in the past. These are critical checks on a person's behavior, performance, and character conducted by the interviewer—it is much less important to check an individual's biographical data.

Remember, when completing these higher authority checks, you are not looking for confirmation on how good a candidate is. Instead, you are looking for reasons not to hire the person. Be a contrarian. Your goal is not to make a great sales hire. Instead, your primary focus must be on avoiding hiring a bad one.

Meeting Outside the Office

One final tool that can be helpful to hiring managers is meeting with candidates, at least once, outside the office. By sitting down with candidates in a less formal yet structured environment (i.e., over lunch or coffee), the interviewer(s) has the opportunity to see how the candidate acts when his guard might be down. Often, this is an ideal setting to examine maturity and judgment.

Building Your Sales Bench

If you have one takeaway from this epilogue, it should be related to the concept of a sales bench.

Ideally, every sales executive and senior sales manager would create a sales bench for their organization as a way to ensure that they have the right people doing the right jobs at any given time. Finding people who have the appropriate sales talents and demand versatility takes time. Therefore, executives with a bench of sales talent to draw upon have a distinct advantage. Without a sales bench, it is nearly impossible to quickly replace lost or fired salespeople. Opportunities and clients are likely to be lost while the void is waiting to be filled. Unfortunately, the result is often a poor hire. Hopes and hurry overrule patience and logic.

Top managers know that the best time to recruit is *always,* especially when they don't need salespeople. Constant recruiting enables an organization to remain steadfastly committed to talent and value rather than need. Need is a terrible burden in the people business.

Experienced managers stay focused on putting high-potential individuals on their bench for the day when a sales position opens up. On that day, the manager goes to her bench to fill the position by choosing an existing member of the sales infrastructure who already understands the business model, the selling framework, and the market.

People hired to be part of a sales bench are typically brought in at lower-level positions. A few traditional examples of these lower-level bench positions include customer service, account management, inside sales, business development (telemarketers), or even sales coordinators (an administrative position). Entry-level outside sales positions that focus on smaller accounts or tactical/transactional offerings (versus your larger and more strategic offerings) can also represent good bench positions.

Be creative. There are endless possibilities for developing new bench positions that will serve as effective launching pads for more critical sales roles.

Creating and implementing a sales bench is advantageous as long as sales managers allow bench players to mature in the bench role, gain valuable experience, and receive adequate training. There are three main benefits of having a bench. First, if a hiring mistake is made with a bench player, the organization probably hasn't invested as much in terms of compensation and training as with a salesperson. Second, when a key sales position becomes available, it can be filled more quickly by a bench player. Market opportunities are less likely to be lost because the hole is filled more quickly. Third, bench players should involve less training and ramp-up time than an external hire because the bench player already has a good understanding of the organization and the offerings being sold. In other words, upgraded bench players should have a faster time-to-production (and a faster time-to-breakeven).

Dave Powell, the corporate sales manager for Harris InfoSource, a Dun & Bradstreet company, recently explained the sales bench in this organization. Harris helps sales and marketing professionals find new customers and grow sales with online and CD-Rom database solutions. Many readers of this book probably use Harris products to generate sales leads and research prospect organizations. Dave illustrated a great example of a powerful bench that has been created for his sales organization.

At Harris, candidates are initially hired into an entry-level position, referred to as the OCAT position. These individuals are responsible for calling on inactive accounts that have not made a purchase with Harris in at least 3 years. Any business gained from these accounts is simply viewed as gravy by Harris. More important, the position serves as good training ground for new hires.

Those individuals who are successful in the OCAT position remain on Harris's sales bench until a retention specialist position opens up. With this position, there is greater responsibility as each specialist is given a book of existing accounts that they are charged with growing.

Finally, those who excel as retention specialists are promoted to the company's top sales position, the ICAT, when such a position becomes available. Like the retention specialists, ICAT salespeople are also responsible for growing a base of existing accounts. However, they are responsible for much larger accounts. In addition, the ICATs receive inbound calls from prospects with *active* needs.

By creating and implementing a strong sales bench, Harris has not only reduced the cost and impact of making a poor hire, it has also offered the people who join the company an opportunity to grow and follow a defined career path with greater rewards.

We highly recommend you build a sales bench for your organization if one isn't already in place. For most large account sales organizations, the cost of maintaining a short but versatile sales bench is less than the high costs of opportunities lost during the sourcing, hiring, and ramp-up processes for external sales candidates. Furthermore, the bench roles should be productive and value-adding to both the organization and the execution of market-facing strategies.

A sales bench also affords you the opportunity to bring aboard less experienced personnel who do not possess a great deal of negative baggage. In other words, you will have the ability to instill solid habits and best-practice methodologies in your bench players. More experienced people, the likely alternative hiring source, are often programmed with bad habits, poor methodologies, and unproductive beliefs about selling. As alluded to in our Harris InfoSource case study, the added bonus is that the bench positions also create a career path within your sales organization. Career paths are effective recruiting and retention tools.

Final Thoughts

We recognize the increasing importance of hiring the *right people*. Consequently, just as salespeople today must develop a *disciplined process* for creating and managing new opportunities, chief growth officers must develop a *disciplined process* for assessing sales talent and potential.

Coaches, managers, and leaders are only as good as the talent levels of their people. Due to this, there is only one competence more important to an organization than selling. That competence is discerning and hiring the right people who are effective sellers, capable of driving the organization's growth.

Notes

1. Gardner, H. (1983). *Frames of mind: The theory of multiple intelligences.* New York, NY: BasicBooks.

Resources

Bosworth, M.T. (1995). *Solution selling: Creating buyers in difficult selling markets.* New York, NY: McGraw-Hill.

Christensen, C.M., & Raynor, M.E. (2003). *The innovator's solution: Creating and sustaining successful growth.* Boston, MA: Harvard Business School Press.

De Bono, E. (1992). *SUR/PETITION: Creating value monopolies when everyone else is merely competing.* New York, NY: HarperBusiness.

Gardner, H. (1983). *Frames of mind: The theory of multiple intelligences.* New York, NY: BasicBooks.

Heiman, S.E., & Miller, R.B. (1985). *Strategic selling.* New York, NY: William Morrow and Company.

Heiman, S.E., & Miller, R.B. (1987). *Conceptual selling.* Berkeley, CA: Miller-Heiman.

Holden, J. (1990). *Power base selling.* New York, NY: John Wiley & Sons.

O'Shaughnessy, J. (1987). *Why people buy.* New York, NY: Oxford Press.

Parinello, A. (Ed.) (1999). *Selling to vito: Increase your commissions by getting appointments with top decision makers today.* Holbrook, MA: Adams Media Corporation.

Rackham, N. (1988). *SPIN selling.* New York, NY: McGraw-Hill.

Rackham, N. (1989). *Major account sales strategy.* New York, NY: McGraw-Hill.

Spencer, L.M., & Spencer, S.M. (1993). *Competence at work: Models for superior performance.* New York, NY: John Wiley & Sons.

Wiersema, F. (1996). *Customer intimacy: Pick your partners, shape your culture, win together.* Santa Monica, CA: Knowledge Exchange.

Counselor Selling was a sales training program taught by Wilson Learning. Some of this work culminated in the following book written by Larry Wilson: Wilson, L., & Wilson, H. (1987). *Changing the game: The new way to sell.* New York, NY: Simon & Schuster.

Index

299